INDELIBLE IMAGES

INDELIBLE IMAGES

Women of
Local Television

Edited by

Mary E. Beadle

Michael D. Murray

Iowa State University Press

A Blackwell Science Company

MARY E. BEADLE is Dean of the Graduate School at John Carroll University in Cleveland, Ohio, and is a Professor of Communications. Dr. Beadle previously founded and chaired the Communication Department at Walsh University in Canton, Ohio. She continues to teach mass media courses in radio-television performance, women and the media, and international media in the undergraduate program and ethics and international media in the graduate program of Communications Management. She has conducted communication seminars in Russia and Latin America. Her publications include articles in media history and international media.

MICHAEL D. MURRAY is author of *The Political Performers* and editor of *Encyclopedia of Television News*. He has written numerous articles on the history of broadcast news. He is a former president of the American Journalism Historians Association, a recipient of a Goldsmith Research Award from Harvard University, and held a Weld Senior Fellowship at Stanford University. He was also elected a fellow of Cambridge University, the University of London, and was named Frank Stanton Fellow by the International Radio and Television Society.

© 2001 Iowa State University Press
A Blackwell Science Company
All rights reserved

Iowa State University Press
2121 South State Avenue, Ames, Iowa 50014

Orders: 1-800-862-6657
Office: 1-515-292-0140
Fax: 1-515-292-3348
Web site: www.isupress.com

Authorization to photocopy items for internal or personal use, or the internal or personal use of specific clients, is granted by Iowa State University Press, provided that the base fee of $.10 per copy is paid directly to the Copyright Clearance Center, 222 Rosewood Drive, Danvers, MA 01923. For those organizations that have been granted a photocopy license by CCC, a separate system of payments has been arranged. The fee code for users of the Transactional Reporting Service is 0-8138-0621-6/2001 $.10.

∞ Printed on acid-free paper in the United States of America

First edition, 2001

Library of Congress Cataloging-in-Publication Data

Indelible images : women of local television / edited by Mary E. Beadle and Michael D. Murray.—1st ed.
     p. cm.
Includes bibliographical references and index.
  ISBN 0-8138-0621-6
  1. Women in television broadcasting—United States. I. Beadle, Mary E. II. Murray, Michael D.
  PN1992.W65153 2001
791.45'082'0973—dc21   2001003974

The last digit is the print number: 9 8 7 6 5 4 3 2 1

To all the women of television whose stories have yet to be told

Women's history is the primary tool for women's emancipation.
                                        —*Gerda Lerner, Ph.D.*

Contents

Preface ix

Contributors xiii

1. Pioneering Women in Television: An Introduction
   Mary E. Beadle, Michael D. Murray, and Donald G. Godfrey 3

2. Adele Arakawa: A Commitment to Professionalism
   Jan Whitt 15

3. Dorothy Stimson Bullitt: Queen of Broadcasting and Her KING
   Val E. Limburg 27

4. Jean Enersen: A Woman of Roots and Wings
   Joanne M. Lisosky 39

5. Dorothy Fuldheim: A Legend in Local News
   Margaret O. Finucane 51

6. Martha Gable: ETV's Pioneer Spokesperson
   Alan R. Stephenson 63

7. Frieda Hennock and KUHT: First in Educational Television
   Susan L. Brinson 75

8. Price Hicks: Stylish Vision
   Mary M. Step 87

9. Lisa Howard (Lisa Thomas-Laury): Philadelphia Television News Anchor
   Betsy Leebron 99

10. Carole Kneeland: Lone Star Legacy
    John Mark Dempsey 109

11. Carol Marin: Chicago's Courageous Newscaster
    Margaret O. Finucane 121

12. Donna Matson: Pioneer ETV Entrepreneur
    Alan R. Stephenson 131

13. Charlotte Peters: One of a Kind
    Michael D. Murray 143

14. Wanda Ramey: KPIX's Girl on the Beat
    Steven Runyon 157

15. Marciarose Shestack: A Broadcaster Who Happens to Be a Woman
    Sarah Sullivan 167

16. Gayle Sierens: Keepin' On
    C.A. Tuggle 179

17. Laurel Vlock: To Be Is to Do
    Margot Hardenbergh 191

18. Alice Weston: Cleveland's "First Lady of Television"
    Mary E. Beadle 203

19. Bobbie Wygant: "They Poured Me in With the Foundation"
    Suzanne Huffman 215

20. Marcia Yockey: A Force of Nature in Evansville, Indiana
    Steven J. Dick 229

    Index 241

Preface

In 1997, ISU Press published *Television in America: Local Station History From Across the Nation.* It was during that project that the idea for a companion book was born; a book that would chronicle the contributions of women to local station development. In recent years, the role of women as a vital force in national television has been recognized in both popular media and scholarly works. But at the same time, little has been written about the history of local television and even less about the contributions that women made to the development and continuing success of local stations.

In *Indelible Images: Women in Local Television,* you will read about 19 women across the country who contributed in a variety of ways to local stations. These 19 broadcasters by no means represent the only women who played a significant role in local television. Rather, we hope this represents a beginning in the systematic documentation of women and their participation in local station development.

From the earliest days, women were providing innovative ideas to the emergence of television. Prior to World War II, Marty Gable worked in the development of test programs for Philco in Philadelphia. Frieda Hennock played a major role in the sign-on of the first educational (later public) television station in the nation operated in Houston, Texas. Dorothy Bullitt provided the leadership to develop a media empire with flagship station KING-TV in Seattle. One of KING-TV's strengths was respected reporter and news anchor Jean Enersen.

Others across the country were also on air from the beginning of local station sign-ons both before and after the television freeze. In Cleveland a few weeks after sign-on in late 1947, Dorothy Fuldheim provided some of the first news commentary and Alice Weston provided some of the first women's programming in the nation. Marcia Yockey in Evansville, Indiana, who was trained by the U.S. Weather

Bureau to serve during World War II while men were overseas, became a weather forecaster. She would often dress in outfits to celebrate a holiday. Charlotte Peters (St. Louis), described as a "female version of Milton Berle," was an entertainer and, like Yockey, often dressed a variety of costumes. Bobbie Wygant was the first woman in the Dallas market to produce and host a general-interest talk show and the first TV critic in the Southwest to review both theater and film. In Philadelphia, Marciarose Shestack became the first woman to anchor prime-time news in one of the top five markets.

In San Francisco, Wanda Ramey was the first woman to anchor the news on the West Coast and the second woman to anchor the news on local television in America. Also on the West Coast, Price Hicks and Donna Matson worked in educational television. Hicks produced shows in the early days of KCET, Los Angeles, and Matson established her own company to provide educational shows for the school programming market. In the process, in 1968 Matson was the fourth woman to become a member of the Directors Guild of America. Her company still provides programming today.

Unlike today, these pioneers were often middle-aged women who brought experience and maturity to the newly evolving medium. Many had opportunities to move to the national level but declined because they were committed to a local area with family and community ties. Often compared to Barbara Walters in their ability to interview, the women who were on air developed an intimate and friendly style, one frequently imitated today. Many remained with the station well into their 80s and were perceived by the audience as an important member of the community. You will read many "firsts" associated with them.

These early contributors to the development of local television laid the foundation for the next group of women: women hired in the late 1970s and early 1980s to meet EEOC requirements. Their contributions span almost half of the time of television's existence. Women began to expand their roles, such as Gayle Sierens in Tampa who was interested in sports broadcasting. Others were concerned about the ethical choices that broadcasters make. Carole Kneeland established a policy on crime coverage for KVUE in Austin that had a national impact on how local stations report crime stories. Laurel Vlock, producer and host of the longest-running television series in Connecticut, was founder of the first television station owned and operated by women who were interested in serving the needs of the local community. She founded the Holocaust Survivors Film Project. In Chicago, Carol Marin fought to maintain integrity in local newscasts. The type of woman hired also became more diverse. Adele Arakawa (Denver) of Japanese American origin and Lisa Howard (Philadelphia) of African American descent represent this trend in local television.

The available written material on the contributions of these women varied greatly. Since many of the records from the earliest days have been tossed out, some authors relied heavily on oral histories, interviews or personal files. Others were able to obtain documentation from the local press or station or university/library archives. Despite these challenges, the histories we present here provide a representation of how women were present and vital to the development and continued success of local stations.

The editors would like to thank all those who made this project possible, especially the authors who contributed their original research. Thank you to Don Godfrey for his work on *Television in America* and for providing impetus for this tome; his encouragement was always appreciated.

Michael Murray especially acknowledges the support of his wife, Carol, who puts up with his peculiarities; and his two daughters, Kate and Ellen; plus Chancellor Blanche Touhill and Dean David Young.

Mary Beadle acknowledges the support of her colleagues in the Communications Department—especially Peggy Finucane, Alan Stephenson, and Erin Demoranville—and in the Graduate Office, Mary Jane Mehling.

We also would like to thank the staff at Iowa State University Press.

Mary E. Beadle
Michael D. Murray

Contributors

DR. SUSAN BRINSON is an associate professor in the Department of Communication at Auburn University. She has recently authored a book on Frieda Hennock that is in press.

DR. JOHN MARK DEMPSEY is an assistant professor of broadcast journalism at the University of North Texas and serves as news anchor for the Texas State Network that includes 175 radio affiliates in the state.

DR. STEVEN DICK is an assistant professor in the Department of Radio-Television at Southern Illinois University, Carbondale. He worked eight years for local television stations including WFIE-TV in Evansville. He has recently published articles on pirate radio and television management.

DR. MARGARET FINUCANE is an assistant professor of Communications at John Carroll University in University Heights, Ohio. She publishes in the area of family communication and media history.

DR. DON GODFREY is a professor at the Walter Cronkite School of Journalism and Telecommunications at Arizona State University in Tempe. He was the co-editor with Dr. Murray of *Television in America* and has recently published the biography of *Philo Farnsworth: The Father of Television*. Dr. Godfrey has authored numerous books and articles and is the former President of the Broadcast Education Association.

DR. MARGOT HARDENBERGH is a visiting assistant professor in the Department of Communication and Media Studies at Fordham University. She writes on media history and the impact of media on social life. She was public affairs project supervisor at WTNH-TV from 1974 to 1979.

DR. SUZANNE HUFFMAN is an associate professor in the Department of Journalism at Texas Christian University in Fort Worth and serves as the head of the broadcast journalism sequence. She is co-author with Dr. C. A. Tuggle of *Broadcast News Handbook: Writing Reporting and Producing*.

DR. BETSY LEEBRON is a professor and chair of Broadcasting, Telecommunications and Mass Media at Temple University in Philadelphia.

DR. VAL LIMBURG is a professor in the Edward R. Murrow School of Communications at Washington State University in Pullman, Washington. He wrote *Electronic Media Ethics* and writes in the area of media ethics.

DR. JOANNE LISOSKY is an associate professor in the Department of Communication and Theatre at Pacific Lutheran University in Tacoma, Washington. Prior to teaching, Lisosky was a woman in local television at Ozarks Public Television in Springfield, Missouri and KNPB-TV in Reno, Nevada.

STEVE RUNYON is general manager of KUSF(FM) at the University of San Francisco, where he has been for over 20 years. Previous to this he worked professionally in San Francisco broadcasting.

DR. MARY M. STEP is a lecturer in the Department of Communication Science at Case Western Reserve University in Cleveland, Ohio.

DR. ALAN STEPHENSON is an associate professor in the Communications department at John Carroll University and serves at the director of graduate program in communication management and co-ordinator of the JCU Media Archives.

SARAH SULLIVAN is managing editor of *Transnational Broadcasting Studies* (www.tbsjournal.com), an electronic journal published by the Adham Center for Television Journalism at the American University in Cairo.

DR. C. A. TUGGLE is an assistant professor of Electronic Communication at the University of North Carolina, Chapel Hill. He is co-author with Dr. Suzanne Huffman of *Broadcast News Handbook: Writing Reporting and Producing.*

DR. JAN WHITT is an associate professor in the School of Journalism and Mass Communication at the University of Colorado at Boulder.

INDELIBLE IMAGES

Chapter 1 ———————————— by Mary E. Beadle
Michael D. Murray
Donald G. Godfrey

Pioneering Women in Television

An Introduction

Women have worked in television from its inception. Their roles, however, are often interpreted as secondary to their male counterparts. There is little argument concerning the fact that the history of television has been written from a male perspective by primarily male authors. No matter how unintentional, this limits our understanding of television history. As Greda Lerner has described the situation, "Men have defined their experience as history and have left women out."[1] The need in historical scholarship is not in overturning historical understanding but in synthesizing history from both male and female perspectives.

Recent studies in journalism history point to the beginning of that synthesis and indicate the important roles that women have played.[2] Especially in print journalism, women are finally being recognized for their significant roles in media development.[3] Horace Greeley alluded to his wife forcing him out of the house and keeping him focused on his career as he provided leadership for the *New York Tribune* from 1845–1872.[4] It was the wife of Joseph Pulitzer who encouraged him to purchase the *New York World* in 1883.[5] The wife of Cyrus H. Curtis helped create the *Ladies' Home Journal*.[6] The wife and daughter of Adolph Ochs were instrumental in the development of the *New York Times,* and *Life* magazine came about at the urging of Clare Booth Luce.[7] Jane Cunningham Croly was a nationally recognized print journalist and in 1889 founded the Women's Press Club of New York.[8] The working women of New England's textile industry established magazines to redefine the traditional descriptions of "true womanhood."[9] The literature is growing and from this base a new understanding is

3

being blended into traditional history. As Susan Henry described, it provides an "added dimension for understanding . . . women in journalism history."[10]

Women in Prebroadcast History

Understanding the roles of the women in broadcasting is beginning to provide that same added dimension seen in journalism history. The literature surrounding women in broadcasting is abundant, especially if one considers the critical studies of gender, race, ethnicity and stereotyping. These studies decry the image portrayed and call for new understanding, but they add little to the historical understanding of the development of the media.[11] The historical roles of women in radio and television history are just coming to light. For example, books such as *Women Pioneers in Television, Women and American Television: An Encyclopedia, Women Behind the Camera* and *When Women Call the Shots* provide some understanding of the contributions of women in television (and film) primarily at the national level.[12] The purpose of this book is to examine the roles women have played in local television. In the way that *Television in America: Local Station History From Across the Nation* looked at the development of individual stations and their contributions to the history of the industry,[13] *Indelible Images: Women in Local Television*, explores roles and contributions of women in television history.

The importance of women in electronic media history actually began before there were studios or stations. The first telegraph message, "What hath God wrought?" was dictated to Samuel Finley Breeze Morse by Annie Ellsworth. The first woman telegrapher, Emma Hunter, worked for $50 a year in 1851 as an office manager.[14] The Civil War, 1861–1864, brought both men and women into wireless service. As telegraphy developed as a means of rapid communication, there were contests for excellence and operation in telegraph messaging. Telegraphy was replaced by wireless, then radio, but women continued handling commercial and military messages through World War I.

The First Lady of Television

The first lady of television was Elma G. "Pem" Gardner Farnsworth.[15] Pem, as she was called by her friends, appeared on the television experimental scene in 1926. "It would be appropriate," according to Arch L. Madsen, President of the Bonneville International Corporation, "to recognize Elma G. 'Pem' Farnsworth [as] the mother of television."[16] George Everson, who worked through the Depression as a fund-raiser for the earliest television laboratory experiments and authored the first publication on the life of Philo T. Farnsworth, noted that "no small part of [Philo] Farnsworth's success is due to his charming and beautiful wife, Elma Gardner Farnsworth."[17] Philo himself put it more directly: "My wife and I started this TV."[18]

The Farnsworths: Working Together in the Laboratories and the Studio

Elma Farnsworth worked with her husband from the beginning of television. The first laboratory was in the dining room of their Hollywood home. "Bang! Pop! Sizzle" was how she described the lead experiment.[19] It had been put together during the summer of 1926 by Philo, Pem, George Everson and Leslie Gorrell. The "bang, pop, sizzle" came after Farnsworth had hooked everything up and started the generator and it sent an electrical surge through the lines, blowing up everything.

The San Francisco laboratory is where the first Farnsworth television pictures were seen on September 7, 1927.[20] By this time Pem was a member of the San Francisco laboratory staff. In the lab her responsibilities included spot-welding the tube elements as they were assembled. She was also taught how to use the precision tools for constructing the elements of the first tubes.[21] Her salary was $10 per month.[22] A photograph of Pem was one of the images transmitted via the Farnsworth television system. Farnsworth's first experiments, in 1927, were transmitting line-drawn pictures of a triangle and a dollar sign. Photographs were transmitted by 1928 and one of several early photos turned out to be of Pem. Quite literally, Pem was the first woman to appear on television. According to Everson, "They [the photographs] televised much better than the solid black triangle and dollar sign."[23]

Farnsworth's greatest triumph came in August 1934. It was the world's first public demonstration of an all-electric television system and Pem was among the first producers. The demonstration took place at the Philadelphia Franklin Institute and opened August 25. The *New York Times* reported, "Tennis Stars Act in New Television."[24] The headline referenced the appearance of two athletes, Frank X. Shield, New

York, and Lester Stoeffen, Los Angeles. They apparently swung their rackets around and demonstrated their techniques.

A small temporary studio was set up inside the Institute and activities were staged outside, where light was more favorable. Inside, speakers praised the system and paraded before the camera. Outside, more sports figures were parading. The Philadelphia Eagles players Kick Lackman and Roger Kirkman talked football and acted out plays called by their coach.[25] According to Pem, the demonstration was scheduled for a week, but was extended for two weeks due to the crowds that it drew.[26]

The demonstrations were broadcast live to an audience anxiously watching in a Franklin Institute auditorium. Programming ran from 10:00 a.m. through to 10:00 p.m. and featured everything from celebrities to trained animal acts. Pem's role in these demonstrations would be parallel to that of a line producer today. In other words, she helped organize various events, making sure there was something in front of the camera.

Farnsworth Television Incorporated filed for a construction permit for station W3XPF in 1936. Pem received her first studio experience at this station. She and her sister, Laura Player, worked with the live performers on the differing stages preparing them for some of the Philadelphia broadcasts. As stage makeup didn't seem to work for television, a representative of Max Factor was brought in to work with the two sisters in developing proper makeup techniques for the new medium.[27] Pem humorously described one of these events as "boxing in the nude." Apparently, the red trunks of the fighter were not visible on the television monitor so it appeared he was fighting without them.[28]

Philo T. Farnsworth died in 1971, and Pem began to promote the credit for her husband's work. She felt RCA had stolen recognition from Philo in the development of television. Even though Farnsworth had won its patent interference case with RCA, RCA had won the public recognition battle. It was a victory she felt the need to try and reverse.[29] The result of her campaign has been that the popular press and scholarly and textbook portrayal of both Farnsworth and Vladimir Zworykin's (RCA's) contribution to the pioneering of television has been balanced.

World War II Brings Women to the Workforce

The end of the Depression and World War II created what Sterling and Kittross called television's false dawn.[30] In other words, the manufacturers, including Farnsworth, RCA, GE, Philco, Westinghouse and others thought they had a system in place ready for commercial marketing, but the marketplace proved unstable. RCA was so sure about its venture that the 1939 World's Fair exhibition was used to launch the RCA system. The patent agreement between Farnsworth and RCA, reached in 1939, paved the way for RCA to push strongly for the RCA 441-line standard. The manufacturers were coming together and recommending standards. Several of the larger manufacturers began to put their first commercial television receivers on the market for home consumption. However, amidst the optimism World War II was spreading.

World War II halted television's development. All technological developments heretofore marked for commercial manufacturing and home sales were redirected toward military applications. Thirty-two televison stations were authorized before the war, but many never reached the air and, of those that did, few remained on the air into 1942.[31] World War II would bring both prosperity and hardship for the manufacturers, but most importantly it brought women into the workforce in great numbers.

Women in Local Stations

Following World War II, television experienced a boom that caused technical problems and challenges the current rules could not handle. To enable the commissioners to study these and other problems, the FCC stopped processing license applications in September 1948. This action by the FCC, referred to as the "freeze," lasted nearly four years. During this time the few stations on the air made significant progress, but no new licenses were granted. It was during the freeze, as television programming schedules expanded, that women in many locales began gaining familiarity with the potential of the new medium to entertain and inform. In the Midwest, WEWS in Cleveland hired Dorothy Fuldheim as a news commentator and Alice Weston to provide programs for women that included cooking tips and household hints (*see* Chaps. 5 and 18). In St. Louis, Charlotte Peters entertained on KSD-TV, the first television station owned by the Pulitzer Publishing Company, and became the premier female performer on the only television station in that town for many years (Chap. 13). Marcia Yockey was one of the first weather reporters in Evansville, Indiana (Chap. 20).

Yockey was brash, plainly attired and well known for unladylike behavior. Although she had no degree, she is identified as one of a "tiny number of bona fide female meteorologists"[32] in the country.

New rules for commercial television were issued by the FCC in April 1952. Known as the *Sixth Report and Order,* it lifted the freeze and allocated 82 VHF and UHF channels for both commercial and noncommercial use. The postfreeze years saw program development move from local stations to networks. There was an increase in network programs, anthologies, dramas, quiz shows and variety shows. Regular network news service was begun. Local stations moved toward syndicated programs and replaced live local programs with film and videotape. Overall, there was a steady decline in local programming.

However, local news became financially successful in the 1960s and resulted in a major programming effort by the commercial stations.[33] Jean Enersen in Seattle and Wanda Ramey in San Francisco are two of the women who began their news career at this time (Chaps. 4 and 14). In 1954, KUHT-TV became the first educational television station in the country to begin regular broadcasts (Chap. 7). Other noncommercial stations began operations in the 1950s and continued strong local programming efforts through the 1960s.

Women were an important asset in the development of educational broadcasting, working both behind the scenes as producers and on camera as talent. Martha Gable in Philadelphia and Price Hicks and Donna Matson in Los Angeles are three of the leaders in this area of local television (Chaps. 6, 8 and 12).

During the 1960s, television stations were also influenced by social movements. Underrepresented groups, especially minorities and women, lobbied to have opportunities that had been denied to them. For example, in the early years of television, women were rejected as news anchors because their voices were not considered authoritative. Some gained on-air employment in meteorology, which evolved as the domain of "weathergirls" in many local markets, while morning television such as *Today* opened doors for a select few.

Employment Opportunities for Women in Television

"Prior to television few women were employed in radio" and those that did primarily worked on women's programs about housekeeping, fashion, or cooking.[34] As women made the transition to television at both the local and national levels, opportunities were limited, but women were present both in front of and behind the camera. Some of these pioneers include Frieda Hennock, the first woman commissioner on the FCC, appointed in 1948; Betty Furness, an on-air spokesperson for Westinghouse; and Ida Lupino, television director and actor. Some movie actresses made the successful transition to television, including Loretta Young, Dinah Shore, Jane Wyatt, and later on, Donna Reed. Comediennes Gracie Allen, Eve Arden, Audrey Meadows, and Imogene Coca made an impact, and Lucille Ball eventually became head of a major production company, Desilu Productions. In news, Pauline Fredrick covered the United Nations, and Marlene Sanders became the first woman to anchor a network evening newscast. Sanders was also the first foreign correspondent who entered news management and directed television documentaries at ABC News.

Employment of women improved in the 1970s. On June 4, 1969, the FCC adopted its nondiscrimination rule prohibiting discrimination based on race, color, religion and national origin. The FCC was urged by many to include women as an affected group and in May 1971, the FCC issued an amendment to its EEO rules and required stations to take affirmative-action steps for women.[35]

This action resulted in the beginning of many famous careers. On a *Phil Donahue Show* entitled "Newswomen" that aired in 1988, the "class of 1972" discussed their entry into national news organizations. This group included Jane Pauley, Carole Simpson, Lesley Stahl and Diane Sawyer. The local stations also began to hire more women who worked both on and off camera.

The second wave of women pioneers in local television hired under EEO guidelines were frequently given jobs in news as news became the primary role of local programming. Adele Arakawa and Lisa Howard are examples of women who began their careers at this time (Chaps. 2 and 9).

Another change that affected the opportunities for women was the development of cable outlets. Paula Zahn now at Fox says she left CBS at the urging of her mentor, Walter Cronkite.[36] In *Broadcasting and Cable*, Rathbun reported that the cable industry had "an 11 point lead on broadcasting when it comes to the percentage of women in professional jobs."[37] In a study, students at Meredith College in Raleigh, North Carolina, found that 12 percent of those profiled on the "Fifth

Estate" page in that magazine between July 1992 and September 1, 1997, were women (31 out of 262 executives). Further, they discovered a lack of representation of women in the trade press. The report notes: "Women have been slow to make inroads in the field of broadcasting and cable. Only in the last twenty years has the presence of women been substantial enough to note as consistent."[38]

Since the early 1970s women have had more opportunity for a variety of careers in broadcasting and cable and have moved beyond women's shows and weathergirls. In the 1990s, they moved into key positions. Some of these leaders are Kay Koplovitz (USA Network), Geraldine Laybourne (Disney cable programming), Margaret Loesch (Fox Kids) and Lucie Salhany (UPN). Others who have been made inroads to top management include Oprah Winfrey, Martha Stewart, Betty Cohen (president of Cartoon Network Worldwide and Turner Network Television International), Pat Fili-Krushel (president of ABC television network), Jamie Tarses (ABC Entertainment president), and Martha Williamson (executive producer, *Touched by an Angel* and the only female producer to executive produce two dramas simultaneously).

In local markets, women also were in key roles. Dorothy Stimson Bullitt owned a media empire in Seattle with KING-TV as its centerpiece (Chap. 3). Laurel Vlock led a group of women in purchasing a local station in Connecticut (Chap. 17). At the time, the only other woman-owned station was in Austin, Texas, held by Lady Bird Johnson.

Women also began to influence the way in which news was reported. At the local stations this was evident in the types of stories covered, including stories about the homeless, childbirth and education. Women who led this effort include Jean Enersen, Carole Kneeland and Bobbie Wygant (Chaps. 4, 10, and 19). "How Women Took Over the News" describes how a number of prominent women news broadcasters have developed a new style of reporting. Described as objectivity with compassion, Katie Couric of NBC calls it compassion mixed with chutzpah.[39] "This has been a slow process. ABC nearly doubled its number of women correspondents from 1991 to 1998. Women are on every beat in every aspect of news. Their influence is undeniable with more emphasis on story topics such as child care, education, health and the moral aspects of politics."[40] Women also were hired to reach more of the audience since women made up about 60 percent of the viewers of these news shows.

Changes concerning hiring practices again occurred in the late 1990s. In April 1998, the U.S. Court of Appeals struck down the

FCC's 27-year-old EEO rules that mandated the hiring of women and minorities at stations. Since women seem to be an accepted part of television, there seems to be little to indicate that this ruling would have an impact on the hiring of women. Then in January 2000 the FCC ordered broadcasters and cable systems to recruit women and minorities for job vacancies. Members of the FCC were still concerned that the new rules faced the same constitutional problems that got the FCC's previous rules thrown out by a federal court. Employment information released by the FCC in 1997 indicated that women held about 41 percent of jobs in the broadcasting and cable industry. This was up just slightly from 1993, when women held about 40 percent of jobs.[41] Today, these employment figures remain about the same.[42]

So from the early days of television when some women were not hired because their voices were not suitable to overall employment of about 40 percent of the broadcasting and cable workforce, women have played an important role in the evolution of television. Although a few books have documented contributions of individual women to local television, a collection of biographies about the diverse contributions in stations across the country has not been written. This book attempts to fill that gap and to celebrate the women who devoted their time and talents to their community and their profession through their work in local television.

Notes

1. Mitchell, C.C. (1990, Winter). The place of biography in history of news women. *American Journalism, 7*(1), p. 24.
2. Henry, S. (1987, Summer-Autumn). Dear companion, ever-ready co-worker: A woman's role in a media dynasty. *Journalism Quarterly, 64,* pp. 301-312; Henry, S. (1976, Spring). Colonial woman printers as prototype: Toward a model for the study of minorities. *Journalism History, 3,* pp. 20-24.
3. Beasley, M.H. (1990, Winter). Women in journalism: Contributors to male experience or voices of feminine expression, how historians have told stores of women journalists. *American Journalism 7*(1), pp. 39-54.
4. Van Deusen, G.G. (1953). *Horace Greeley: Nineteenth-century Crusader,* p. 154. Philadelphia: University of Philadelphia Press.
5. Swanberg, W.A. (1967). *Pulitzer,* p. 69. New York: Scribners.
6. Playsted, J.W. (1956). *Magazines in the United States,* p. 105. New York: Ronald Press.
7. Swanberg, W.A. (1972). *Luce and His Empire,* p. 120. New York: Scribners; Talese, G. (1955). *The Kingdom and the Power,* p. 55. New York: World Publishing Company.
8. Gottlieb, A.H. (1995, Winter). Network in the nineteenth century: Founding of the woman's press club of New York City. *Journalism History, 21*(4), pp. 156-163.

9. Cronin, M.M. (1999, Spring). Redefining woman's sphere: New England's antebellum female textile operatives' magazines and the response to the "cult of womanhood." *Journalism History, 25*(1), pp. 13-25.

10. Henry, S. (1979-1980, Winter). Private lives: An added dimension for understanding journalism history. *Journalism History, 6*, pp. 98, 102.

11. For a recent example, *see* Furham, A., and Farragher, E. (2000, Summer). A cross-cultural content analysis of sex-role stereotyping in television advertisements: A comparison between Great Britain and New Zealand. *Journal of Broadcasting and Electronic Media, 44*(3), pp. 415-436.

12. O'Dell, C. (1997). *Women Pioneers in Television.* Jefferson, N.C.: McFarland and Co.; Lowe, D. (1999). *Women and American Television: An Encyclopedia.* Santa Barbara: ABC-Clio; Krasilovsky, A. (1997). *Women Behind the Camera.* Westport, Conn.: Praeger; Seger, L. (1996). *When Women Call the Shots.* New York: Henry Holt and Co.

13. Murray, M., and Godfrey, D. (1997). *Television in America: Local Station History From Across the Country.* Ames, Iowa: Iowa State University Press.

14. Moreau, L.R. (1989). The feminine touch in telecommunications. *A. W.A. Review, 4*, pp. 70-83.

15. Godfrey, D.G. (2001). *Philo T. Farnsworth: Father of Television.* Salt Lake City: University of Utah Press. pp. 182–184.

16. Madsen, A. (1979, Dec. 12) Resolution from Bonneville International Corporation. Godfrey Papers, Arizona State University Library Special Collections.

17. Everson, G. (1949). *The Story of Television: The Life of Philo T. Farnsworth,* p. 70. N.Y.: W.W. Norton.

18. Farnsworth, P.T. (c.1960). Speech to Indiana College. Meeks/Farnsworth Papers, Arizona State University Library Special Collections.

19. Farnsworth, E. (1989). *Distant Vision: Romance and Discovery on the Invisible Frontier,* p. 53. Salt Lake City, Utah: Pemberly Kent.

20. Hofer, S. (1979, Spring). Philo Farnsworth: Television's pioneer. *Journal of Broadcasting, 23*, pp. 153-165; Farnsworth, P.T., and Lubke, H. (1930) The transmission of television images. *California Engineer,* pp. 12-22.

21. Farnsworth, P. (nd). Handwritten pages, Box 61, FD #4. Philo T. Farnsworth Papers, Manuscript Division, Special Collections. University of Utah Marriott Library. Salt Lake City, Utah.

22. Early television laboratory personnel. (nd). George Everson and Philo T. Farnsworth Papers, Arizona State University Library Special Collections.

23. Farnsworth, P.T. (1927, Feb. 27). Correspondence from Philo T. Farnsworth to George Everson, Box 2/1. Philo T. Farnsworth Papers, Manuscript Division, Special Collections. University of Utah Marriott Library. Salt Lake City, Utah.

24. Tennis stars act in new television. (1934, Aug. 25). *New York Times,* p. 4.

25. Televising football. (nd). Philadelphia Record Morgue V72272. Historical Society of Pennsylvania. Philadelphia, Pa.; Moon makes television debut in pose for radio snapshot. (1934, Aug. 25). *Christian Science Monitor;* Utah lauded for progress of television. (1934, Sept. 3). *Salt Lake Tribune,* pp. 4-5; Television is near as adjunct to radio, young inventor says. (1934, Aug. 30). *Philadelphia Evening Public Ledger,* p. 10; Farnsworth, P.T. (1934, Oct.). Television by electron image scanning. *Journal of the Franklin Institute, 218*(4), pp. 411-444.

26. Farnsworth, E., 1989, p. 154.

27. Farnsworth, E., 1989, p. 172.

28. Farnsworth, E., 1989, p. 172.

29. Farnsworth, E., 1989, p. 214.

30. Sterling, C., and Kittross, J. (1990) *Stay Tuned: A Concise History of American Broadcasting* (2nd ed.). Belmont, Calif.: Wadsworth.

31. Sterling and Kittross, 1990, pp. 632–633.

32. Henson, R. (1990). *Television Weathercasting: A History,* p. 81. Jefferson, N.C.: McFarland and Company.

33. Murray and Godfrey, 1997. p. xxv.

34. Lont, C. (1995). *Women and Media: Content/careers/4criticism,* p. 172. Belmont, Calif.: Wadsworth.

35. *Window Dressing on the Set: Women and Minorities in Television.* (1977, Aug.). A Report of the United States Commission on Civil Rights, p. 75. Washington, D.C.

36. How women took over the news. (1999, Oct. 2-9). *TV Guide,* p. 18.

37. Rathbun, E.A. (1998, Aug. 3). Women's work still excludes top jobs. *Broadcasting and Cable,* p. 25.

38. Rathbun, 1998, p. 24.

39. How women took over the news, 1999, p. 17.

40. How women took over the news, 1999, p. 18.

41. Rathbun, 1998, p. 27.

42. Eggerton, J. (2000, July 3). TV news is diversifying. *Broadcasting and Cable, 130,* pp. 4-5.

Other Sources

Acceptance and dedication of the statue of Philo T. Farnsworth. (1990, May 2). Proceedings in the Rotunda of the U.S. Capitol, Washington, D.C.: U.S. Government Printing Office, p. 58.

Barnouw, E. (1968). *The Golden Web* (Vol. 2) of *A History of Broadcasting in the United States* (Vols. 1-3). New York: Oxford University Press.

Beasley, M., and Gibbons, S. (1993). *Taking Their Place: A Documentary History of Women and Journalism.* Washington, D.C.: American University Press.

Head, S., Sterling, C., and Schofield, L. (1994). *Broadcasting in America* (7th ed.). Boston: Houghton Mifflin.

Hosley, D., and Yamada, G. (1987). *Hard News: Women in Broadcast Journalism.* New York: Greenwood.

Marzolf, M. (1977). *Up from the Footnote: A History of Women Journalists.* New York: Hastings House.

Sanders, M., and Rock, M. (1988). *Waiting for Prime Time: The Women of Television News.* Urbana: University of Illinois Press.

Streitmatter, R. (1994). *Raising Her Voice: African American Women Journalists Who Changed History.* Lexington, Ky.: University of Kentucky Press.

Adele Arakawa. (©*9News/Andy Schaeffer*)

Adele Arakawa

A Commitment to Professionalism

Adele Arakawa, co-anchor of the weeknight KUSA Channel 9 news team in Denver, had just finished having an early lunch with her husband on the morning of April 20, 1999. When she arrived at home, she turned on the television and heard a special report that made her catch her breath: There were gunmen at a high school in Littleton, Colorado.

Arakawa was on the scene an hour after the shooting began, and she would report live for much of the day, not leaving the scene until 2:30 a.m. As the story unfolded, viewers were horrified to learn that two Columbine High School students, Eric Harris and Dylan Klebold, had shot 12 of their classmates and one teacher to death and had wounded 23 others. It was the worst school shooting in U.S. history.

In spite of her compassion for the victims and her concern for the survivors, she focused on her professional responsibility to the public. "You are doing your job. Later, you go home and maybe hug your child more and tell him you love him. You talk to your spouse about the experience. But on the scene, you do your job."[1]

Because of Arakawa's commitment to journalism, her coverage of the Columbine High School tragedy was praised by viewers, fellow journalists and state media critics. Joan Ostrow, television and radio critic for *The Denver Post* said, "Channel 9 was first on the air with the story and set the pace . . . in terms of meaningful reporting, graphics, helicopter footage, photography and calm anchors. . . . Arakawa most astutely covered the TV angle, noting the need for media discretion in giving details and strategies. . . . She refrained from discussing numbers of fatalities until they could be confirmed."[2]

Arakawa believes her job is to relay information as calmly and neutrally as possible, even if the news is terrifying. "I was taught years

15

and years ago that the primary function of a journalist is to inform and educate."[3]

The Columbine High School shootings and their aftermath were not the only devastating news stories Arakawa has covered. She also reported live after the bombing of the Alfred P. Murrah Federal Building in Oklahoma City in 1995. She was there for three days, working 18 hours a day. "Later, you wonder why you can't sleep and realize that you have to deal with your feelings in some way."[4]

Arakawa compares her reaction to a crisis such as the Oklahoma City bombing with that of medical personnel called to the scene. "When I am in that kind of a situation, I become like one of the paramedics, detached and deep into my job. I know that I am there to inform and report the facts. I am not there to react to them. I can tell you that the tears came days later when I got home."[5]

Largely because of her professionalism during crises such as the shootings at Columbine High School and the bombing of the federal building in Oklahoma City, Arakawa is today the top female anchor in the Denver television market. She is also a proud representative of the Japanese American community.

Arakawa's mother, who lived in Hawaii and was of Japanese descent, met Adele's father, an American soldier, during the war. Adele Arakawa was born in Knoxville, Tennessee, August 31, 1957, but grew up in both Hawaii and La Follette, Tennessee. When she was a child, she was one of only a few Japanese students in La Follette, a town of approximately 12,000 near the Kentucky border. It was here she realized she was "different" from all the other kids when one day a couple of other second graders called her "Nip" and "Jap." Her mother told her to ignore the taunting and eventually it did stop.

Arakawa's mother believed so strongly that Adele and her sister should assimilate that she did not teach them to speak Japanese, nor did she talk with them about Japanese culture. "We were raised as 'all-American' kids," Arakawa said. "I understand her reasoning—and I know she understands my desire to keep in touch with my Asian heritage."[6]

Being on the receiving end of taunting has given Arakawa what she calls a "perspective of tolerance." Occasionally, she still receives an unsigned hate letter from someone asking why a "slant-eye" or a "Jap" is doing the news.[7]

That pain is mitigated by the positive experiences Arakawa has had with Asian American viewers in Denver, especially children. In

July 1999, for example, Arakawa conducted an interview with 12-year-old Ashton Do and 15-year-old Angie Blum. Do is a Vietnamese American; Blum is half Vietnamese and half Caucasian American. She told the children, "My mother was a war bride. She was born and raised in Maui, which is where her family lived. So I'm what they call in the islands 'Hapa-Haoli,' which means I'm half white."[8]

When she worked at WBBM-TV in Chicago, she was especially engaged in activities involving members of Asian American communities. "In that circle of acquaintances, you do learn a lot about these local communities' commitment to their ethnic background. They contacted me and sought me out. And I've had the opportunity to help them, and they have helped me in return."[9]

Arakawa celebrates her connection to the Asian American community, although she balances that allegiance with the tenets of fairness in broadcasting. "While a primary function must be to remain unbiased in this business, I believe it is acceptable for a journalist to encourage and pursue stories of personal interest. . . . All the while, we have to remember the cardinal rule of fairness and balance."[10]

Channel 9 often integrates Asian Americans into larger subjects. In the weeks before the October "Race for the Cure," a national fundraiser for breast cancer research, Channel 9 ran a different story each night about breast cancer. Arakawa's contribution to the series was a story about a Chinese American woman who had been diagnosed with breast cancer six years before. The story was designed to remind viewers that Asians also develop breast cancer and that the topic must be discussed with their families. The women of Channel 9 were chairpersons of the 1998 and 1999 races and participate in the event each year. Arakawa said of the event: "It's one of the most uplifting experiences I have ever been involved with."[11]

In addition to her visibility as an anchor on Channel 9 news, Arakawa is often featured in publications of the Japanese American community. She was the subject of a cover story in the January-March 1994 issue of "Mile-Hi Notes," a newsletter of the Japanese American Citizens League (JACL). In addition to the JACL, Arakawa is a member of the National Association of Asian American Professionals and the Japanese American Service Committee. She is also former president of the Chicago chapter of the Asian American Journalists Association.

As one Denver broadcast critic said, Arakawa "doesn't buy into the notion that her steady rise in the industry is based primarily on being an attractive woman who happens to be half Japanese."[12] Instead, she attributes her success to a great deal of hard work and a hefty dose of luck. "I'm very competitive, but while I'm competitive, I've learned that this is a business of lucky breaks. No matter how competitive or talented you are, it takes lucky breaks to get somewhere in broadcasting." She also said that she has never tried to hide the fact that she is one-half Japanese but she has not "tried to capitalize on the fact."[13]

Bringing ethnic and gender balance to the anchor team at Channel 9 is not Arakawa's only contribution. She is also a role model for young women in journalism schools across the country, and her contributions to women in the industry are often noted by viewers, fellow journalists, educators, and students in Colorado and elsewhere.

Lee Hood, a member of the broadcast faculty at the University of Colorado at Boulder and a former news producer at several Denver television stations, said of her:

> She has elevated the stature of female anchors in Denver. She is extremely credible and an excellent communicator, whether at the news desk or in the field. . . . Behind the scenes, Adele is a serious journalist who stays on top of news events and takes on an editor's role. That kind of preparation and command of the news add to the credibility viewers see and make her one of the most important forces—male or female—in Denver television today.[14]

Marguerite Moritz, associate dean of the School of Journalism and Mass Communication at the University of Colorado, believes that having accomplished women anchors as role models is essential for her students.

> The majority of students in journalism programs today are women. Many aspire to be anchors, and I'm always happy to point to Adele Arakawa as a role model—someone who is very open and available to an audience but also a solid journalist. . . . Any time you watch her, it's clear that she knows the news. There is no fluff and a lot of substance.[15]

Arakawa is 43 years old and was recently awarded a six-year contract. Some women in television believe that such contracts mark a new trend in television news history. One of those women is Christine Craft. She filed a lawsuit after losing her job at KMBC-TV in Kansas City and wrote *Too Old, Too Ugly, and Not Deferential to Men.* Craft said that there are now "several stations savvy enough to figure out that the population is aging, that news audiences will accept older men and women at the anchor helm. . . . In some environments experience is a valued and saleable commodity."[16]

Ed Sardella, who recently retired as Arakawa's seven-year co-anchor at KUSA, believes that the industry still bases its evaluation of the talent of individual anchors largely on gender. "I believe that Adele has transcended the standard anchor talent gender categorization and can now be considered the leading news anchor in the Denver market, regardless of gender, virtually without debate. Adele, almost immediately after her arrival, became the number one female anchor talent in the market, demonstrably and significantly superior to any other female talent at the time or since."[17]

When Arakawa started her career, television and radio were seen as career choices for men and the industry was male dominated. Today there is more equality both in front of and behind the scenes, but Arakawa still sees a need for more women in upper management. In her 27 years in broadcasting she has only worked for four female news directors. She also is concerned about salary equity but is encouraged by female anchors and reporters working well into their 40s and 50s.[18]

Arakawa's inspiration is her mother, Katsuko Arakawa Hausser, 75. Recently retired from teaching elementary school, her mother works in a church library; tutors; teaches Sunday school; visits shut-ins; and takes care of her father-in-law, making daily trips to a nursing home out of town. Arakawa speaks highly of her mother. "My hero is my mom. She is the person who deserves the credit or blame for making me who I am. She always told me: Whatever you do, just do it to the best of your ability. I'm sure she had reservations about my career choice . . . but she encouraged me to pursue it because she knew I liked it."[19]

Her other hero is her older sister, who recently retired as a lieutenant colonel in the U.S. Army's military police branch and now lives in Alabama. Arakawa admires her "strength, resilience, fortitude, independence, sense of humor, intelligence, and inner beauty."[20]

Arakawa was only 16 when she became a disc jockey and anchor at WLAF-AM, a radio station in La Follette. Soon after, Arakawa skipped her senior year in high school, although she earned her high school degree in 1975. Arakawa surprised her parents by telling them that she wanted to leave school and work full time in radio, and at the age of 18 she became news director at WYSH-AM in Clinton, Tennessee. In 1977, Arakawa moved to Knoxville, where she became the first female disc jockey at WRJZ-AM. Arakawa began a major in secondary education with a minor in journalism at Tennessee Tech University, but she dropped out of college after attending both Tennessee Tech and the University of Tennessee.

Today Arakawa cautions young people not to follow in her footsteps and reminds them how competitive the industry is, but she also has no regrets about her decision to move into the industry without a college degree. "At that time, very few women were in broadcasting," she said. "The opportunities were there. At the age I would have graduated from college, I had almost three years of full-time experience in a field that women were just breaking into."[21]

One of the reasons she now recommends that journalists graduate from college is that she and others at KUSA demand strong grammatical skills and a solid knowledge of world events. "My pet peeve is those who cannot spell and have a weak command of the English language," Arakawa said. "If we are charged with the responsibility of informing and educating through the English language, how can we do so without knowing the difference between 'its' and 'it's' or 'there,' 'they're' and 'their'? Communication is a skill. Our language is the tool."[22]

By 1981, Arakawa was working in Knoxville as an anchor, reporter and producer at WTVK-TV, then an NBC affiliate, where she had begun as a weekend weather forecaster on the 6 and 11 p.m. weekday newscasts. She gradually gained experience in photography, editing, and production. From 1983 to 1989, Arakawa worked in Raleigh, North Carolina, anchoring two weeknight newscasts at WRAL-TV.

Then Arakawa moved to Chicago and worked for WBBM-TV from 1989 to 1993. She was co-anchor of the 4:30 p.m. news and later co-anchored the 6 p.m. news with Bill Kurtis, formerly host of *CBS Morning News* and now seen regularly on the Arts and Entertainment Network. She also shared anchoring duties with Lester Holt, who is now with MSNBC. Arakawa was the primary reporter for the 10 p.m. news at WBBM. Eric Ober, former news director at WBBM and later president of CBS News, spoke highly of Arakawa in a 1994 interview with *Rocky Mountain News* media critic Dusty Saunders. "She not only had great camera presence, but her experience as a reporter and editor made her a valuable news asset."[23]

Since 1993, Arakawa has been co-anchor of the 5 and 10 p.m. news on weeknights at KUSA, breaking the 35-year, all-male anchor tradition at the station. In spite of her longtime success at Channel 9 in Denver, Arakawa continues to believe what she recently told reporter Andrea Jacobs: "Broadcasting is a 'flighty business.' If you're lucky enough to land some place where your family's happy and you can stand to work out the rest of your career, then you've got the best of both worlds. And that's all I've ever wanted in this business."[24]

Arakawa thinks the gathering and disseminating of news is a high calling that demands the best of those who enter the industry.

> I believe the focus of the industry has changed over the years. In the beginning, I believe the intention was indeed to inform and educate. Now, local stations and national outlets must compete for portions of a pie that keep getting smaller and smaller. To effectively compete, stations must sell a product. They must entice viewers.
>
> I guess what disheartens me most as the years go by is the callousness of the young people getting into the business. Many could not care less. They don't read a newspaper, watch television news, or know the number of congressional districts in this state, much less the name of the candidates. They're in it to feed off the business, not to make a contribution to it.
>
> I worked for an assistant news director who actually told me: "It's time you got that big 'J' off your chest" ("J" stood for journalism.). I almost quit the business at that point. Fortunately, I found a station in a smaller market that still had a journalistic conscience, although still admitting that news is a product that must be marketed. It becomes a compromise."[25]

According to Arakawa, the anchors at KUSA maintain some editorial control, especially over individual scripts.

> Our nightside executive producer, Jene Nelson, is from the "old school" and the best around; she controls content. With such controls in place, the end product is something I often feel proud of. How many people in this business can honestly say that?
>
> There is too much emphasis on performance and cosmetics versus content and knowledge. There is not enough accountability. That said, the industry still has much to offer—and it's my deepest desire to see responsible, impassioned young people carry on a strong journalistic tradition for all of us who pass the torch.[26]

Viewers and media critics have recognized Arakawa's talent and have rewarded her with praise and with awards. Joanne Ostrow, *Denver Post* television and radio critic, believes Arakawa set the standard for a local newsperson.

> She is not only a poised anchor presence behind the desk but she performs well in the field. From the first, Denver viewers could tell there is a brain at work behind this face, something we can't say for all local anchors. Arakawa knows how to be accessible in a visual medium while holding onto old-fashioned notions like good journalism.[27]

In a June 18, 2000 article about the retirement of Arakawa's co-anchor, Ed Sardella, Ostrow called the team "the most authoritative anchor pair in town." In that article, Ostrow again pays tribute to Arakawa: "In late 1993 . . . Sardella was paired with Chicago import Arakawa, who immediately impressed viewers as a star in her own right. The team of Sardella and Arakawa took the station's late newscast to new ratings heights, last year scoring the highest audience levels for any network affiliate in the country."[28]

Arakawa's awards have been plentiful. Named Best Female TV Anchor by *Denver Post Online* in 1999, Arakawa "has been perceived as a smart, likable newswoman with a good delivery and a very strong presence, able to ad lib or read a script, hold down the anchor desk or go live from the field." She has been chosen Best Local TV Anchor by *Westword's* "Best of Denver" in 1996, 1997, 1998, and 2000. She was first runner-up as Best Local Television Personality in the Colorado Community Newspapers (CNN) in 2000.

Named top anchor in an eight-state region, Arakawa earned a Heartland Emmy Award in 1999, bringing KUSA's total number of awards to 15 that year. Nominated as Outstanding News Anchor in the Heartland competition in 1994, 1995, 1997, 1998, and 1999, Arakawa won best anchor in 1997 for her reporting of the Oklahoma City bombing and trial and again in 1999 for her coverage of the tragedy at Columbine High School. Arakawa's sense of humor surfaced after winning the 1995 Hottest Female Reporter Award from *Quest* magazine, a gay monthly in Denver. Bill Husted, a columnist for the *Rocky Mountain News,* said that an editor at *Quest* magazine had called her selection a "nearly unanimous decision." When Husted asked Arakawa her reaction to the editor's statement, she replied: "Is that right? The best part is they called me a reporter. But I thought I was too old to be 'hot.' I'm getting past the 'hot' age. I'll be lukewarm in a few weeks."[29]

Now the mother of a 16-year-old son, Arakawa has been married for 23 years. She protects the identities and privacy of both her husband and son by not using her married name, although it is her legal name, and says that her family has always been her first priority. "While I'm competitive, I'm not driven. There is a difference. I've seen too many women put their job ahead of family life. I won't do that."[30]

Arakawa, who loves Colorado and enjoys playing golf, racing cars, and being outdoors, is pleased with the contract and confident in her commitment to the station. She believes that her determination to balance her personal life and her career has helped her to succeed in an increasingly competitive television news market.

It has been a long time since Arakawa sent out 50 audition tapes and received 10 rejections and 38 "no responses" to her application for a job in broadcasting. Although Arakawa expresses concerns about the future of television news, she is characteristically optimistic about its contributions. "It's competitive and there are a lot of young people getting into the business for the wrong reasons right now, so it's a little frustrating for people who have been in it a long time. But the payoffs are that I do feel like I'm making a difference sometimes, and I feel like I am fulfilling an obligation. I do have a large responsibility, and I want to do it right."[31]

Notes

1. Pomeroy, A. (2000, June/July). After the shooting stops. *Media Human Resources Association News,* p. 8.
2. Ostrow, J. (1999, April). Horror tests media mettle. *The Denver Post Online* [On-line]. Available: www.denverpost.com.
3. Jacobs, A. (nd). Arakawa's strength anchors 9News' efforts. *Colorado Media* [On-line]. Available: www.coloradomedia100.com.
4. Pomeroy, 2000, p. 8.
5. Johnson, W. (1999, April 22). La Follette native on school scene. *The (Knoxville) Sentinel Weekend,* p. 22.
6. Arakawa, A. (2000, Sept. 28). Personal communication.
7. Arakawa, 2000, Sept. 28.
8. Do, A., and Blum, A. (1999, July 11). Interview with Adele Arakawa. *Asia Press* [On-line]. Available: www.asiaxpress.com.
9. Do and Blum, 1999.
10. Arakawa, A. (2000, Oct. 3). Personal communication.
11. Brandorff, D. (1998, Sept. 20). Race for the cure selects honorary chairs. *The Denver Post.*
12. Saunders, D. (1994, Feb. 6). Colorado people. *Rocky Mountain News,* pp. 7M, 8M.
13. Saunders, 1994, p. 8M.
14. Hood, L. (2000, Oct. 15). Personal communication.
15. Moritz, M. (2000, Oct. 6). Personal communication.
16. Craft, C. (1988). *Too Old, Too Ugly, and Not Deferential to Men,* Rocklin, Calif.: Prima Publishing. p. 208.
17. Sardella, E. (2000, Oct. 13). Speech. Metropolitan State College, Denver, Colorado.
18. Arakawa, A. (2000, Oct. 3). Personal communication.
19. Arakawa, A. (2000, Sept. 19). Personal communication.
20. Arakawa, 2000, Sept. 19.
21. Arakawa, A. (2000, Sept 22). Personal communication.
22. Arakawa, 2000, Sept. 22.
23. Saunders, 1994, p. 8M.
24. Jacobs (nd).
25. Arakawa, A. (2000, Oct. 11). Personal communication.
26. Arakawa, 2000, Oct. 11.

27. Ostrow, J. (2000). Personal communication.
28. Ostrow, J. (2000, June 18). Sardella departure, bittersweet. *The Denver Post,* p. 7H.
29. Husted, B. (1995, Aug. 8). Magazine honor surprises TV celebs. *Rocky Mountain News,* p. 2.
30. Saunders, 1994, p. 8M.
31. Do and Blum, 1999.

Other Sources

Sanders, M., and Rock, M. (1988). *Waiting for Prime Time: The Women of Television News.* Chicago: University of Illinois Press.

Dorothy Stimson Bullitt, KING-TV (Used by permission of the Bullitt family)

Dorothy Stimson Bullitt

Queen of Broadcasting and Her KING

The first television station in the Northwest was shaped and developed into an institution dedicated to serving its community of Seattle and the Puget Sound. That shaping was accomplished by Dorothy Frances Stimson Bullitt, perhaps the first and foremost woman in the history of broadcasting. Her active work in the leadership of KING-TV and its subsequent broadcasting empire, which can be used as a classic text in successful broadcast management, offers lessons in character and values.

Dorothy Bullitt was the first to transact the sale of a television station, buying the newly made television station that was to become KING-TV in 1949. She was a powerful business executive who was deeply involved in her community of Seattle and wanted to give to it the benefits of public service of her broadcasting stations. She was a friend of powerful political figures and the daughter of a wealthy timber baron. She began the management of her family's station as a widow and mother of three and ended overseeing its broadcast activities at the age of 97. In many respects, she was a remarkable woman but the genius lay in the details of her administration. Only a glimpse of her management of the stations can be cited here, but perhaps there is some insight into the keen leadership and business genius of this grande dame of broadcasting.

Dorothy Stimson, the daughter of a pioneer lumber entrepreneur in the Northwest, was born to wealthy parents in 1892, just three years after Washington had become a state. Her father, C.D. Stimson, was owner of an expansive acreage of timberland in the Cascades and president of a mill that had become one of the largest producers of lumber. Later, that wealth was invested in a number of successful business ventures, including real estate holdings in Seattle. Her mother, Harriet, became a force in Seattle social circles. She helped found the Seattle Children's Home, medical facilities, and the Seattle Symphony. Young Dorothy was to acquire the talents and affinity for the goodness of both her mother and father—a shrewd sense of business from her father and a heart for charity, the arts and community development from her mother.

As a girl, Dorothy exhibited leadership qualities. At age 10, after she became local marble-playing champion, her father ordered her to get rid of her marbles. She negotiated with the owner of the local soda fountain and got a line of credit for ice cream sodas and the right to make them herself.[1]

As a young woman, she attended finishing school in New York and then returned to a thriving Seattle. In 1922, when radio had begun to storm across the country, Dorothy heard music late one night from a choir hundreds of miles away. She marveled and was curious about this phenomenal invention. It was a curiosity that would spawn into an interest in the medium's ability to inform, entertain and, of course, make money.

In 1918, she married Scott Bullitt, a promising law school graduate with an active interest in politics. She was 26, he was 40. In 1926, the aspiring politician ran for the U.S. Senate and lost. But politics seemed to run strong in his veins, a determination that did not go unnoticed by Dorothy, now a mother with a young son and two little girls. In 1928, he ran for governor against a populist. Again, Bullitt lost. Still, he stayed active in politics and was elected national committeeman for the Democratic Party. A few years later, while attending a party meeting in Washington, D.C., Scott took ill. It was only a matter of months before his death. Dorothy was left with three young children and no husband. Her father and brother had died not long before.

It was the onset of the Depression and Dorothy Bullitt was shouldered with the responsibility of raising her family and managing the family businesses in an era when women rarely ran businesses. Fortuitous breaks came that allowed the sale of some properties. Carefully, she was learning business skills, talking openly with associates, sizing up deals, and coming to understand something about cash flow and the bottom line. But perhaps the most important talent she was developing was the people skills that came to make her a renowned and trusted business legend. She became active in social and political circles, and her presence became an expected sight at high-level occasions.

In a self-description contained in a family-authorized biography, Dorothy Bullitt is quoted as admitting "it was difficult being a woman in the financial world during those days. I didn't know what I was doing."[2] The biographer went on to note that "Dorothy could see that the passive role of a society matron would never work for the challenges before her. She knew that a privileged upbringing would have to be supplemented with a firm stance, strategic thinking, and straight talk. She would have to combine a soft voice with hard decisions and an ingratiating smile with a will of iron." In her later years, she noted in an address to career women that she "had some men friends who counseled me and gave me support that I would never have [had] if I'd been a man. . . . Men gave me every help I ever asked for. And they still picked me up for lunch, picked up the tab afterwards, paid the taxi fares—which kept expenses down—and I hope it stays that way."[3]

Dorothy Bullitt may have used some of the wiles of a charming woman. She didn't want to look dominant, but she had subtle ways of suggesting ideas. She seemed passive but was no-nonsense and kind. She often did that which was unexpected of a woman of that day, keeping her associates just a little off guard. She was punctual in her meetings. Her style was subtle, quiet and unobtrusive, not strident. She understood male territoriality; she let men think that her subtle suggestions were theirs. They could take the credit; she got the business at hand accomplished.

Dorothy Bullitt first came into broadcasting when her cousin, Frederick Stimson, spoke to her of the promise of radio technology. Although it was the 1940s and there were many radio stations in existence, the idea fascinated her. She applied for an FM license in a medium that was mostly unknown. But the year was 1941 and the government put a freeze on the spectrum space used for FM stations. She settled for an AM radio station that had almost no listening audience. This became her first big challenge in the business of broadcasting: to turn the ho-hum into success.

One of her first steps was to change the call letters. Since she was in King County and since the call letters had to be four letters starting with K, it seemed logical to use the identification of KING. But the letters were held by a U.S. shipping-board freighter, the *Watertown*. Mrs. Bullitt negotiated with the ship's owner and acquired the letters.

It was a one of the first demonstrations of her skill in negotiation. KEVR became KING.

Bullitt began to create an image for the station, even hiring Walt Disney to draw a cartoon microphone with a king's crown to symbolize the station. The station's format featured a little something for everyone. The station began broadcasting Seattle Rainier baseball games with Leo Lassen, who became the city's first sports broadcast personality. His announcing was so compelling that soon the station's audience grew. The enterprise was becoming financially viable.

Perhaps one of the most compelling stories about the remarkable Dorothy Bullitt is her move into television. It began in 1947. Bullitt had already acquired a reputation for being a shrewd, creative and reputable businesswoman. After some research into this new, unknown and altogether chancy medium and after some advice from inside professionals such as Hugh Feltis, who worked for Frank Stanton's Broadcast Management Bureau, she was convinced to buy into television. In the meantime, Palmer K. (P.K.) Leberman operated an AM and FM station, KRSC, and held the license for an unbuilt television station. He had as an expert assistant, Lee Schulman, who urged him to develop TV. Seattle's first TV station began its broadcasts in late November 1948 with a state championship football game played on Thanksgiving Day. Not only was it a first broadcast, it also was a *remote* broadcast.

Leberman's station had beaten the FCC freeze imposed upon the growth of TV and was the only TV station in town. If Dorothy Bullitt wanted to invest in television, she could acquire KRSC-TV or wait until the FCC freeze was lifted. The larger looming question was one of good business: could this medium, with such expensive apparatuses and such a voracious scheduling appetite be profitable? Bullitt thought that it could be.

After just two years in radio broadcasting, Dorothy Bullitt was ready for the venture in television. At a time when a television station had never been sold from one owner to another, Leberman had estimated the value of the station to be somewhere between $350,000 and $400,000. Perhaps this was low, but he was anxious to get out from underneath the mounting debt of the enterprise. Or perhaps this price was high; not many people had that much money to invest in an operation that was demonstrating itself *not* to be profitable. No one really seemed to know the value of the station.

Arrangements were made for Leberman to come to Bullitt's home. After dinner, Bullitt began negotiating for the station. Even though Leberman's broker, who was present, urged him to sell at a higher price than Bullitt's offer, Leberman was anxious to sell. According to one account, Mrs. Bullitt looked at Leberman and said, "Now we've talked about this, and we'd like to know exactly what we are talking about—a little more exactly than the $350,000 to $400,000 which Hugh [Feltis] tells me you quoted." Leberman tried the bluff: "How's $375,000?" She looked at him sharply and said, "How's $350,000?"[4] Leberman knew he had that much in hand from a reputable businessperson. He agreed.

It was reportedly the first sale of a television station in the United States, and a woman, Dorothy Bullitt, had made the transaction. Her standing in the community, her financial assets, her increasing prominence as a business head, and her highly skilled managers brought her to this unique achievement. But powerful as she was becoming, she would still take the leap of faith into the unknown aspects of the new medium. This, together with her reputation as a community leader, built the expectation of the new station to serve the community and at the same time be a successful and profitable business venture.

As the station began its operation, the call letters became KING-TV. It got a running start as a powerful presence in local news and captured the ever-increasing audience of viewers' fascination with this new visual medium. Early in its schedule KING-TV ran the hydroplane races from Lake Washington, a popular event of the area. It brought viewers to TV and a reputation for the station of serving the public's interest.

Local news was being shaped. Bullitt hired a dynamic young news reporter, Charles Herring, who undertook events with a film cameraman and showed himself on the spot. In addition to news, Dorothy Bullitt brought attention and favor to her station by hiring the best people in public affairs programming and children's programming. She cultivated them to produce imaginative programs that both reflected the community and was interesting to them. Not everyone knew the prominent political figures in Seattle, but everyone, it seemed, knew the characters on *KING's Clubhouse,* the popular afternoon kid's show. Another show, *Televenture Tales* won national awards and furthered the station's image of prestige. Mrs. Bullitt's personal interest in children's shows and her work with the shows' stars demonstrated her personal touch in the station's programming. In 1958, KING's children's show *Wunda Wunda* was given recognition by winning a Peabody Award, the first non-network children's show to be given this distinction.

Since 1952, KING-TV had had commercial competitors and could no longer take the pick of the best programming from four networks. It was left with a failing DuMont and a weak ABC network, usually third in the program ratings. The enterprise was still not profitable. Could she survive? With the flurry of interest in television as a national medium, Bullitt was able to interest the Hearst newspaper empire in buying into the station. Two years after her original purchase, she sold 25 percent of its stock for more than her purchase price: $375,000. Needless to say, it added stability to the business and still allowed control by her and the family.

The Hearst company encouraged Bullitt to expand, and she did. She applied for a TV station license in Portland and in so doing acquired a long-reputable radio station, KGW, from the *Oregonian* newspaper. Later, her company was to acquire stations in Spokane and Boise. The KING empire was beginning to spread.

About this time, Dorothy worked to become the Seattle affiliate of the better-positioned NBC network. She wined and dined NBC executives, including David Sarnoff himself and kept notes on his top aides. After many trips to New York for discussions and after meeting Sarnoff in Seattle on a trip to visit KOMO-TV's O.D. Fisher, Dorothy convinced NBC executives that KING-TV was more in keeping with the innovative traditions of the network. The results turned out to be a major shake-up of a 32-year affiliate relationship of KOMO with NBC.

Spurred by the kinds of investigative news documentaries aired on the networks by the likes of Edward R. Murrow, KING-TV looked at the local scene and found issues to be uncovered at its doorstep. Dorothy watched as her station boldly took on the issue of corruption and theft by organized crime in the port of Seattle and along its docks. With unprecedented hype, a 90-minute documentary, *Lost Cargo*, aired. The community and the nation sat up and took notice. It was the first documentary of its kind at a local station, much to the credit of its producer/host, Robert Schulman. Because of the business and economic clout behind the show, most notably Dorothy Bullitt, investigations triggered by the exposé cleaned up the corruption and put the business of the port on a healthy track.

Such news efforts were not the only precedents for KING-TV news. In 1954, years before they were popular, the station acquired a helicopter for news-gathering purposes. Some of new reporter Herring's stories caught national attention, such as when he interviewed Teamster's Union President Dave Beck and got a concession from him. Also, KING-TV was first with news commentaries. Although they were dull at first, they were Dorothy Bullitt's way of trying to educate the community and serve the public interest.

Ironically, although Bullitt was from an elite, prosperous family, she encouraged the development of a news documentary, *Bitter Harvest.* It was a program about the poor and the migrants, so advertisers were not anxious to place ads on a program where they wouldn't have much economic influence. But it was the year of Murrow's *Harvest of Shame* and heroic efforts in politics and journalism. This was Dorothy's idea of an unselfish, if not heroic, effort in business.

Other programs not forgettable to the Seattle audience included *The Volcano Named White,* a tale of a black man convicted of killing two people. The sympathetic treatment seemed controversial enough that no advertisers could be found for the program. Dorothy Bullitt felt it to be so powerful that she decided to run it without commercials. The program drew the attention of other parts of the country, and it aired in New York City. Reactions were mixed, but it achieved the recognition of an Alfred Dupont Award for programming. *Newsweek* cited it as "unlike anything ever done in television."[5] The magazine quoted Dorothy Bullitt as stating that her stations could make more money by simply buying programs but that she would rather see her station do such striking programming. It was a model of public service and responsibility that was rare because it chose to subordinate profit to broadcasting's ideals. It was a high watershed for the industry, put there by a woman who became nationally recognized by her professional broadcasting colleagues.

In 1961, Dorothy decided to turn the daily management over to her son, Stimson. He was a quiet man with the trappings of an intellectual. During the decade that he ran the station, he made some decisions that caused many to question his good judgment. After several frictions and a decade at the helm, Stimson Bullitt eventually left the overseeing of the station to his mother.

Even though she was at the age when many had long since retired, she gladly took on the challenge. Dorothy suggested to the board that

Ancil Payne become manager. He could work well with people, especially with Dorothy and her two daughters, who were on the board. Payne was to run the station in close collusion with Dorothy from 1972 until 1986.

One of KING-TV strengths came to be its respected female reporter and news anchor, Jean Enersen. She was popular with viewers, and worked well with Payne and Mrs. Bullitt. Although Dorothy was no modern-day feminist, she knew that women were often underestimated and underchallenged. She had experienced that herself dozens of times. She seemed to see in Jean Enersen a fulfillment of the challenge that she had begun back when men thought that businesses and critical administrative duties could not be done by women. Enersen's tenure at KING-TV surpassed nearly everyone's except, of course, Dorothy Bullitt's.

As Dorothy grew older, her style at the station seemed to mellow. She was often seen chatting with employees. Those who knew her felt a genuine kindness from her, even though she would not intervene or persuade Payne to play favorites. She trusted her manager to carry on her interests and even her approach to responsible broadcasting. They seemed to rise to the occasion together.

After Stimson left the station's management, editorializing stopped. But Dorothy wanted it to continue as a means of contributing to the community and showing courage by taking stands. She asked Payne to undertake the editorials and—to further make them part of the station's institutional image—to have him do the on-air editorializing. After agreement on the stands to be taken, Payne began the task and the station returned to an image that had previously been dwindling.

Dorothy gave Payne almost complete autonomy. He invested in the latest equipment. He became chairman of the NBC affiliates board, the liaison between the stations and the network that fed them programming and national advertising revenues. In all these tasks, he showed skills and management know-how. Dorothy had found a gold mine in Ancil Payne for continuing the legacy that she had started.

Dorothy Bullitt carefully observed the rigorous, independent efforts of the news operation. She liked the journalistic tradition of independence and respected that, although on more than one occasion she didn't like the approach of a story. Once she tried to urge Payne to fire a reporter when it was alleged that he had visited the family of a murder victim and had gone through the victim's personal belongings. The reporter denied the claims. Payne believed him and convinced Dorothy to give the reporter the benefit of the doubt.

On another occasion, Dorothy's grandson Ben had apparently been partying on Lake Washington and disappeared. A serious and expensive effort was undertaken to find him or his body. When the local media got wind of the search, it made headlines. Even KING news got in on the story. Neither Mrs. Bullitt nor any of the family members sought to censor or even dictate how to handle the story.

Dorothy once told her granddaughter her formula for success in business: "Set the overall goal; hire good people; then step aside and let them get the job done."6 It was an ideal that she managed to hold to and show her commitment to that which went beyond personal convenience.

KING-TV news was the first in the Puget Sound area with footage of the horrific explosion and damage from the eruption of Mount St. Helens in 1980. In 1985, KING and Soviet Gostel radio produced *A Citizens' Summit,* a two-hour discussion between audiences in Seattle and Leningrad. Phil Donahue and Vladimir Pozner were the hosts. It was really a star in KING's crown. It was one of many shows about the Soviet Union in the 1980s. One observer commented that perhaps KING was one of the instruments that helped bring about an end to the Cold War.

By the mid-1980s, total pretax profits had grown to $44.5 million annually on net revenues of $134.7 million. Its annual growth was 12–15 percent. Payne indicated that although the business was capital intensive, it was very lucrative.

Toward the end of the tenure of Ancil Payne, the company was still acquiring broadcasting properties. Although Mrs. Bullitt seemed satisfied with its current size, she'd get excited when she'd see new opportunities. The venture of business opportunities was still in her heart.

By the end of the 1980s, Dorothy Bullitt seemed ancient, nearly as old as the state of Washington, which celebrated its centennial in 1989. She had attended the funeral of her good friend, Warren Magnuson. Stories circulated about the effect of her age. How competent could a 97-year-old person be? According to one biographer, "Stories circulated at KING that the old woman had become senile. She closed her eyes and seemed to drift from the conversation. But in fact, when she didn't want to deal with someone, she occasionally pretended to be senile."[7] Still she stayed on her daily routine of going to the station and chatting with the employees. Eventually she cut back on her contact with others, perhaps because of her ever-slipping memory. Dorothy Bullitt passed away on June 27, 1989.

While Dorothy had been less active in the day-to-day operation of the station in her final years, nevertheless, could the station truly survive without the energy and inspiration of Dorothy Bullitt? Her daughters, members of the station's executive board, tried to allay the fears of an age-old institution falling apart. But doubts continued. The charisma of her leadership was absent. Management changes began to unfold, and new management saw things differently than when Dorothy was alive. Some saw stridence in contrast to the KING family harmony that Dorothy appeared to have engendered. Some observers thought that the company was so devoted to the bottom line that the rigor, the courage and the aggressive position of its news faded. Soon firings began to take place in a way that was unthinkable during Dorothy's tenure. One trade publication reported that KING made "major bonus payments" to those leaving in exchange for a three-year silence about the station.[8]

Earlier, everyone had talked of Mrs. Bullitt's station, in much the same way that the British might refer to government matters belonging to the Queen. But the Queen of this enterprise was gone, and there was no successor to the throne. In 1990 the Bullitt daughters announced the station would be sold, and in 1991, the Providence Journal Company bought it.

The radio stations were not part of the deal; they were sold to other buyers with a reputation for responsibility. The FM station was bought by Mrs. Bullitt's daughters, who later donated it to a consortium of nonprofit arts organizations: the Seattle Symphony, the Seattle Opera, and the Corporate Council for the Arts.[9] The family also formed a foundation to help serve environmental issues, causes dear to the heart of Dorothy's daughters. Also out of the deal grew Northwest Cable News, a connection of regional cable news from the property's stations. It was a good source for revenues while serving news and public affairs, now to a broader region of the Northwest. Perhaps Dorothy would be pleased at such arrangements.

Notes

1. Corr, O.C. (1996). *KING: The Bullitts of Seattle and Their Communications Empire,* p. 13. Seattle: University of Washington Press.
2. Haley, D. (1995). *Dorothy Stimson Bullitt: An Uncommon Life,* p. 156. Seattle: Sasquatch Books.
3. Haley, 1995, p. 157.
4. Feltis, H. (1991). Oral history interview conducted by Hugh Rundell in March 1976. Transcribed in Burt Harrison (ed.), *They Took to the Air: An Oral History of Broadcasting in Washington* (abridged). Pullman, Wash.: Washington State University, Murrow School of Communication.
5. Radio and television. (1962, Apr. 9). *Newsweek,* p. 71.
6. Corr, 1996, p. 222.
7. Corr, 1996, p. 257.
8. Top 20 markets: Year in review. (1992, Jan. 13). *Electronic Media,* p. 32.
9. Taylor, C. (1994, May 13). KING-AM purchase provides "critical mass". *Seattle Times,* p. E1.

Other Sources

Boss, K. (1990, Aug. 21). It's time to grieve, whoever the new owner might be. *Seattle Times,* p. A5.

Boss, K. (1990, Nov. 30). Sweeps bring KING-TV a ratings victory—of sorts. *Seattle Times,* p. B1.

Broadcasting and Cable Yearbook. (1993). p. C-71.

Duncan, D. (1990, Aug. 22). Pioneers in broadcasting. *Seattle Times,* p. A1.

Geehan, J. (1991). Oral history interview conducted by Hugh Rundell in July 1977. Transcribed in Burt Harrison (ed.), *They Took to the Air: An Oral History of Broadcasting in Washington* (abridged). Pullman, Wash.: Washington State University, Murrow School of Communication.

Gregory, N. Norm Gregory's Pacific Northwest time line [On-line]. Available: http://gregory.com/shn/tvtl.html.

Haas, D. (1991). Oral history interview conducted by Hugh Rundell in June 1976. Transcribed in Burt Harrison (ed.), *They Took to the Air: An Oral History of Broadcasting in Washington* (abridged). Pullman, Wash.: Washington State University, Murrow School of Communication.

KRSC-TV takes air tomorrow with grid game. (1948, Nov. 24). *Seattle Times,* p. 28-G.

Priebe, R.E. (1991). Oral history interview conducted by Hugh Rundell in June 1977. Transcribed in Burt Harrison (ed.), *They Took to the Air: An Oral History of Broadcasting in Washington* (abridged). Pullman, Wash.: Washington State University, Murrow School of Communication.

Richardson, D. (1981). *Puget Sounds: A Nostalgic View of Radio and TV in the Great Northwest.* Seattle: Superior Publishers.

Jean Enersen covering the news. *(©KING 5. Reprinted with permission.)*

Jean Enersen

A Woman of Roots and Wings

Nestled in the hills between Lake Washington and the Puget Sound, between the Olympic and Cascade mountains, the Seattle area is uniquely endowed, if not defined, by its distinctive geographic features. As the largest city in the state of Washington, Seattle reigns as the cultural and commercial center of the region. Settled by loggers and fishermen, the city has also been championed by pioneering women—especially in the television industry. In fact, Seattle's most famous broadcast pioneer, Dorothy Stimson Bullitt, amassed a Pacific Northwest television empire in the 1950s that included stations in Seattle, Spokane and Portland.

On the high heels of Dorothy Bullitt, television today in Seattle remains distinctive in that its most revered and award-winning television journalist is not a silver-haired 60-year-old man, but a blonde 50-something woman: Jean Enersen. Enersen, who began her broadcast career as a newsroom note-taker, has been recognized for the last three decades as not merely Seattle's quintessential *female* television journalist but also as the most renowned television personality in the Puget Sound area. Enersen has been part of the evening news at KING-TV in Seattle since the early 1970s and has lived up to the label "anchor" in a marine town that understands the definition of the word.

Jean Marie Stanislaw Enersen's early years were spent not far from where she makes her home today in the Seattle area. She credited her supportive and loving family with providing the initial preparation for her celebrated career as a television journalist. She said this training began when she was a child at the dinner table, where her parents encouraged her and her siblings to read newspapers and magazines and keep up with contemporary issues. She said her father encouraged his children to discuss the pressing issues of the day and he would often play devil's advocate to keep the debate going. "Contemporary issues were always part of our dinner."[1]

In addition to her father's coaxing, Enersen said she also gained an appreciation of narrative prose by listening to her mother's fantastic Irish storytelling. Her mother also reminded Jean that she should use two things in her life: one was roots, the other, wings. "By roots she meant know where you came from and what your values are and by wings she meant you have lots of people telling you to try this and go there, so be adventurous."[2]

Initially, Enersen chose a career in teaching and attended Stanford, where she was completing a Ph.D. in political science during the Vietnam War. Unfortunately, her fellowship from the government was cut short because of the war effort. With the help of her faculty advisor at Stanford, she parlayed her other advanced degree, in broadcasting and film, into a writing position at KPIX-TV in San Francisco. Enersen said she was never disappointed because she left academe for broadcasting or that her teaching career was never realized. In fact, she believed "television to some extent is teaching to a large audience."

Her position at KPIX included collecting notes for other male television reporters. "It was a very hands-off job at the beginning," she explained. She worked the overnight shift in the Tenderloin district in San Francisco at KPIX. Her job included riding along with a photographer "who liked to jump out of buildings and interview prostitutes." She said this was quite an eye-opener for someone who grew up rather sheltered in an academic household in the Pacific Northwest, but she was testing her wings as her mother had recommended. "I think to some extent they thought this would either kill me or cure me."

The cure didn't take because when a position opened up in her hometown at KING-TV, she took it and moved back to Seattle. She started at KING as a secretary in news operations, doing clerical and filing jobs—anything to stay close to the newsroom.

Enersen's move back to KING-TV had been remarkably fortuitous. The philosophy of the station under its president, Dorothy Bullitt's son, Stimson Bullitt, was significantly ahead of its time in its attention to controversial political and social issues. Stimson Bullitt was considered a maverick when he read the nation's first television editorial against the Vietnam War in 1966.[3]

Bullitt also promoted another relatively unpopular agenda at the time by consistently hiring women and minorities for responsible positions at his station. In his book on the history of KING-TV, Daniel Jack Chasan reported, "In the mid-1960s virtually no one was hiring [women and minorities]—and KING Broadcasting Company wouldn't have hired them either, if Stimson Bullitt hadn't insisted."[4]

Ancil Payne, who took over the helm of KING in 1972 from Stimson Bullitt, agreed Stimson was very pro-female: "He was really a driving force in hiring women and was able to make a difference because he was an upcoming owner of the company that had a big share of the business."[5] Payne continued this practice when he took over as president of KING in 1972, although advocating for women in television was hardly a new approach for Payne. A few years earlier in Portland, Oregon, he had hired the first woman anchor on the West Coast.

Payne recalled how he explained his rationale for hiring females to a male colleague who objected to Payne's hiring the first female radio news reporter in Seattle. The colleague remarked there was no way he could hire a woman to do news on the radio because he could never ask a woman to cover a murder on Skid Row. Payne explained to his colleague: "We're not asking her to cover a murder in Skid Row; she's asking *us* to cover a murder in Skid Row. There's a big difference."[6]

Enersen admitted she was lucky to be at KING in the late 1960s. "We were all aware that we worked with and for a very special family. Many times when they hired us, they were taking a real risk. . . . What they looked for in the beginning were young people . . . with a natural curiosity or intelligence, without necessarily the experience in television. They supported us and provided us with the tools and opportunity and vision."

Her good fortune and tenacity paid off when, in her mid-20s, she worked her way up to an on-air reporting position at KING-TV. Not long after she began working on air, Ancil Payne decided to move Enersen over to the programming department to co-host the talk show *Telescope,* which was the local continuation of the *Today* show. "I thought it would help her with her voice levels and help her become more animated in her voice, and it did."[7]

Payne's idea to bring Jean over to the talk show offered her more opportunities than developing her vocal skills. She learned to perfect her interviewing skills as well. She said, "One of the lessons I learned from the talk show was that no matter what your stature or your profession, you are nervous or uncomfortable or lack confidence in some area or another." As a new interviewer in this talk-show format, she gained an appreciation for what her guests went through on the air. She used this experience to develop a genuine rapport with the people she interviewed.

For a while, Enersen shuttled between both the programming and news departments at KING: "I did a talk show in the morning and reporting in the afternoon." The mastery of her skills as an interviewer did not go unnoticed at the station. O. Casey Corr reported in his book about the Bullitt communication empire that "previously in news she [Enersen] had been a little stiff, a little clumsy, and not very good—sent to do vegetables at Pike Market. But in the talk format, she was relaxed, warm, and attractive. The camera loved her. It brought out her natural personality and brains."[8]

This was a difficult time financially for KING-TV. Cigarette advertising had been pulled from the air, and the networks had relinquished a half-hour of programming back to the affiliates. As a result, local affiliates had additional programming expenses at the same time a major revenue source had been unplugged. KING-TV was struggling to regain its foothold in the ratings, battling neck and neck with KOMO-TV. Under the direction of the general manager, Eric Bremner, KING-TV took steps to re-establish its leadership in the market. To do this Bremner proposed the station launch a major initiative to regain its strong position in news.[9]

In 1971, Norm Heffron, the news director at KING-TV, took the mandate from Bremner and proposed a bold new idea for his 11 p.m. broadcast. The idea came from a public television show he had seen in San Francisco where reporters casually discussed the news of the day as if they were in someone's living room.[10] He wanted Enersen to be part of the anchor team because he felt she was qualified. Ancil Payne agreed.

Payne noted, "Jean was recognized for her spark. Among other things she had an excellent educational background. She was charismatic, and from the first, she was a believable person, a local person. And though she's not Scandinavian, she looks it and that doesn't do any harm in this market."[11] Payne thought this was a good idea not just because it was time to promote women to prominent areas in the television business, but also because it was simply good television business. "We realized that women did a different job on the air and had a different attraction, and you always tried to broaden your offerings as much as you could to draw the widest variety of people to your station."[12]

Enersen was excited about the notion of anchoring the late news, but she also realized this venture had its hazards. She said, "It was something I had pursued for a long, long time. I guess I had to prove that if it was risky, then it was a risk worth taking." The idea had its share of detractors. Initially, many were convinced the idea would flop because few women were anchoring the news anywhere in the United States, and no women were anchoring in the Seattle market. Additionally, this new format was shocking: no anchor desk and no formality— just chatting between the two anchors. "Some in the KING news department asked how could a third-string reporter, a personality from the entertainment side of KING, be given a senior journalistic position? And the format? They sneered that it was 'Chatty Cathy and Her Boy Friend.'"[13]

But Bremner did not see the prospect of putting a woman on the anchor desk as much of a gamble: "It was certainly something very overdue, and we recognized that not only could women fully contribute on any level, they represented in some ways a relatively untapped resource. I don't remember having any trepidation about the strength of Jean as a co-anchor. . . . Jean is a survivor and a treasure."[14]

From the start, the new anchor and the new format were a success. Enersen was teamed with several new hires until the station found Jim Harriott in New York. Their chemistry clicked. Corr reported, "No one credited the set or Harriott. It was the blonde. People liked her. There was something sincere, sexy, and intelligent about her. Both men and women liked her."[15]

Enersen continued to hone her skills in those early years on the anchor desk. She admits to sometimes being treated differently because of her gender, "but once I was accepted, the guys were a lot of fun and very encouraging." She said she responded to bias or discrimination by just working harder and being herself.

> I worked with an anchorman, Jim Harriott, who had been in the business for quite a while and was very encouraging and very supportive. When I would fill in, I would sit next to him and he would be very helpful, and I would try to be like him because I thought he was very good. But he was more than six feet tall and he had a great big voice. Early on I realized that I couldn't be like him. That I wasn't really big and tall and I didn't have a big voice. So I had to be like me and that was a breakthrough.

Not long after her success on the late night news, Enersen was introduced to the main news broadcast at 5:30 p.m. but not immediately as the anchor. She said, "I would go on and fill in and they would see how it went, then I would go on and fill in more frequently and finally it became a regular job." The station's ratings grew and so did Enersen's popularity.

In 1974 Jean Enersen was recognized in *The New York Times* as one of a handful of women who anchored a daily television news program in an article about how women were changing the face of local television.[16] Enersen was reported to "sit on the anchor desk because ratings indicated that she pulled women in the 18-to-34 age bracket with 'real buying power.'"[17] The article also supplied national statistics from government records for 1973 showing 23 percent of the full-time employees of the country's 614 commercial television stations were women. Of these, 69 percent were clerical or office workers. Jean Enersen was among the few women working not in the television typing room but in the television newsroom.

Enersen also retained her presence in the programming department after she began anchoring. Under the auspices of the programming department, she helped produce documentaries that received local, national and international critical acclaim.

Even *The New York Times* noticed, just two years after she began anchoring, how Enersen was promoting her values and spreading her roots through program content at KING-TV. In 1974, Enersen co-anchored a series on breast cancer detection during the 6 p.m. news. She said the program ran despite some male executives' misgivings that the subject might be wrong for the dinner hour. The station conducted a survey after the series ran that revealed 80 women mentioned the program when they subsequently sought treatment for breast cancer and of those 80, 76 required surgery.[18]

Ancil Payne suggests that Enersen's work on controversial subjects has been her greatest contribution to local television. He recalled that it was Jean who brought area television audiences their first look at the AIDS epidemic. "It was when people were afraid to shake hands with people who were HIV positive. Jean did a wonderful half-hour documentary with a person who was suffering from AIDS."[19] He added that Enersen went to the home of the AIDS victim and had coffee with him. By doing this, he said, she broke down some of the hysteria surrounding the dreadful disease. For this work, she won a Special Jury

Award from the San Francisco International Film Festival (1986) and a Public Enlightenment Award from the Greater Seattle Business Association (1986).

More recently Enersen has promoted her own values when in 1998 she hosted what Seattle newspaper critic John Levesque called "a thoughtful, powerful documentary," *Poverty in the Land of Plenty,* on poverty in the Seattle area.[20] Levesque added that the program was a call to action and a rich addition to the KING-TV's library of responsible programming.

During her career, Enersen has tested her wings by pursuing a number of extraordinary stories both geographically and fundamentally beyond the purview of the average *local* television reporter. Payne credited Enersen with contributing to the end of the Cold War when, in 1988, she was the first U.S. journalist invited to appear live on Soviet television to provide commentary on Soviet society. Her commentaries were presented live and uncensored to Soviet citizens for five days on the nationally broadcast Soviet program *120 Minutes.* "Such freedom of comment on Soviet television by an American journalist was unprecedented."[21] Earlier in 1987, Enersen had joined a U.S. high school teacher and his wife on a visit to a Russian artist in Leningrad. She subsequently hosted the program that resulted from this historic visit, *Face to Face: U.S./U.S.S.R.*[22]

Enersen again ventured into international waters in 1993 when she became the co-host of a weekly series, *Asia Now,* which was co-produced by Seattle's public television station KCTS and NHK in Tokyo. The program was seen on 62 public stations in the United States as well as in Thailand, Singapore, Hong Kong, South Korea and Japan.[23]

When the Kosovar refugee situation heated up in Albania, KING-TV again turned to Jean Enersen to report from abroad. She traveled to Albania in 1999 with a team of volunteers who treated the refugees. A Seattle television critic commented on Enersen's live reports from Albania, saying they included information that was not readily supplied by the networks. The critic added that Enersen's stories were vivid and too few.[24]

Enersen believes she has been lucky to experience such adventures and to work for a station with such a global vision. She added, "You see bumper stickers that say 'think globally, act locally' but the people I work for really believed that and understood Seattle's unique geography and unique opportunity to connect with the rest of the world. . . . That's the thing that makes KING so special." Another thing that makes Enersen an anomaly in local television news is her loyalty to her hometown station despite her vast resume. In a business known for its mutability, Enersen has remained at her hometown station for over 30 years. Ancil Payne recalled when Jean went to *Today* in 1986 to fill in for vacationing Barbara Walters. At that time, NBC would routinely invite an anchor from one of the large-market affiliate stations to replace the vacationing national talent. But this practice posed a recurring problem when the local anchor returned and became increasingly difficult to work with because she felt she belonged in New York. Jean just wanted to have the experience and then return home.[25]

Eric Bremner posited that Enersen's greatest achievement has been her ability to retain her stature as the region's foremost television journalist for so many years. "She has worked hard not only to preserve but also to increase her skills and talent. She is just as strong a personality on camera, just as effective a communicator, and just as respected and trusted in the community today as she was six months after we put her on the air as an anchor."[26]

Ancil Payne agreed that Enersen has remained absolutely unchanged. He stated, "She is no more a prima donna today than when was when she started. The way she has grown shows in the work that she has done."[27]

Much of what Enersen's audience sees everyday is her continued enthusiasm for what she does. She said she still enjoys her job because of the people she meets. "You think you've seen it all; then along comes something that you've never seen and once again you're surprised and amazed by human kind and I'd say it happens on a weekly basis." Enersen also credits the people she works with for contributing to her success. "I'm very sure that one of the things that makes an anchor successful is to work with a good team of people, for example, our team at KING. We all get along well and have a lot of fun on the air, in the office and during the commercial breaks. I think that teamwork and that conviviality comes through."

Yet, despite all of her accomplishments, Enersen admits that her greatest achievement as a woman in local television doesn't have anything to do with television but her ability to balance her work and her family. "It has always been my main goal to have a balanced life and to have a family and to take the responsibility to give back to the community and to constantly be learning and to share with other people what I was learning, whether it was teaching or reporting."

It was her quest for a balanced life that compelled Enersen to scale back her hours at KING in 1998 and relinquish her anchor chair at the 11 p.m. newscast, the spot she has held since 1972. "I want to spend more time with my family, and this affords me that chance."[28]

And it seems Enersen has also made the Puget Sound residents her extended family. She has given back to her community through community service that has included serving as president of the YWCA, volunteering at battered women shelters, participating in the annual Northwest AIDS Walk, and contributing to the King County Boys and Girls Kids Auction. Not surprisingly, she is also a member of the Washington World Affairs Fellows.

Enersen continues to be recognized for her contribution to the field of broadcast journalism both in and outside the Seattle area. The July 2000 *RTNDA Communicator* acknowledged Jean Enersen as one of the nine women and minorities who changed the face of news in the United States.[29] Some of her other awards include Silver Circle (1994), two Seattle regional Emmys (1988, 2000) and an Excellence in Electronic Journalism Award (1992) from the Radio Television News Directors Association (RTNDA) for the series *Where Has All the Water Gone?*

Enersen says she has witnessed many changes in the nearly three decades she has worked in television. Her time at the helm at KING has spanned from the 1970s, when only 23 percent of the total workforce in the television industry was female, to 1999, when an RTNDA/Ball State University survey showed the number of women in television *news* had reached an all time high of 40 percent.[30]

Following the legacy of other strong women like Dorothy Bullitt, Enersen has become an integral part of the history of television in Seattle. Following her mother's advice, she planted her roots and promoted her values through the stories she tells. She has used her wings to pursue significant stories in her backyard and to fly to remote areas of the world to witness and tell these stories to her hometown family.

Notes

1. Enersen, J. (2000, Aug. 9). Personal communication. (Note: All undocumented quotes in this chapter are from this source.)
2. Dunnewind, S. (1999, May 9). Things their moms told them: How these Seattle notables achieved prominence. *The Seattle Times* [On-line]. Available: http://archives.seattletimes.newsource.com.

3. Chasan, J.C. (1996). *On the Air: The King Broadcasting Story.* Anacortes, Wash.: Island Publishers.
4. Chasan, 1996, p. 151.
5. Payne, A. (2000, Oct. 10). Personal communication.
6. Payne, 2000.
7. Payne, 2000.
8. Corr, O.C. (1996). *KING: The Bullitts of Seattle and Their Communications Empire,* p. 204. Seattle: University of Washington Press.
9. Bremner, E. (2000, Sept. 9). Personal communication.
10. Corr, 1996.
11. Payne, 2000.
12. Payne, 2000.
13. Corr, 1996, p. 204.
14. Bremner, 2000.
15. Corr, 1996, p. 204.
16. Dullea, G. (1974, Sept. 28). The women in TV: A changing image, a growing impact. *The New York Times,* p. 18.
17. Dullea, 1974, p.18.
18. Dullea, 1974.
19. Payne, 2000.
20. Levesque, J. (1998, Oct. 6). KING-TV's look at poverty is a powerful documentary. *Seattle Post-Intelligencer,* p. F6.
21. Caulfield, D., and Weinstein, S. (1988, Apr. 25). Morning report: TV and video. *The Los Angeles Times,* p. 2.
22. Chasan, 1996.
23. Enersen to do international show. (1993, Mar. 18). *The Seattle Times,* p. F8.
24. McFadden, K. (1999, July 4). Anchorwomen who hold sway on the Northwest shows offer their perspectives on the profession. *The Seattle Times,* p. M1.
25. Enersen, 2000.
26. Bremner, 2000.
27. Payne, 2000.
28. McFadden, K. (1998, Jan. 30). Enerson (*sic*) inks new contract. *The Seattle Times,* p. F2.
29. Papper, B., and Gerhard, M. (2000, July). Women and minorities: Nine who changed the face of news. *RTNDA Communicator,* pp. 28-35.
30. Women and minorities in radio and TV news. (2000, July). *RTNDA Communicator,* pp. 36-37.

Other Sources

KING5. The Home Team: Jean Enersen [On-line]. Available: http://www.king5.com/local.
McFadden, K. (1999, Apr. 15). Reporting from Kosovo—and pitching for dollars. *The Seattle Times,* p. C1.

Dorothy Fuldheim on her news set at WEWS-TV. *(Courtesy of John Carroll University Media Archives, University Heights, Ohio)*

Dorothy Fuldheim

A Legend in Local News

When WEWS in Cleveland signed on in December 1947, few of the early staff believed the medium would last. One of those disbelievers was Dorothy Fuldheim, a pioneer in Cleveland television history. Dorothy Fuldheim was the first female newscaster in the United States.[1] Whether it was her flaming red hair, her love of clothes and jewelry, or her distinctive interview and commentary style that attracted viewers' attention, she was unmistakably a legend in local television. She kept her hair bright red because she knew that when she walked down Euclid Avenue, people would recognize her.[2] Bianculli wrote, "She is an individual in a business that thrives on conformity."[3]

As Hickey, a television critic for *The Cleveland Plain Dealer,* wrote in his article celebrating 30 years of WEWS, there were no manuals, no directions as to how it was to be done, no one with experience; it was pure trial and error.[4] WEWS was the first television station in the Cleveland market and one of the first stations in the United States.[5] The early employees often made up procedures as they went; there were no guidelines for them to follow. Initially, Fuldheim did not quit her other employment when WEWS hired her. She was too unsure of the future of television. As her doubts about the future of television began to fade, she gradually focused her energies on the development of WEWS.[6]

Dorothy Fuldheim began her career as a television news anchor at an age when most people are beginning to think about retirement. At age 54, Dorothy Fuldheim signed on with the Scripps-Howard Broadcasting Company two months prior to the station going on the air.[7] The station manager, James Hanrahan, hired Fuldheim, in part,

51

because of her local popularity and notoriety as a book reviewer. Mote wrote, "Dorothy's unique style of reviewing a book could enthrall an audience. She used no notes. Not satisfied to only relate the story to her audience, she dramatized the character roles."[8] Her dramatic flair led listeners on an adventure with every talk she gave. Drawing on her expertise as a book reviewer, teacher, and stage actress, Dorothy Fuldheim fascinated, repelled, intrigued, and rankled viewers on a daily basis. Known for her intellect and quick wit, she was said to be the consummate interviewer.[9] In some years of her television career, she conducted over 250 interviews.[10]

The Early Years

Dorothy Violet Schnell Fuldheim was born in New Jersey in 1893; she was one of four children, three of whom survived to adulthood. Her family moved to Milwaukee, Wisconsin, in search of a better life. The family was very poor and lived in the central city area. Despite their poverty, her parents emphasized finding a talent and developing it. Fuldheim found she possessed an overwhelming desire to learn and use the power of language. Her siblings nicknamed her "dictionary-swallower." She also was an avid reader and read daily.

Her love of the language and reading led to a career as a schoolteacher. Fuldheim graduated from the Milwaukee Normal School and began teaching. After three years, she was drawn to the stage.[11] Fuldheim's first appearance was with the Little Theater in Milwaukee. Fuldheim soon moved on to Chicago to pursue her career in the theater. Three years later during a performance of the anti-war play *The State Forbids,* Jane Addams, the famed social reformer, spotted Fuldheim. Addams was organizing a lecture for the peace movement and she asked Fuldheim to speak in Philadelphia. Although Fuldheim was unsure of what she was supposed to speak about and unsure of her public speaking abilities, she agreed. According to Winfrey, this speech launched her career as a lecturer.[12]

Fuldheim traveled extensively throughout the midwestern United States as a lecturer. Her fee: $10.00. Fuldheim's ability to read, analyze, digest, and present information served her well throughout her career. Fuldheim read as many as 12 books a week in preparation for book reviews, lectures, and news analysis.[13]

Early Broadcasting

Fuldheim's first venture into broadcasting was with WJW radio in Cleveland, Ohio.[14] She was later hired by the Brotherhood of Railroad Trainmen for a biweekly radio show on ABC Radio. Every other week she traveled to New York and presented a news commentary and analysis show. Fuldheim's forthright style as a lecturer transferred to her role as a news analyst.

Initially, Fuldheim was hired in 1947 at WEWS to anchor the evening news. At this time, major advertisers sponsored most television programs. Duquesne Beer, the original sponsor of Fuldheim's news commentary and analysis objected to "her interpretations of the news—something nobody was doing on the new medium." Fuldheim's response was, "Maybe nobody is doing it because you haven't found anybody qualified to do it!"[15] Fuldheim's popularity in the Cleveland community and the support of WEWS' management convinced Duquesne Beer to sponsor Fuldheim's commentaries. Fuldheim's relationship lasted 17 years, making Fuldheim the longest sponsored personality on air.[16]

Not only was Fuldheim the sole news commentator in this new industry, she also was the only woman. She said, "He [Hanrahan] was the only man in the country willing to give a woman a chance to anchor a news show."[17] This career opportunity Hanrahan provided was not lost on Fuldheim but she reported feeling very lonely as the only female newscaster in a male-dominated industry; she always felt like an outsider. Fuldheim told Nancy Gray in an interview that despite a public persona that was quite outspoken, she never asserted herself with the men who worked behind the cameras.[18]

Dorothy Fuldheim anchored the local news for WEWS for 10 years. According to Hickey, Fuldheim set a standard within the industry and for women everywhere: "A half-century before Gloria Steinem appeared on the news scene, Dorothy Fuldheim was a liberated woman. She said her piece and said it well. . . . [Her unique contribution to the station which has employed her this past 25 years is that she gave it a priceless gift—a personality and soul of its own."[19]

In addition to anchoring the evening news, Fuldheim co-hosted a live variety show called the *One O'clock Club* with Bill Gordon. The *One O'clock Club* was an hour and a half show that combined talk, cooking, book reviews, and interviews. Gordon described Fuldheim as "the consummate professional. . . . [W]e didn't have teleprompters. Back in those days we ad-libbed everything off the top of our heads. She was unusual and incredible. And people have been copying that format ever since."[20]

During this time, Fuldheim sparkled. "She would sit on stage without a note and literally bring a book to life. It was not so much a critique as it was a dramatization."[21] Book reviewing became an art when presented by Dorothy Fuldheim. Regine Kurlander, a writer for the *Plain Dealer* commented, "Although she has the uncanny ability to retain every scrap of information that she unearths, Dorothy Fuldheim is an Impressionist. When she has absorbed a volume, it comes forth, without notes, accurate to the last detail but distinctly her own, colored by her vital personality, and enriched by the background of her tireless reading."[22]

The *One O'clock Club* lasted for seven years on WEWS. Designed to attract a female audience, in the earliest years of the show Fuldheim appeared in elegant gowns; men wore morning suits and striped trousers.[23] Even when men changed to business attire, Fuldheim continued to dress in elaborate costumes. Mote described the interaction between Fuldheim and co-host Bill Gordon as vaudevillian in nature. The two personalities played off one another very well. The show was all live—they did not rehearse their act prior to airtime. Gordon wrote about Fuldheim, "The queen of England never did better. I'm not kidding. She would sweep in (although short in stature, she somehow managed to 'sweep in') and stroll (that's the word, sort of a combination of strut and flaunt) toward the stage and there would be a feeling of awe from the audience. I actually saw people sitting there with their mouths agape."[24] Fuldheim's "overall contribution to the station cannot be measured. . . . [S]he has given every one in the medium [a] target of excellence to aim for."[25]

Over 20 years after her death, director Jim Breslin spoke fondly of her. Dorothy "was one of those people everybody wanted to see and hear, even if they didn't like her."[26] He was delighted to share tales of bringing his wife's homemade tomato soup in for Dorothy's lunch on a regular basis. He recalled her fondness for chocolates—lots of them. Former cameraman Charlie Step's wife, Bev, laughed about having baked gingersnaps for Dorothy on a regular basis also.[27]

According to Bill Gordon they called her "Big Red" behind her back. He noted her presence was such that she was "Queen of all she surveyed."[28] "Nobody ever said she couldn't do something; it was 'my way or not all' with Dorothy."[29] Jim Breslin also recalled when Fuldheim was interviewing then-President Jimmy Carter. Breslin was sitting in his office preparing for the show when he heard, "Pardon me Mr. President, . . . JIM, where's my coffee??!!"

In an article in *Ms.*, Nancy Gray wrote, "Before Barbara Walters there was Dorothy Fuldheim."[30] Fuldheim's vast experiences included interviews with every president of the United States from Franklin D. Roosevelt through Ronald Reagan. Her interviews with world leaders included Hitler, Anwar Sadat, the Duke of Windsor, and Pope Pius XII. Her favorite interviewee was Helen Keller. Fuldheim also interviewed Albert Einstein, Jerry Rubin, Madame Chiang Kai-shek, Gypsy Rose Lee, Charlton Heston, Tennessee Williams, Carol Channing, Jimmy Hoffa, Helen Hayes, and Martin Luther King, Jr., among others. Perhaps her favorite tale about an interview was the day she threw Jerry Rubin off her show. "I threw Jerry Rubin off my show because his manners were bad and his arrogant attitude offensive. . . . [H]is manner, his attitude, his indictment of everything that was decent and disciplined made me sick. I was filled with wrath at the so-called hippie who disclaimed everything the establishment stood for."[31]

A show that moved Fuldheim greatly was her commentary about the shootings at Kent State University on May 4, 1970. After visiting the campus earlier that day, Fuldheim shared with Clevelanders her pain and anger for what had happened. "As I recounted their deaths I called it murder, for these four were no housebreakers, they were no killers, no drug addicts, no muggers, no rapists. . . . There were no guns in the hands of the four who were killed and the nine who were wounded—they had no weapons."[32] Fuldheim's indignation over the shootings did not strike a chord with Cleveland viewers' sentiments. Many were appalled at her support of the students and through phone calls and letters condemned her statements. Few viewers supported her position and Fuldheim offered to resign from WEWS. The station manager refused to accept her resignation.

This genuine concern for others translated into her interactions with her viewing public. Fuldheim always answered her own phone. If she were unable to speak with the caller at that moment, she would ask them to call back later. She said the people with important issues always did, the others often forgot. Fuldheim told Terrence Sheridan, "I'm really a very simple person and I think that is my strength, that common people can confide in me, can feel free to call me."[33] J. Kerekes, a longtime WEWS employee, referred to Fuldheim as "the champion of the little man. She always spoke with people who called during each day, regardless of their social stature."[34]

In addition to being accessible to her viewing audience, Dorothy Fuldheim was committed to the community and a generous supporter of social causes. A typical schedule for Fuldheim might include speaking at a banquet to raise money for Israel, visiting with a March of Dimes poster child, helping a friend who worked with underprivileged children, and speaking to a rural group about the importance of alternative fuels.[35]

Fuldheim's strong commitment to the community and WEWS was demonstrated when she refused job offers from the networks and cable companies. Don Perris, former station manager for WEWS, told Russell Cook that NBC and ABC both extended offers at different times.[36] Despite offers that would quadruple her salary, Fuldheim remained in Cleveland. She felt "a curious sense of loyalty [to WEWS]. . . .[T]hey took a gamble with me."[37] Fuldheim's sense of loyalty to WEWS and the Cleveland community was an important component of the many awards and honors she received during her long career.

One of the most notable honors Fuldheim has received, the Overseas Press Club Award, came as a result of an interview done in Formosa in 1955. Fuldheim was able to get the only sound recording of an interview with the first two prisoners released from communist China, Martin Bersohn and Adele Rickett. The extent of their brainwashing astounded all the reporters present. None of the other reporters had sound equipment with them. The Library of Congress holds the tape of the interview and Fuldheim earned the Press Club Award because of it.

In 1956, a Gallup poll reported Fuldheim as one of America's most admired women.[38] Other awards and honors she has received include First Lady of Television from *The Ladies Home Journal.* Fuldheim also was nominated as one of 50 women across the country for a special article on American heroines in *The Ladies Home Journal.*[39] Locally, Fuldheim was voted Favorite Cleveland Newscaster for 10 consecutive years, 1947 through 1957.[40]

Family Life

Although Fuldheim grew up in poverty, her parents believed in education. "[N]othing was allowed to interfere with our school. My parents, like thousands of other immigrants, were deeply determined that their children were to be educated. Were they not now in the land of the free, the land of hope, where all men were promised equal opportunity?"[41] Fuldheim held onto these strong values instilled by her parents. From analyzing her commentaries, both Cook[42] and Reisman[43] conclude that the premise of most of her commentaries was rooted in a strong belief in the American dream and in activism in journalism. "She had the speaking skills, the drive, the public affairs knowledge, and the fervent American ideals required to take advantage of the opportunity created by a new mass medium to promote her activist causes."[44]

Fuldheim met and married her first husband, Milton Fuldheim and they came to Cleveland, where he established a law practice.[45] The young couple struggled financially. The Fuldheims had one child, also named Dorothy. Dorothy Fuldheim's life revolved around her daughter.

One day as Dorothy Fuldheim was pushing her infant daughter in her pram they met Jeanette Silber, a neighbor and friend. When Silber inquired why Fuldheim appeared disturbed, Dorothy opened her purse and said, "I have 15 cents, I have to decide whether to buy milk for the baby or bread." Dorothy decided to become a book reviewer because "I know I am good at reviewing books and I can't depend on Milton."[46] Fuldheim's speaking commitments as a book reviewer helped them to become more stable financially. She soon was speaking to 1800 listeners for Monday afternoon book reviews at Higbee's (department store) auditorium in downtown Cleveland.

Eventually, Dorothy's daughter graduated from the Carnegie Institute of Technology and soon married. Her husband, Hal Urman, was immediately shipped overseas to fight in World War II. While he was overseas, a daughter, Halla, was born. Tragedy soon struck.[47] First, Halla was found to be permanently disabled. Then shortly after Hal returned to Cleveland, he committed suicide in his grief over Halla.[48]

Milton Fuldheim died in 1952. The following year Dorothy Fuldheim married William Ulmer. Dorothy Fuldheim's mother, Bertha Schnell, lived with the family until her death in 1959. Daughter Dorothy Urman and granddaughter Halla also lived with them. Ulmer died in 1971 at age 86.[49]

According to Jim Breslin, mother and daughter were inseparable, despite their constant disagreements.[50] Dorothy picked her mother up from work each evening. In 1980, Dorothy Fuldheim suffered perhaps her greatest loss, that of Dorothy Jr. Fuldheim presented a tribute to her only daughter both on the air and in print in the *Cleveland Press*. Fuldheim noted, "Much of my happiness depended on my daughter, Dorothy, who made my days and my years rich with affection and laughter."[51] Dorothy Fuldheim was perceived to never be whole again.[52]

Conclusion

Dorothy Fuldheim's lasting impact on television news and the local Cleveland market can never be truly measured. Barbara Walters, in an interview with the Associated Press at the time of Fuldheim's death noted, "Dorothy Fuldheim was the first woman to be taken seriously doing the news."[53] J. Kerekes said about Fuldheim's 40 years with WEWS, "She was a vital force of the WEWS TV5 news department and was held in high esteem by not only her colleagues but just about any-one who ever met her. I thought she was the most interesting and com-passionate person I ever met. She was a legend that I don't think will ever be matched in female television personalities and newsmakers."[54] In her years on Cleveland television, Fuldheim left an indelible impression on most viewers. In an editorial in the *Cleveland Plain Dealer* shortly after her death, editors wrote, "Imagine. She worked until she was 91 in a highly visible job that called for stamina, intelligence, wit, erudition, and verbal agility. She had those gifts, as those who had the pleasure of forming her nightly WEWS-TV (Channel 5) audience will attest."[55] Fuldheim's pioneering style, her ability to ad-lib, and a deep commit-ment to her beliefs produced a lasting impact, not only for Cleveland viewers but also for the television industry. Ted Henry, WEWS news anchor and commentator said,

> Dorothy Fuldheim was a great gal (her term, not mine). . . . [She] taught me fire in the belly; she had it by the truckload. . . . [It was her] single greatest asset. . . . She helped define us because she gave us a face, we were the Dorothy channel, . . . she was TV5."[56]

Notes

1. Cook, R.J. (1991). Dorothy Fuldheim's Activist Journalism and the Kent State Shootings. Paper completed in partial fulfillment of Ph.D. degree, E.W. Scripps School of Journalism, Ohio University, Columbus.
2. Silber, J. (2000, Oct.). Personal communication.
3. Bianculli, D. (1983, June 19). Dorothy. *Beacon Magazine,* pp. 4, 6.

4. Hickey, W. (1977, Dec. 11). Thirty years of memories: WEWS-TV. *The Cleveland Plain Dealer.*
5. Beadle, M.E. (1997). In the public interest: WEWS-TV, Cleveland. In M.D. Murray and D.G. Godfrey (eds.), *Television in America: Local Station History From Across the Nation,* pp. 268-281. Ames, Iowa: Iowa State University Press.
6. The non-retiring ways of a nonagenarian newswoman. (1993, July 4). *Broadcasting,* p. 103.
7. Hickey, W. (1972, Oct. 1). The redhead sets a record. *The Cleveland Plain Dealer,* p. 6F.
8. Mote, P.M. (1997). *The First Lady of Television News,* p. 43. Berea, Ohio: Quixote Publications.
9. Sheridan, T. (1973, Apr.). Dorothy Fuldheim and mother news. *Cleveland Magazine,* pp. 48-60.
10. WEWS News Release. (1952). John Carroll University Media Archives, University Heights, Ohio.
11. Hickey, 1972.
12. Winfrey, C. (1939). She started Clubwomen. *Cleveland Plain Dealer,* p. 3.
13. Mote, 1997.
14. Gray, N. (1976, Dec.). Before Barbara Walters there was Dorothy Fuldheim. *Ms.,* p. 43.
15. Sheridan, 1973, p. 50.
16. WEWS News Release. (1962, January 25). John Carroll University Media Archives, University Heights, Ohio.
17. Hickey, 1972, p. 6F.
18. Gray, 1976, p. 45.
19. Hickey, 1972, p. 6F.
20. Seifulah, A.A.A., and Strassmeyer, M. (1989, Nov. 4). Dorothy Fuldheim, TV news legend, dies. *The Cleveland Plain Dealer,* pp. 1A, 2A.
21. Hickey, 1972, p. 6F.
22. Kurlander, R.U. (1935). *Cleveland Plain Dealer Magazine,* p. 1.
23. Mote, 1997.
24. Gordon, B. (1990, Feb.). Dorothy. *Cleveland Magazine,* p. 22.
25. Hickey, 1977.
26. Breslin, J. (2000, Aug. 23). Personal communication.
27. Step, B. (2000, Apr.). Personal communication.
28. Gordon, 1990, p. 23.
29. Breslin, 2000.
30. Gray, 1976, p. 43.
31. Fuldheim, D. (1974). *A Thousand Friends,* p.69. Garden City, N.Y.: Doubleday and Co., Inc.
32. Fuldheim, 1974, pp. 75-76.
33. Fuldheim, D. (1973, July 13). Dorothy's first 25 years were the hardest. *The Cleveland Press,* p. 49.
34. Kerekes, J. (2000, Oct.). Personal interview.
35. Mote, 1997.
36. Cook, R.J. (1991).
37. Hosley, D.H., and Yamada, G.K. (1987). *Hard News: Women in Broadcast Journalism,* p. 96. New York: Greenwood Press.
38. WEWS News Release. (nd). John Carroll University Media Archives, University Heights, Ohio.
39. Fifty American heroines. (1984, July). *Ladies Home Journal, 101,* p.85.
40. WEWS News Release. (nd).

41. Fuldheim, D. (1966*). I Laughed, I Cried, I Loved: A News Analyst's Love Affair with the World,* p. 3. Cleveland, Ohio: World Publishing.
42. Cook, 1991.
43. Reisman, J. (1979). A Rhetorical Analysis of Dorothy Fuldheim's Television Commentaries. Unpublished Ph.D. dissertation, Case Western Reserve University, Cleveland, Ohio.
44. Cook, 1991, p. 16.
45. Mote, 1997.
46. Silber, 2000.
47. Mote, 1997.
48. Silber, 2000.
49. Mote, 1997.
50. Breslin, 2000.
51. Fuldheim, D. (1980, Dec. 3). Dorothy Fuldheim's tribute to her daughter. *The Cleveland Press.*
52. Mote, 1997.
53. Seifulah and Strassmeyer, 1989, p. 1.
54. J. Kerekes, 2000.
55. The end of the Fuldheim era (1989, Nov. 4). Editorial, *The Cleveland Plain Dealer,* p. 6B.
56. Henry, T. (2000, Oct.). Personal communication.

Other Sources

Larronde, S. (1982). At 89, she's still the queen of TV news. *Modern Maturity,* p. 58.

Martha Gable

Martha Gable

ETV's Pioneer Spokesperson

At a time when most Americans had never seen television, Martha (Marty) Gable was already doing two shows a week on a station in her home city of Philadelphia. While most people would be happy with one successful career and delighted with two, Marty Gable found time and energy to become well recognized in four. One of these would make her one of the founding forces in the development of public broadcast, known in the 1950s and 1960s as educational television (ETV).

The Early Years

This 4-foot, 11-inch bundle of energy was born in 1905, one of four children. She set out to become a teacher and graduated from the University of Indiana, later adding an M.Ed. from Temple University. Very athletic, she made a mark as a gymnast at a time when women's gymnastics wasn't even a part of the Olympic Games. The "Turners" were gymnastics and fitness clubs spread across the country. She competed for the Philadelphia team, which won the national championship three years in a row, receiving a special Golden Wreath Award for this accomplishment.[1]

Although she never competed in one, Marty Gable had an interest in the Olympics that grew far beyond her expectations. In 1932 she visited Los Angeles and attended the games there, and, as she said, "that gave me the Olympic Fever."[2]

The games were forced into hiatus by the war until 1948. As the plans to resume them were coming together, Marty got a surprise phone call inviting her to judge the women's gymnastics, now part of the events. She found that the Federation of International Gymnastique had decided that there must be women judges and coaches. Marty's earlier accomplishments in gymnastics and the fact she had already done some judging led them to her. So, she was off to London in 1948. This, in turn, led to her appointment to the National Committee for Gymnastics. Her Olympic judging continued in 1952 in Helsinki, in 1956 in Australia, then Rome in 1960 and Tokyo in 1964, after which the other challenges kept her too busy and she retired.

The "other challenges" had been building since before the start of World War II. Her education degrees and accomplishments in sports led her to be appointed head of physical education for the Philadelphia schools. As the American war effort began in 1941, President Franklin Roosevelt appointed John B. Kelly, father of Princess Grace, as head of a national fitness program. Kelly, himself twice an Olympic gold medal winner, knew of Marty's accomplishments and stature. He asked her to take a year's leave of absence and work with him on the women's activities in his undertaking.[3]

Television on the Horizon

Philco Corporation had activated one of America's few prewar television stations in Philadelphia. The company had a receiver factory in the suburbs. Fitness and television connected when Philco decided they would like to have some sports programs on their new station. They invited Gable to do an hour on women's sports on Tuesdays and an hour on men's sports on Thursdays. An instinctive programmer, she drew in many local sports stars, covering everything from how to hold a golf club to how to get into shape.[4]

She commented that "people don't realize how it was to go into a television studio and perform. The lights were so hot I used to take a complete change of clothing, because the perspiration would run down into my shoes."[5] She also experienced the use of extreme makeup because of the insensitivity of the early cameras. She described the base as looking like "powdered cocoa" and the lipstick as "melted chocolate." This was to avoid having the talent's features completely washed out. Occasionally forgetting to take off the makeup before leaving the studio led to some very strange stares out on the street.[6]

Everything was done live and all the accidents went on the air. In one instance a roller skater, being swung by her partner, nicked scenery stored behind a curtain and caused it to come crashing into the shot. Marty calmly stepped to the microphone and said, "Well, we brought down the house with that act. We'll have the next act ready in a minute."[7]

As it did with virtually every nonessential activity, the all-out effort behind World Was II brought the telecasts to an end in 1942. In 1946, the war over, she was back on the air, this time in much better facilities, as a women's sports reporter and commentator on a broader sports program. Philco was programming sports heavily because they felt that men would be the ones buying the television sets. Soon Marty was pushing the station management to program for women and children as well, pointing out that they were an important part of the market. The Channel 3 manager decided to start moving into daytime and asked Marty to do a 5 p.m. children's show. One of her primary sources of program material was the various activities of the schools. Occasionally, she even used a student as a co-host.[8]

There were three stations in Philadelphia by the end of 1947, and the managers watched each other's actions, as they do today. Because commercial programming was still embryonic, public service programming was welcome because of its low cost. The three managers went to School Superintendent Alexander Stoddard (who would later become quite a figure in educational television) and suggested they all would like to do something for the schools. When Stoddard balked because no one in the schools knew anything about television, the managers called his attention to all that Marty Gable was doing, on her own time, at night. Promptly, she was pulled out of physical education and put in charge of radio and television under the associate superintendent for community relations.

The Philadelphia schools began efforts on all three commercial stations. The focus was on content that related to what was being done in the classrooms. The programs flourished into 1951, at which time Marty had 12 teachers presenting televised lessons. In the summer of 1951, the national interconnect was completed and the networks began claiming the daytime hours and the schools' programs were dropped. Only WFIL continued its instructional broadcasts until 1968. Although it would take six more years to fruition, the activation of Philadelphia's first noncommercial station was, in part, the result of Martha Gable's efforts over the previous years. Additionally, she would play a bigger role in the future of public television.

Certainly all that was to follow began quite innocently when Martha was asked to do a television demonstration at the University of Pennsylvania for their annual Schoolmen's Week. Philco agreed and a remote facility was set up in the gym of the local high school. Although gymnasium acoustics are hardly ideal, she created eight or nine areas where different activities were to be displayed, ranging from a band to gymnastics to a baking demonstration. "Finally we were ready to go with the program. So I blew the whistle . . . and I said, 'This is history-making, and if you people make one sound when you're not on the air, you'll ruin the whole thing. [We'll] come around and start talking and then you will do your thing. In the meantime, keep quiet. Don't drop anything.'"[9] Philco had set up three receivers in the University auditorium and Marty soon got word that the hall was jammed with 500 people with another 500 outside trying to see. At this time many people still did not have television, so curiosity was undoubtedly a factor. It all was a big success and Philco's comment was that they had "sold" more receivers with that program than any of their other promotions.[10]

This successful demonstration began a road show of presentations that continued for several years. She quickly received an invitation to do something similar for a national physical education conference in Boston, where her show played to a jammed Statler Hotel ballroom. Then it was on to Atlantic City for the American Association of School Superintendents (AASS) convention. In this case her program was microwaved in from Philadelphia, an early use of that relay technique and one which some superintendents doubted was genuine, accusing her of showing them a film on the sly. This production soon evolved into annual demonstrations at the convention, where superintendents could observe the television production and see the impact on a class in an adjoining area.[11]

The next stop was the West Coast, where for a month she put programs on KRON and spoke at area colleges and public schools about the potential of television in education. This effort can be viewed as an early contribution to the founding of San Francisco's public station, KQED.[12]

Penn State

As one of the true pioneers, Gable was doing demonstrations for various groups before many had even heard of educational television. Others had little sense of what was needed to do a demonstration. In 1962 she was called to Penn State to do a show the next day for a conference of some 90 college and university presidents. When she arrived she was ushered into a huge armory and shown two cameras, related equipment and a switching device, none of which was even connected. She was provided with two student assistants who had never seen a camera before and a man from RCA who was waiting for instructions. Snapping into action, she got the technician moving, connecting the equipment, and began coaching her students on camera use. She asked her Penn State guide to round up some flats or something she could hang things on. When the flats arrived she marked out a space and began planning the program. Well-known ETV pioneer Keith Tyler from Ohio State dropped in, looked around and exclaimed, "How in God's name are you going to get a program together by tomorrow?" "Only by the grace of God," she replied.[13] Not only was she to do the show, but also her audience of presidents would be there in the armory watching how she put it together.

Marty rounded up three Indonesians, a doctor, an artist and a young girl who could dance. "So we put it together. We had the little dancer, and this physician talked about something—and the artist. At least it worked well enough so they saw how it worked; they sat there watching what we were doing and watching the pictures on the camera.".[14]

Testifying

From 1948 to 1952, the Federal Communication Commission (FCC) instituted a moratorium on new applications for station construction (the "freeze") to give itself time to reexamine problems related to television. Over the four years of the freeze many educational leaders would go before the Commission to testify in support of proposed educational channels. One of these leaders presenting testimony would be Martha Gable.

Gable's extensive speaking, combined with her success in Philadelphia, made her a logical expert to appear before federal bodies to discuss and support federal action on things related to televised instruction. She made her first appearance before the FCC in December 1950. She worked in conjunction with Frieda Hennock, first woman commissioner on the FCC, who was an ardent supporter of educational television. "We had to go down and say what we were doing and the results. We zoomed in on the values that the children were learning and that the parents were for this," Gable said.[15] She recalled that Paul Walker was the chairman of the FCC and, though a supporter, was prone to ask tough questions. "He was on our side, but he would ask questions as though he was the devil's advocate to convince the other people who were listening. We kind of had a little thing going."[16]

The Joint Council for Educational Television (JCET) was set up in 1950 to coordinate testimony and educate the public about the potential of television in education. JCET director Ralph Steeple asked Gable to make a speech at Georgetown University. To her surprise, she was preceded at the podium by a commercial broadcaster who disparaged the idea of educational television and the waste of money it would be, and made other standard criticisms of the period. When Gable's turn came, she was upset.

> So I got up and I went at it. I told them what we were doing, how the
> children were learning, how the parents were devoted to it, how they bought
> the television sets, how the stations were solidly behind it, that the teachers
> thought is was a tremendous tool. I went at it, you know, because my Dutch
> was up then! And everybody stood up and cheered! And this poor guy, he was
> defeated, and he knew it.[17]

Ralph Steetle, who was responsible for her being there, said, "It was worth your railroad fare down here."[18]

In the summer of 1965, Congress was considering a revision of the Copyright Law. Educational broadcasters had encountered considerable difficulty in getting permission to use books, literature and film clips on the air. The proposed law would make the use of copyrighted materials even more difficult. Among those called to testify against the proposed changes was Martha Gable.

Gable pointed out how the manufacturers and producers benefitted from the exposure their materials received when used on instructional programs. She noted that showing clips from a film invariably resulted in demands from the classrooms for the entire film, resulting in more purchases. She said that libraries were overwhelmed by demand when a book was featured on a program, adding that librarians begged for advance notice when such a recommendation was to occur. Gable also noted that the producers had a widely varying set of rules so that anyone attempting to get permission was invariably discouraged. Ultimately the laws were changed to provide more amenable requirements.[19]

Two years later she testified before committees of both the Senate and the House on the legislation that led to the establishment of the Corporation for Public Broadcasting and the Public Broadcasting System. Part of the legislation called for a study of the future direction of instructional broadcasting. Gable took particular pains to urge that groups involved in the examination have an intimate knowledge of the field. She also urged that the observers be given adequate time to learn about an operation and not just briefly observe it. Instructional programs were often relatively simple in terms of style and production values because many educators thought these were expensive distractions. There was considerable concern that the "observers" would take one brief look and decide that the programs were so simple that they couldn't be of much worth.[20]

Large Classes

One of the biggest challenges faced by educators in the late 1950s and the 1960s was the baby boom. The unprecedented tidal wave of students overwhelmed many districts, which could not seem to build classrooms and hire more teachers fast enough. While many schemes were devised as a possible way to meet the challenge, none was more creative or controversial than the one put forward by Martha Gable's former boss, ex-Philadelphia schools superintendent Dr. Alexander Stoddard. He proposed two approaches, one for elementary and one for secondary schools, that were essentially the same. In the elementary version, 300 students would move among the resources room, the auditorium and the playground in 45-minute blocks, while another 300 would meet in 12 traditional classes with individual teachers. Those in the resources room would receive televised instruction. Then, in the afternoon, the two groups would exchange. He projected significant savings on a quantitative basis but seemed to give little consideration to quality.[21]

Philadelphia became one of the systems to test this "large classroom" approach to mass education, and it was Martha Gable's job to make the television end of it work. The first thing she did was to set out to rationalize the proposal. With her experience in training teachers to use television she knew that hour-long broadcasts would never be accepted. "I said, 'Dr. Stoddard'—and he had been my former superintendent so I felt I knew him well enough to really level with him.

'Dr. Stoddard, this isn't going to work. The teachers are going resist you. The parents are going to resist you. They're going to think we have a machine-made education. If you will let me work it out, I think we'll make this a success.'"[22] Gable replaced Stoddard's five-day-a-week plan with shorter broadcasts three days a week and shortened the broadcast lessons to 20 minutes. She knew that televised instruction packed so much material in a program that the shorter broadcasts would be all the pupils and teachers could handle. Using Ford Foundation money to pay teachers to come for meetings on afternoons and Saturday mornings, she guided them to developing curriculum and television programs for the large classes.

The Atlantic City Show

Gable's demonstrations for the superintendents' conventions in Atlantic City took a new form when, in 1963, a new executive director of the AASS called her in and inquired how they could do a series of programs based on discussions of issues by superintendents attending the convention. Her response was, "No problem. You get a room for a studio. We get a couple of cameras."[23] Undertaking a project that some would feel was not possible, she set out to produce and direct a day-long series of discussions done live with inexperienced talent and no rehearsal that would originate from her little studio and be sent to all the hotel rooms in the city by cable. Topics and superintendents were settled on well in advance and a separate television guide booklet was distributed.

After a sign-on logo and an announcement of the first topic and the participants, they were on their way, with a new show every 30 minutes. At first they had only one set and went to a logo while the new batch of superintendents replaced those who had just finished. Eventually they graduated to two sets so changes were easier. This continued for 17 years. Her retirement came before those years were over, but she still was called in to run the show.

Her programs made it possible to cover many special interests that wouldn't fit in the regular convention schedule. Gable commented, "It got a lot of people to come to the convention because they were on the program. It increased their participation, their attendance and it gave people something to watch in their rooms."[24]

Activation of WHYY

Although Martha Gable is not listed among the founders of WHYY, she played a significant role in its activation. When the first educational stations came on the air in the middle 1950s, there was no network to assist them, and little programming was available. Also, with no significant source of revenue for evening programming, the shows frequently resulted in dull, static talk-based programs. The school broadcasting services were the backbone of many early stations. Through their connection to the school districts, the school broadcasters had a relatively reliable source of funds to support them. These funds used, in part, to pay for airtime and production services became the primary source of funds for station operations.

When Philadelphia's WHYY signed on in 1957, Gable's operation moved to the new station, partly because the commercial stations had sharply reduced the time they would provide and partly because of the potential for more programming hours. Gable said, "They couldn't have done it without our money . . . that UHF station. But the fact is . . . our teachers, our programs, our curriculum and our audience were ready, you see, so we didn't have to start from scratch. We were well underway when we got our channel."[25] Broadcast pioneer James Robertson, the former general manager of Los Angeles's public station KCET, has rated Gable's school program service as one of the best in the country at that time.[26]

Literacy

One of Gable's contributions falls in an area often overlooked. She supervised the development of a series called *Operation Alphabet*. These half-hour programs were recorded by a means known as "kinescopes," which, though of low quality, preserved them and made repeats and sharing with other stations possible. They were used widely for many years. The instructor got letters from all over the country expressing appreciation for the series. Gable told of one day when she was visited by a woman who was extremely grateful for the programs. She said her husband was a capable man who was kept in low-level jobs because he couldn't read or write. She said, "This has opened up whole careers to him."[27] Marty was very proud of this series, which, though neither fancy nor crisp and clear on the receiver, helped many people improve themselves.

Changes

In 1968 she retired from the school system and shifted her efforts to Washington, joining the American School of Superintendents Association, with which she had a long relationship. Here she edited publications for the AASS and continued her annual television shows at the convention for the next five years.

She had an understandable interest in public relations and became active in the Philadelphia Public Relations Association (PPRA), where she served as a member of the board of directors until her death. In 1974 she was inducted into the PPRA Hall of Fame. In the ceremony, her effigy, dressed in Superman tights, a blue cape and a big G on its chest, swooped across the Benjamin Franklin Hotel ballroom amid the smoke from several canisters. She is remembered as having more energy in her 60s and 70s than a woman much younger. The director of public relations of the Philadelphia Art Museum said, "She would jump into a project and get it done immediately. She did so much and she did it so quickly and so well."[28]

One of Gable's enduring joys was the Women of Greater Philadelphia, a group dedicated to polishing the city's image and making it more attractive to tourists. Alma Jacobs, former regional head of the U.S. Department of Health and Human Services said, "She gave her all to improve the cultural image of Philadelphia."[29] Friends remember Gable's many efforts, from the publication of guides highlighting the city's many museums to progressive dinners, to the restoration of a famous mansion, to appearing in colonial costume at a variety of public affairs.[30]

Martha Anna Gable died January 11, 1991, in the city she loved. In athletics, in the creation of a public television system and in community service, she left a record of which anyone could be proud.

Notes

1. Robertson, J. (1981). Recorded interview with Martha Gable. Public Television Oral History Project. Madison, Wisconsin: The State Historical Society of Wisconsin.
2. Robertson, 1981, p. 47.
3. Robertson, 1981.
4. Robertson, 1981.

5. Robertson, 1981, p. 2.
6. Robertson, 1981.
7. Robertson, 1981, p. 2.
8. Robertson, 1981.
9. Robertson, 1981, p. 7.
10. Robertson, 1981, p. 7.
11. Robertson, 1981.
12. Robertson, 1981.
13. Robertson, 1981, p. 10.
14. Robertson, 1981, p. 11.
15. Robertson, 1981, p. 32.
16. Robertson, 1981, p. 34.
17. Robertson, 1981, p. 35.
18. Robertson, 1981, p. 35.
19. U.S. Congress/House. (1965). *Copyright Law Revisions Before the Committee on the Judiciary.* 89th Congress, 1st Session.
20. U.S. Congress/House. (1967). *Public Television Act, Hearings Before The Committee on Interstate and Foreign Commerce.* 90th Congress, 1st Session.
    U.S. Congress/Senate. (1967). *Public Broadcasting Act, Hearings Before the Subcommittee on Communications.* 90th Congress, 1st Session.
21. Costello, L., and Gordon, G. (1969). *Teach With Television: A Guide With Instructional TV* (5th ed.). New York: Hastings House.
22. Robertson, 1981, p. 13.
23. Robertson, 1981, p. 36.
24. Robertson, 1981, p. 38.
25. Robertson, 1981, p. 32.
26. Robertson, 1981.
27. Robertson, 1981, p. 33.
28. Wallace, A. (1991, Jan. 11). Martha Anna Gable, women's sports backer. *The Philadelphia Inquirer,* p. 14B.
29. Wallace, 1991, p. 14B.
30. Stephenson, A. (2001, Feb. 4.). Oral history interview with Carolyn Anchor. Gable Project, Tape 2. The John Carroll University Media Archives, University Heights, Ohio.

Other Sources

Gable, M. (1972, Sept.). "Are you ready for cable TV?" *Today's Education, 61,* np.

Oslin, J. (1999). Celebrating the past: A century of challenge, Part IV: The war and post-war years, 1940-1952. *Journal of Physical Education, Recreation and Dance, 70,* p.16.

Pfleiger, E. (1961). *The National Program for the Use of Television in the Public Schools.* New York: The Fund for the Advancement of Education.

Philadelphia educational TV tops, thanks to Martha Gable. (1962, Dec.). *Center City Philadelphian.*

Robertson, J. (1983). *Televisionaries.* Lake Charlotte, Fla.: Tabby House Books.

Stoddard, A. (1957). *Schools for Tomorrow.* New York: The Fund for the Advancement of Education.

Frieda Hennock. *(Courtesy of Library of American Broadcasting, University of Maryland)*

Frieda Hennock and KUHT

First in Educational Television

Monday, June 8, 1953, was an auspicious day for Frieda Hennock. The guest of honor at the opening ceremonies for educational television station KUHT in Houston, Texas, FCC commissioner Hennock celebrated the realization of a dream. For four years she fought against the commercial broadcast interests and fellow commissioners who argued that educational television was both impractical and a waste of valuable and scarce resources. Yet she stood at a podium surrounded by flowers and supporters, to welcome KUHT on the air. "Here in Houston," she claimed, "begins the practical realization of the tremendous benefits that television holds out to education."[1]

KUHT began broadcasting Hennock's address live on Channel 8 to the greater Houston area.[2] However, the audience for this great educational experiment extended far beyond that auditorium and the Houston television audience. Hennock referred to that larger audience when she spoke at the commencement ceremonies for the University of Houston nine months earlier and warned attendees that, with regard to educational TV, "not only the eyes of Texas but the eyes of the entire country are upon you."[3] In spring 1953, the eyes of Texas and the country were on KUHT and Hennock. The Hennock-inspired experiment in noncommercial broadcasting was underway.

As the first and only female member of the Federal Communications Commission, Hennock became a highly visible public servant committed to serving the public interest. She served on the Federal Communications Commission from 1948 to 1955, years that saw the establishment of television allocations for education and the development of the educational television.

Her appointment to the FCC afforded the opportunity to focus interests, particularly in the form of educational television. She was a strong believer in the power of education to transform individuals; her life as a young immigrant to the United States was testament to the gift of education. She wanted to share that gift by offering educational alternatives to Milton Berle and Howdy-Doody. In Hennock's eyes there was no greater good she could accomplish than establishing educational television. Guided by this motivation, Hennock joined the Commission in 1948 and became the moving force behind the creation of educational television.[4] As a result of tenacity and dedication to its creation, Hennock played a pivotal role in the start of KUHT, Houston, the first educational television station in the country.

Hennock's story is one of a young woman who took full advantage of unusual opportunities and challenged expectations. Frieda Barkin Hennock was born into a middle-class Jewish family on September 26, 1904, in Kovel, Poland, the youngest of eight children. The family immigrated to the United States in 1910 and settled in Manhattan. Only six years old at the time of her immigration, young Fritzie (her family nickname) entered public school. Unlike the vast majority of female Jewish immigrants, who left school by age 12 to work for wages, Hennock completed her primary education and graduated from Morris High School in 1921. Unlike others, Hennock eschewed marriage and convention by entering Brooklyn Law School in 1922 (one of few schools of law in the United States to admit Jews or women). She graduated in 1924 at age 20 and was admitted to the New York bar in 1926.[5]

Over the next 20 years, Hennock's professional life was split between acting as counsel for the underprivileged and working for wealthy clients who provided access to a greater income and passage to inner circles of political power. Beginning in the early 1930s Hennock became a devoted New Deal Democrat, active in New York politics, and she became a formidable fund-raiser for the Democratic Party. The Party repaid devotion when President Harry Truman nominated her to fill an FCC position vacated by Clifford Durr in 1948. Against considerable odds, the Republican-controlled Congress confirmed her and she assumed her seven-year position on July 1, 1948.

When Hennock accepted her FCC position she had no expressed intentions regarding educational television. Nearly a year after joining the Commission, in early May 1949 she was invited to attend a meeting of the Institute for Educational Radio and Television at Ohio State

University.[6] She discovered a cause. She learned first-hand problems inherent in providing educational material on radio, anticipating challenges of TV.[7] She became very involved in the meeting, and participants were impressed by her interest.[8]

Stanley Neustadt, her first legal assistant, asserted that Hennock returned from that meeting with an interest focused on educators.[9] A commitment to educational broadcasting was apparent. She commented: "I feel that it is my duty to do everything in my power to spread education over the air wherever possible and that means helping the educational institutions get more stations."[10]

Between May and July 1949 Hennock's vision crystallized. By July 11 she supported reserving TV channels for noncommercial use. On that date the FCC issued a "Notice of Further Proposed Rule Making," in which it offered initial plans for allocating channels.[11] Again, there was no mention of noncommercial television channels. In a lone dissent, Hennock asserted that the notice "should include a provision for the reservation of a specified number of frequencies in the ultra-high frequency band for the establishment of a noncommercial educational television service."[12]

Hennock said that failure to make a set-aside would result in waste from the standpoint of public interest and education.[13] By this time she developed a definition of educational television, describing it as providing classroom instruction, both at school and home. Viewers could watch lectures on television. Additionally, ETV would provide "a higher type of cultural programming."[14] To this end, Hennock organized a campaign to secure allocations; her goal became television channels for education.

The FCC was required to schedule hearings during which interested parties could respond to allocation plans. The task of organizing the hearings fell to Hennock. She had to accomplish two things: organize witnesses to testify at hearings and build both educational and public support for her plans.[15] Those whom she invited to testify recognized the role she played. One person wrote that she would "be pleased to testify at *your* [emphasis added] hearings on educational use of television."[16] Journalists also understood. Hennock would conduct a campaign engaging educators and general public to reserve television bands for education use.[17]

Hennock realized she needed educators testifying before the hearings. As a result, she had to quickly create and maintain educator interests in developing noncommercial television, and cajole them into communicating this interest. Hennock used several methods to accomplish that goal. On the same day the Notice was issued, Hennock embarked on a letter-writing campaign in which she alerted interested parties "that it [would] be necessary for the educators to file their comments by August 8, 1949, in order to appear at the hearings."[18]

Richard Hull, president of the National Association of Educational Broadcasters (NAEB), responded to her appeal by sending an urgent letter to all members asking them to show their "appreciation of Commissioner Hennock's efforts in our behalf" by notifying the national office of their interest.[19] A second form letter was created by Hennock's office to respond to correspondents who commented on her first ETV dissent. In this letter Hennock asserted that she felt "very strongly that educators have a responsibility to utilize the tools for mass communication in the cause of education."[20] She also encouraged educators to think about television and share ideas on the subject. Hennock's efforts were successful. By August 1949 several educational organizations filed formal proposals for educational broadcasting services and expressed a willingness to participate in the hearings.[21]

Behind the scenes, Hennock also worked with the Joint Committee on Educational Television (JCET), formed in August 1949 as a result of Hennock's appeal for educators to contact the FCC.[22] The JCET was a group comprised of seven educational organizations, most notably the American Council on Education, the National Education Association, the National Association of Educational Broadcasters, and the Association of Land Grant Colleges and Universities.[23] The goal was to unify some clout under one banner and lead an ETV reservation appeal.

Hennock labored to persuade educators to join the battle to reserve frequencies for noncommercial use, promising rewards for participation; threatening failure for inactivity. She appealed to educators' ability to extend their pedagogical touch to large groups of people,[24] while challenging them to take responsibility to make their wishes clearly known to the FCC. "You must come out swinging," she said, to "make the strongest showing possible."[25] Noticeably absent from these speeches are indications of how educators would pay for costly equipment, or *what* they would broadcast. Hennock's first priority was to simply persuade educators of the need for the FCC to allocate channels strictly for noncommercial TV programming.

When the hearings opened in November 1950, Hennock was ready. She amassed more than 60 witnesses to testify in support of noncommercial television. This included four senators, a member of the House of Representatives, the commissioner of the U.S. Office of Education, several professors and university presidents, leaders of labor and civic organizations, the former president of the NBC network, and numerous others.[26] The testimony of these witnesses was buttressed by dozens of letters from additional educational institutions unable to send representatives to Washington, D.C., all of whom pledged support for ETV. She received the silent support of President Harry Truman.[27] In less than 18 months on the FCC, Hennock developed a passion for the possibilities of educational television. She motivated supporters and organized the hearings to guarantee allocations of noncommercial television channels.

Despite formidable and influential opposition from the broadcast industry and intellectuals concerned with the spread of mass culture, Hennock waged an imposing campaign supporting noncommercial television, both during the hearings and to the public as well.[28] She made at least two nationally broadcast appearances during the hearings period. On November 28, 1950, she was a guest on the ABC radio program *Town Meeting of the Air,* during which she claimed that television could "be put to better use as an electronic blackboard than as an electronic billboard, bringing roadside advertising messages into the home."[29] On January 21, 1951, she was Eleanor Roosevelt's guest on NBC's *Mrs. Roosevelt Meets the Public,* during which she promoted channel reservations.[30] In a guest editorial for *The Saturday Review of Literature,* she outlined arguments supporting noncommercial television.[31] For *Variety* she boldly predicted that television could "become one of the greatest forces America [had] ever known for personal improvement, mass public education, and a resulting rise in our general standard of living."[32]

Hennock amassed more supporters than she realized. One such person eventually became pivotal in helping her realize her dream of educational television. He was Dr. W. W. Kemmerer, who was the acting president of the University of Houston. In early 1951, while the ETV hearings were still underway, Kemmerer became aware of the enormous educational potential television offered while watching Senator Estes Kefauver's organized crime hearings, televised nationwide.[33] A few months later, in April 1951, Kemmerer attended the JCET meeting in Pennsylvania where he learned in great detail of ETV's potential.[34] By this point, one of the leading goals of the acting president of the University of Houston was to develop an educational television station at the University of Houston. Frieda Hennock's passion for educational television, envisioned from a national perspective, was matched by Kemmerer's fervor for ETV in Houston.

Hennock insisted that 25 percent of the newly allocated VHF and UHF channels should be reserved for noncommercial programs. Between the end of the hearings, in January 1951, and the release of the allocation decision, in March 1951, it became clear to Hennock that she would not achieve that 25 percent goal. Indeed, as part of its overall television assignments plan, on March 22, 1951, the Commission set aside approximately 10 percent of television frequencies for noncommercial stations.[35] Hennock was "in complete agreement with the Commission's action in adopting reservation of television channels for non-commercial education,"[36] and she was disappointed at the Commission's failure to reserve 25 percent of channels. "[T]he Commission has grievously erred," Hennock said, "in not providing education with the reservations it needs and deserves."[37]

Disappointment aside, the stage was set for the emergence of educational television. Among the hundreds of noncommercial allocations created by the FCC was Channel 8 in Houston, Texas. Sitting in the middle of the VHF bandwidths, this was a plum channel assignment for ETV. VHF channel assignments were highly coveted, especially by commercial broadcasters. Television signals transmitted on VHF channels were received over greater distances than UHF signals and resulted in clearer pictures. More significantly, at that time all of the existing television sets in the United States received only VHF transmissions (an adapter was required to receive UHF). The fact that a VHF channel was reserved for noncommercial use in a metropolitan area was a plus for supporters, and a disappointment for commercial interests.

Indeed, when given the opportunity to respond to the Commission's reservation of Channel 8 for educational purposes, several broadcasting organizations attempted to persuade the FCC to reallocate Channel 8 for commercial purposes. They argued that there was no evidence of a demand for educational television in Houston.[38] The Commission was persuaded to the contrary, however, by letters from the University of Houston preparing to submit an application for a construction permit for an educational television station.[39] Additional supporting letters came from the Houston Independent School District and the JCET. These were not empty promises. As early as April 17, 1951, barely a month after the allocation decision was released, the University Board of Regents permitted application.[40] A month later, on May 22, 1951, the regents instructed President Kemmerer to invite Houston educational institutions to participate in the educational television project.[41]

Through the remainder of 1951 and into 1952 Hennock fought to persuade educational institutions and local governments to take advantage of the reserved channels. This required extensive traveling on her part, as she toured the country speaking to local community organizations. Throughout 1952 and 1953 Hennock's journeys ranged from San Francisco to Houston to Atlantic City. Wherever she traveled, Hennock stressed that educators and government leaders had to get started on educational programming.[42]

Although frequently forced to take a defensive position to protect development, Hennock recognized the need to make offensive moves to nurture growth. The single greatest obstacle to the progress of ETV was lack of funding for building stations and producing and/or purchasing programming. In 1952 Hennock persuaded Emerson Corporation—a major television manufacturer—to create a fund from which the first 10 ETV stations on the air would each get $10,000.[43] Hennock went on to act as the intermediary between that company and eligible stations, as when she informed Emerson that KETC in St. Louis was on the air and available for a $10,000 award.[44] She similarly pursued support from the Ford Foundation.[45] Recognizing the second most difficult problem facing educational programmers, that of producing and/or acquiring quality programming, she considered ways in which noncommercial stations could share programs by distributing kinescopes of locally produced shows.[46]

As Hennock traveled, focusing on metropolitan areas such as New York City and San Francisco, Kemmerer went about planning for an educational television station. On April 15, 1952, the University Board of Regents authorized FCC application and a construction permit. The board was impressed with his vision of creating a "television center," facilities funded and used by the university and the Houston Independent School District, therefore serving the educational needs of that metropolitan area.[47] Within six months of authorization to pursue a construction permit, he had an approved a site for station location, architect and attorney, bids for equipment, and an appropriation of $300,000.[48]

By midsummer 1952, Hennock was aware of the progress made by the University of Houston toward the creation of the educational television station. On August 20, 1952, the Commission approved the university's application for a construction permit, thereby granting the ninth application for construction of an educational television station.[49] Ten days later Hennock presented the university's commencement address, congratulating the school and its president for committing to serve "spiritual, educational and cultural" needs in that Texas community.[50]

The period between August 1952 and May 1953 resulted in a flurry of activity. The studio was constructed in a classroom building, a 325-foot antenna was erected, and a $70,000 transmitter was purchased and installed. John Schwarzwalder was appointed station supervisor. W.T. Davis became chief engineer.[51] After testing and FCC nods, KUHT went on-air May 25, 1953 becoming the first ETV station in the country.[52]

Frieda Hennock was overjoyed as this moment represented attainment of a personal goal. Almost exactly five years to the day after Hennock joined the Federal Communications Commission as its first female commissioner, the goal toward which she labored for the previous four years came to fruition: a noncommercial, educational television station. But the work was not done. As important as the station was to the University of Houston, she called it a "keystone" for educational TV.[53]

It was a gratifying, defining moment. When she retired from the FCC in 1955, Kemmerer recognized her role in the creation of KUHT.[54] Despite corporate opposition and apathy of fellow commissioners, Hennock's dream of a nationwide system of educational, noncommercial television was finally on the air.

Notes

1. Hennock, F.B. (1953, June 8). Station KUHT opens the new frontier of educational TV. KUHT archive, University of Houston, Tex.
2. Militello, J. (1993, June). Past, present, and future: The story of Houston public television. *Houston Metropolitan*, pp. 88-99.
3. Hennock, F.B. (1952, Aug. 30). Educational television: A new force in Houston. Frieda H. Simons Collection, Box 8/Folder 105, Schlesinger Library, Radcliffe College, Cambridge, Mass. (Hereafter cited as FHS.)

4. Brinson, S.L. (1998). Frieda Hennock: FCC activist and the campaign for educational television. *Historical Journal of Film, Radio, and Television, 18,* pp. 411-429.

5. Brinson, S.L. (1999, winter). Frieda Hennock. *BLS [Brooklyn Law School] Law Notes,* pp. 42-43.

6. Novik, M. (1978). Recorded interview with Harrison, B. Series 1/Box 4/Folder 4. Harrison Papers, Oral History Project, National Broadcasting Archive, University of Maryland, College Park, Md.

7. Hennock, F.B. (1950, Oct. 27). Dedication of Station WKBW. FHS 8/104.

8. Broderick to Hennock, F.B. (1949, May 17). Frieda B. Hennock Collection: Box 2/Folder: Cor-Bo, Harry S. Truman Presidential Library, Independence, Mo. (Hereafter cited as FBH).

9. Neustadt, S. (1996). Personal communication.

10. Hennock, F.B. (1949, May 17). Letter to Brower, R.C. FBH 2/Cor-Bo.

11. Notice of further proposed rule making. (1949, July 11). 49 FCC Report 948.

12. Notice of further proposed rule making, 1949.

13. Notice of further proposed rule making, 1949.

14. Topical outline for informal talks. (nd). FHS 7/97.

15. Stambler, A. (1996, May 16). Personal communication.

16. Gordon, D. (1950, Nov. 29). Letter to Hennock, F.B. FBH 4/Cor-Go.

17. Brandon, D. (1950, May 14). Blackboard of future? *New York Herald Tribune,* Sec. 2, p. 4.

18. Hennock, F.B. (1949, July 14). Letter to Bartlett, K. FBH 1/Cor-Ba.

19. Hull, R. (1949, July 21). Letter to National Association of Educational Broadcasters. FBH 4/Cor-Hu.

20. Hennock, F.B. (1949d, Aug. 3). Letter to Abbot, W. FBH 1/Cor-A.

21. Hennock, F.B. (1949e, Aug. 29). Letter to Carpenter, C.R. FBH 2/Cor-Ca.

22. Hull, R. (1979). Recorded interview with Robertson, J. Series 1/Box 2/Folder 6, Robertson Collection, Oral History Project, Broadcast Archive, University of Maryland, College Park, Md.

23. Taylor, T. (1951, Jan. 28). Finding a place for education on TV. *New York Times,* Sec. 6, p. 9.

24. Hennock, 1950, Oct. 27.

25. Hennock, F.B. (1950, Apr. 20). The 37th Annual Schoolmen's Week. FHS 8/104.

26. U.S. Congress/Senate. (1950-1951). *Official report of proceedings before the Federal Communications Commission,* 82th Congress, 1st Session.

27. Hennock, F.B. (1949, Sept. 1). Letter to Truman, H.S. FBH 121/Ha-He.

28. Crosby, J. (1950, Dec. 10). The time is now. *New York Herald Tribune,* p. 27; McGrath, E.J. (1951 January). Safeguarding television channels for education. *School Life,* pp. 33, 51; Taylor, 1951.

29. Hennock, F.B. (1950, Nov. 28). Who should be responsible for education on television? FHS 15/152.

30. Hennock, F.B. (1951, Jan. 24). Letter to E. Roosevelt. FBH 8/Cor-Ro.

31. Hennock, F.B. (1950, Dec. 9). TV conservation. *The Saturday Review of Literature, 33,* 22-23.

32. Hennock, F.B. (1951, Jan. 3). The 3 R's on television. *Variety.*

33. Hawes, W. (1996). *Public television: America's first station, An intimate account.* Santa Fe, N.Mex.: Sunstone Press.

34. Hawes, 1996.

35. Third report and order. (1951). 41 FCC Reports 158.

36. Third report, 1951, p. 588.

37. Third report, 1951, p. 588.

38. Sixth report and order. (1952). 41 FCC Reports 426. p. 426.

39. Sixth report, 1952, pp. 428-429.

40. Minutes of the Board of Regents. (1951, Apr. 17). Book 2, University of Houston Archive, University of Houston, Houston, Tex.

41. Minutes of Board of Regents. (1951b, May 22). Book 2, University of Houston Archive, University of Houston, Houston, Tex.

42. Hennock, F.B. (1953, Feb. 19). Address to the American Association of School Administrators. FHS 8/105.

43. U.S. Congress/House. (1958). *Hearings for the investigation of regulatory commissions and agencies,* 85th Congress, 2nd Session.

44. Hennock, F.B. (1952, Oct. 18). Letter to Abrams, B. FBH 1/Corresp-A.

45. Tannenwald, T. (1953, January 8). Letter to Abrams, B. FHS 3/32.

46. Hennock, F.B. (1955, Oct. 31) Letter to Abramson, M. FHS 6/76.

47. Minutes of the Board of Regents. (1952, Apr. 15). Book 2, University of Houston Archive, University of Houston, Houston, Tex.

48. Minutes of Board of Regents. (1952, Sept. 16). Book 2, University of Houston Archive, University of Houston, Houston, Tex.; Minutes of Board of Regents. (1952, Oct. 21). Book 2, University of Houston Archive, University of Houston, Houston, Tex.

49. Hennock, 1952, Aug 30.

50. Hennock, 1952, Aug 30.

51. Militello, 1993; Nystedt, B. (1952, Oct. 24). $300,000 UH TV plant started. *University of Houston Cougar,* p. 1.

52. Militello, 1993.

53. Hennock, 1953, June 8.

54. Kemmerer, W.W. (1955, July 20). Telegram to Hennock, F.B. FHS 6/75.

Other Sources

Beadle, M.E., and Stephenson, A. (1997). Frieda Hennock: Leader for educational television. *Techtrends,* pp. 42, 45-49.

Brinson, S.L. (In press). *Personal and Public Interests: Frieda Hennock and the F.C.C.* Westport, Conn.: Greenwood Press.

Hennock, F.B. (1949, May 17). Letter to Tyler, T. FBH 8/Cor-Tu.

Morgenthau, H. (1996). Dona Quixote: The adventures of Frieda Hennock. *Television Quarterly,* 26(2), pp. 61-73.

Smith, R.F. (1967-1968). Madame commissioner. *Journal of Broadcasting,* pp. 12, 69-81.

Price Hicks

Price Hicks

Stylish Vision

Price Hicks considers herself a lucky woman. When asked to comment on the climate toward women at KCET, the station where she interned and later worked, Price remarked, "Those were the best of times for a producer, especially a woman producer. I was very lucky to be where I was when women were trying to get on that side of the television fence."[1] Hick's story is not one of fighting for gender equity; it is a story of fighting for the best possible quality in a climate of limited resources.

Price Hicks began to develop her vision of quality from a very early age. She grew up in the 1930s and 40s the daughter of John and Maude Pendergrass in Birmingham, Alabama. Her father was a contractor and her mother was a traditional homemaker. The youngest of three children, Price enjoyed a household full of conversation and energy and read anything and everything. Even then, she was experiencing the involvement that comes with a good story telling. She stated, "I think a story is good if the reader . . . just has to see how it all comes out."[2]

Price also loved the movies. Many young women of the time may have found themselves infatuated with the likes of Clark Gable or Norma Shearer, but Price noticed the others. "I loved the movies but my early interest was in the people behind the scenes. I actually read the credits and knew all the names of the great costume designers, art directors and music people. I did have daydreams of being another Helen Rose or Adrian."[3]

Price Hicks developed an appreciation for the supporting cast. She was drawn to the specifics of set design, lighting, and writing. In other words, Price noticed that the final product on the screen was the outcome of a vast coordinated effort.

There was one more element that completed Price's early media experiences. This was the interplay between photography and news. Some of Price's earliest recollections are of news events. As an eight year old she remembered the Lindbergh baby's kidnapping and the tragic air crash of the plane carrying Will Rogers and Wiley Post. These were dramatic events made more vivid by intense media coverage. Most importantly, World War II galvanized the news experience for Price. "I was in my teens during the war and its effect on me and everyone I knew was enormous. Even though the battlegrounds were far away, I certainly had an acute sense of how small the world really was and how vulnerable we all were."[4]

Following World War II, Price loved the black-and-white photography of the weeklies *Life* and *Look*. The photos taken by Margaret Bourke-White, Robert Capa, and Edward Weston prompted her to consider news as a stylistic expression rather than just information. She admired the news giants of the day—Edward R. Murrow, Eric Sevareid and Walter Cronkite—but gravitated toward the study of art when she began college. There were no women on the news at that time, but her vision of style was being formed. "I got caught up in theater where my art studies were helpful in designing sets and lighting, which I did a lot of."[5]

Price earned a bachelor's degree in art with cum laude honors from the Alabama College for Women. Now known as the University of Montevallo, it enrolled approximately 850 young women while Price was there. "I learned so much from being in a school where no one could ever say, 'you can't do that because you are a girl'. I would never have been allowed, for example, to do stage lighting in a coed school."[6] However, similar to many women of the day, Price did not pursue a career in art or theater. She married.

Price began the next phase of her life with her husband, Paul Hicks, the day she graduated from college. They moved north to Providence, Rhode Island, where they raised two daughters, Pamela and Leslie. In 1959, Paul began work for the Rand Corporation, which required the young family to transfer to the then sleepy town of Santa Monica, California. In New England, Price had become involved with community theater, where she continued to develop her "behind-the-scenes" talents, especially lighting. However, it wasn't until Paul and Price came to Southern California that all her interests came together and found a creative outlet.

For a scholarly minded homemaker, accessibility to intellectual pursuits is tantalizing. By this time, the girls were in elementary school and Price had a bit of free time. She attended what is now California State University at Northridge and was allowed to create a program of study that began in creative writing, evolved into journalism, and ultimately became television news. Paul and the children were encouraging and supportive. "Paul gave 120 percent of his support. He was the biggest fan for all his girls."[7] Price doesn't recall them ever quarreling over careers.

During this time, Price became a full-fledged "news junkie." Southern California was quickly becoming the focus for much of the social upheaval that would come to define the 1960s. Although her passion for news had been there for some time, she finally found a place to express it. She became assistant editor at the campus radio station but quickly realized her future belonged to television. "I think producing was just in my veins."[8] With a letter of recommendation in hand, she went in search of an internship.

Price found it difficult to secure an internship where she could actually work and develop her skill as a news producer. The internship was a technical necessity. There was no television equipment at CSUN at the time; students were taught entirely out of books and through lectures by television professionals from local network stations. Although several stations were willing to let her in, she could only observe the process. She knew she couldn't learn that way. The only station that was willing to let her get into production work was KCET, the Los Angeles Public Television outlet.

KCET, located on Sunset Boulevard in Los Angeles, sits near a string of Hollywood movie lots. "KCET allowed me to do anything and everything I was capable of, even some things I wasn't capable of."[9] All the alternative news writers found their way to KCET. While commercial outlets maintained the status quo for television news, public television was willing to experiment. Price quickly had to sink or swim. She was the only intern and she was also 41 years old. Price never felt that age or gender was a hindrance. She maintains that working hard, focusing on task, and not acting negatively or defensively about your minority position alleviated any age- or gender-based tension.

KCET was growing quickly and needed personnel. Price was put in the news and public affairs department. She learned how to produce her own and other people's ideas into words and images that engaged people's attention just like the stories she read as a child. Typical of many new interns, Price was at first afraid to ask questions in fear of betraying her lack of experience. "Hardly anyone even spoke to me unless they had to. Actually, I found out later that no one in the news department had been told why I was there or what I was supposed to be doing."[10] She was hired as a part-time producer at the end of the internship.

Price quickly found out that her liberal arts academic experience served her well. Television production requires familiarity with all the different languages found behind the scenes. Her art background enabled her to have meaningful dialogue with art directors. Her theater background enabled her to discuss options with lighting directors and set designers. Her creative writing and journalism training brought knowledge of the writing process.

During her first years in public broadcasting Price had few negative experiences with male co-workers. KCET was equitable when it came to hiring and promoting women, an unusual quality for the time. "When I became a full-fledged producer . . . some crew guys would give me little tests, but I think they were more bemused than anything else. I learned that if you do your homework, do first rate pre-production, take care of your staff and crew and run the show efficiently you'll be fine, male or female."[11]

Price produced a variety of television programs during her tenure at KCET, including musical showcases *(Rosemary Clooney, with Love, Presenting Nelson Riddle)*, cultural issues *(The Eames Design, The Russian Avant-Garde)*, and public affairs *(The Venice Town Council, LA Collective)*. "I liked studio work for music shows and talk shows. You have more control, obviously . . . [but] I never felt as connected to [a] performance as I did to public affairs and news shows."[12]

Her most influential and rewarding experience was *Citywatchers.* *Citywatchers* was a local public affairs program that began in the studio at KCET. The show was hosted by venerable *LA Times* columnist Art Seidenbaum and film critic Charles "Chuck" Champlin. Price described the show: "I think *Citywatchers* had the look and feel of the city, its bigness and smallness, depending on the show. Someone once compared us to a trolley wandering around town, picking up and dropping off passengers rather randomly."[13] *Citywatchers* was a remarkable chemistry of personalities and talent.

When Price took over *Citywatchers,* she and her colleagues made an innovative decision: to broadcast remote. It was a program that introduced the city of Los Angeles to its residents.[14] The program took advantage of the remote truck and went around the city where things were happening. Each program had a single topic but showed a variety of perspectives that documented the growth and challenges facing the city. The format also changed according to the nature of the topic. "What we are trying to do is make Los Angeles approachable. We are looking at the city from a personal journalistic point of view, concentrating on what is unique to Southern California, not solely on its problems."[15]

The traveling version of *Citywatchers* debuted in February 1971. Price and her team started the show where the city started, Olvera Street. No place was off limits, including flophouses, rooftops and alleys. Price reserved a single pair of sneakers for remote shoots. An eight-hour day might only end up with two hours of shooting. The rest of the time was spent getting to the location, setting up and troubleshooting. All this was done with big noisy generators and large studio cameras hauled out to all these exotic locations. One of the more significant problems was baffling the generator so the sound didn't register on tape. By the sixth and final year, those shoes were falling apart.

Citywatchers was a great success. It was nominated for seven Emmy Awards and won three. The awards were for Best Community Affairs Series (1971); a special, *The Metropolitan Opera Auditions, L.A.* (1973); and Best Information Series (1974). Also, in 1973, she received a Golden Mike Award for another KCET special, *Venice Town Council*. Price Hicks attributes that success to two primary factors: the chemistry of her production team and the quality of production.

The *Citywatchers* team consisted of Art Seidenbaum and Chuck Champlin as hosts; Jerry Hughes, the program's first director; Price as producer; and Nancy Salter as production assistant. Price recalled that she, Chuck and Art all moved to LA in the same year. "These guys knew each other, were friends, had so many contacts and knew so much. The show opened with Art and Chuck doing 'the walk.' We went to wherever the show was filming that week and [Art and Chuck] walked and talked the opening of the show. We used a long lens and remote mike."[16] This opening became the *Citywatchers'* trademark.

Jerry Hughes was responsible for the look of the show and, fortunately, was a technical wizard. When he became program director at KCET, they employed Allan Muir (later director of *Austin City Limits*) and then Bruce Francini. Price described production assistant Nancy

Salter as "the queen of research." She had the knack for getting people to talk about anything and was a "true artist" at editing. In fact, Price attributes much of the show's success to thorough research. "The research had to be fast and thorough. . . . We always had three shows in some stage of production at the same time—one in pre-production, one in production, and one in post-production—so it was really a matter of keeping three shows in my head at once."[17]

But it was not just the research that was important, it was maintaining quality. Price describes a quality production as the outcome of the best of all physical elements in a program that create a "visceral response" in the viewer. That response is a deep emotional or personal reaction to what is on the small screen. She identified several skills as being important to creating quality.

Price believes the ability to recognize a good story is crucial to quality programming. "I think if you start out with fresh material you have a better chance of staying fresh longer. Sometimes doing funny material seriously or serious material funnily works."[18] However, just being able to recognize a good story is not enough. Quality production involves making good choices about how to get the job done. Her experiences shooting two shows on location at Catalina Island demonstrate the need to make good choices. Price had two days to complete the project.

Price and her crew of nine were familiar with the trials of field production, but water was soon to present a new set of challenges. All the video equipment was precariously arranged on a small dive boat bobbing in the Pacific Ocean, the best vantage point from which to photograph diving practices.

> Our first shots of the first day were to be of two divers under water demonstrating safe and unsafe scuba practices. We were the first show to use an underwater camera in the ocean and we were very excited. We sent the cameraman and the camera down to get some beauty shots before we shot the divers and we were standing in the control booth waiting for that first shot to come up on the screen, and there it was, beautiful! Then, in horror, we saw bubbles appearing at the bottom of our screen, and the director was yelling, "Pull it up! Pull it up!" The camera housing had sprung a leak and it was filling up with water.[19]

The technicians emptied the seawater, rinsed the camera with freshwater, and with the boat skipper's wife's hair dryer tried to dry out the camera. Fortunately, they had a backup camera and were able to shoot the programs and get everything except the underwater shots. But the shooting that was left to do was not easy with only one camera. There was a midocean rendezvous at a specific moment with a county helicopter, a *Baywatch* rescue boat with two lifeguards, and people at the island's resuscitation chamber to simulate an actual scuba rescue and treatment situation. The crew accomplished that in two very long tracking shots from the helicopter to the *Baywatch* boat, loading the "victim" onto a stretcher and up to the chamber. Then they had to reset to get the shots of the chamber treatment and the audio, and there was still another show to shoot.

Price decided to shoot the second show in what remained of the first day and hope for good weather and a working underwater camera the next day. She called all the people who were going to be on the second show, rescheduled them for the first day and did the entire shoot for the second show. The next morning, they went out to sea with the dried out camera, completed the shooting and came home with two shows ready for editing.[20]

Price was adept at finding ways out of restrictive situations and made the most of her resources. She was an excellent producer. This contributed to *Citywatchers'* reputation as a cutting-edge program.

Citywatchers was almost always done on location. In the early 1970s, this required some logistical finesse. Not only can weather be a factor, but also time and light are no longer controlled variables. Forgetting something can halt production. Even getting the talent and guests to the location can be problematic. Price boasts that she has made more maps for how to get around in LA than anyone she knows! Amazingly, *Citywatchers* was not rained out once in six years on the air. But rain wasn't the only threat. Since there were no remote cameras, they used the big studio cameras. After finishing an interview on the street, the cameraman stepped back from his camera just as a stiff little gust of wind came. It caught the $85,000 camera and knocked it into the gutter, where it lay in pieces.[21]

Price Hicks was tremendously successful at KCET. She and her team received a total of 15 Los Angeles area Emmy nominations and won four. Three of those were for *Citywatchers,* the fourth for a program called *28 Tonight.* Although *28 Tonight* was never as successful as *Citywatchers* with the public, it also benefited from Hicks' signature style. "If I had a certain style, I know that I had a reputation for being almost insanely prepared, for working long, hard hours, for fighting for every dollar and hour and crews. Once in a while I would hear the word 'classy' attached to our work."[22]

Price believes that the key to beng inventive is collaboration, a style that some call "feminine."[23] She also attributes some of her success to the nature of the television industry in the late 1960s and early 1970s. Hicks described the climate of those times as having three main features that made public TV women-friendly. First, public television had a great need for affordable talent. Public television was beginning to create a unique identity with the broadcast of such landmark shows as *Sesame Street* and *Electric Company.* People were noticing and watching. Second, public television was more community centered than national outlets. Women could identify with the mission of public broadcasting, which understood the needs of their community. Local issues were more immediate and accessible to women balancing career and/or home in a rapidly changing social climate. Finally, public television was more child-centered. Not only did they produce programming for children, but they recognized the challenges faced by female employees with children. In sum, it was easier for a woman to move into a position of authority at a public TV outlet.[24]

In the 1980s, the television industry began to change, and Price decided to leave KCET in 1982. She spent a few years as an independent producer for clients around the world, but by 1985 she made a move that brought her full circle to her beginnings in television.

The Academy of Televison Arts and Sciences (ATAS) is most famous for the Emmy Awards they bestow annually. However, ATAS organizes conferences and colloquia for industry professionals and academics. They explore current media topics, trends in broadcasting, public service efforts, and maintain the ATAS Archive of American Televison. The organization has an elaborate network of services for its members, most notably, an arm that creates and coordinates educational programs and services. In 1985 Price Hicks came onboard to direct these activities.

ATAS was beginning to recognize the need for mentorship in the television industry. Colleges and universities began graduating thousands of telecommunications majors each semester. Although an internship and awards program was in place at ATAS, Price recognized the dual needs that could be served by a high-quality program. Just as she needed hands-on experience when she was trying to break into the industry, so did the burgeoning telecommunications industry need quality personnel. Clearly, the future of television would be created by today's interns.

Price found a way to distill her early experiences in public television into a structured opportunity for new people in the field through The College Student Internship Program. This competitive program offers 40 paid summer internships in 27 categories of telecommunications work. All the internships are in Los Angeles. Price believes a good internship includes "a dedicated host in a place that is welcoming to an intern, a situation where the intern can participate at almost every level of activity, and ongoing support for the intern from the intern managers." Students who are successful in this program "give 100 percent . . ., roll with changing situations, have great aptitude and know that every aspect of the internship is an opportunity to learn something you didn't know already . . . good or bad. A sense of humor helps a lot."[25]

She has also made learning opportunities available to other professionals. ATAS sponsors a four-day faculty seminar for college professors to learn about the industry. Additionally, the Academy also makes professionals available to colleges and universities for lectures and workshops. It is evident that the early efforts Price made in being prepared and willing to work have developed into a philosophy and style that now benefit students, faculty, professionals, and the television industry as a whole. This philosophy is grounded in the idea that practical experience is crucial to creating an individual style that allows creativity and innovation to develop. In Price's view, no industry task is too small or insignificant to gain insight on the overall process.

Perhaps one of Price's most enduring contributions to local television may be in providing a source of well-trained novices to disseminate throughout the field. The ATAS summer internship program has repeatedly been lauded as one of the best in the country. Price has also forged a partnership between telecommunications faculty and industry professionals. Today it is a standard expectation for a new hire to possess at least a bachelor's degree and have some structured experience in the field. So faculty members are faced with preparing students for a diverse and rapidly changing industry they often know little about. The ATAS faculty/industry seminar provides a link between these entities and bridges this knowledge gap. To complete the process, Price makes an annual fall tour promoting her programs. She encourages faculty and students alike to work together with ATAS to produce a better experience for all involved. She promotes the value of a liberal arts education. She encourages students to take courses in art, theater and philosophy and tells them about how she used those skills in her career. She asks the students to create their own vision of style.

In sum, Price Hicks has made many contributions to broadcasting on the local level and broadcasting as an industry. Her experiences at KCET helped establish a credibility for Public Television and showed many women that they could bring their own style to television. Her experiences at ATAS are showing many future broadcasting professionals what it means to be professional and what is required to be successful. Price is an excellent role model who possesses those attributes that make quality television—creativity, diversity, and style.

Notes

1. Hicks, P. (2000, Sept. 11). Personal communication.
2. Hicks, P. (2000, Nov. 21). Personal communication.
3. Hicks, 2000, Nov.
4. Hicks, 2000, Nov.
5. Hicks, 2000, Nov.
6. Hicks, P. (2001, Jan. 4). Personal communication.
7. Hicks, 2000, Nov.
8. Hicks, 2000, Nov.
9. Hicks, 2000, Nov.
10. Hicks, 2000, Nov.
11. Hicks, 2000, Nov.
12. Hicks, 2000, Nov.
13. Hicks, 2000, Nov.
14. Murphy, M. (1972, Apr. 3). New breed of TV producers. *The Los Angeles Times*, p. 16.
15. Murphy, 1972, p. 16.
16. Hicks, P. (2000, Dec. 6). Personal communication.
17. Hicks, 2000, Dec.
18. Hicks, 2000, Dec.
19. Hicks, 2000, Dec.
20. Hicks, 2000, Nov.
21. Hicks, 2000, Nov.
22. Hicks, 2000, Nov.
23. Seger, L. (1996). *When Women Call the Shots: The Developing Power and Influence of Women in Television and Film*. New York: Henry Holt.
24. Hicks, P. (Apr. 1999). Women's Roles in Public Broadcasting. Paper presented at the annual meeting of the Broadcast Education Association, Las Vegas, Nev.
25. Hicks, 2000, Nov.

Other Sources

Academy of Television Arts and Sciences. (nd). Price Hicks biography. Los Angeles, Calif.
KCET [On-line]. Available: http://www.kcet. org/ inside_kcet/history/ index.htm

Lisa Howard (Lisa Thomas-Laury)

Lisa Howard (Lisa Thomas-Laury)
Philadelphia Television News Anchor

Lisa Howard began to think about women on television as early as age 11. She remembered that through her early teenage years, there was a woman on network news that she admired. Ironically, her name was Lisa Howard. She would come on the air at noon and present a five-minute newscast. Young Lisa Howard identified with this woman because she thought someday she would like to do the same thing. Howard also admired Carol Simpson for her good diction, enunciation and a certain presence when dealing with the camera. Howard remembered thinking as a young girl, "I could do that."[1]

Howard pursued her interest in broadcast journalism during the second semester of her freshman year at Marshall University. She had won a most promising student journalism award to help defray some of the expenses of college. She also had a financial aid grant, but Howard knew she needed to find employment.

She learned, from a classmate, that a local NBC affiliate was interviewing for a weekend weathergirl. Howard was majoring in English at the time and was available on weekends to work so she auditioned and got the job, becoming West Virginia's first black woman weathercaster. The experience as weather anchor was challenging, but Howard was eager to expand her broadcast experience. She asked management at the station where she was anchoring if it would be possible to pursue an internship in reporting and was given permission to do so. Many of the pieces she did were voice-overs, so the reporter was not always seen in the story, but each piece helped strengthen her writing and videography skills. Howard continued as the weekend weatherperson until her graduation in 1975.

Howard interviewed for television positions in Kentucky, Oklahoma and North Carolina. There were few blacks and few women on the air at the time. When she graduated, she was in the right place at the right time. Howard selected Oklahoma station KTVY because they offered the highest salary, $185 a week.[2]

Experience as a television cameraperson enabled Howard to move to the next position with some ease. She shot her own stories with a CP 16 (one of the first news cameras in the business), which was heavy and bulky by today's standards. She worked with Dave Smith, who would shoot Lisa's stories so that she could report, and Lisa would shoot Dave's stories. Then each reporter would edit his or her own story for air. It is rare today that a news director would send two reporters out together unless it was a very big story.

The news director in Oklahoma City at that time was Ernie Shultz, former president of the Radio Television News Director's Association. Darryl Barton, chief of photography, made an impact on Howard. He wanted her to be a television news photographer and to make her the first (and best) woman TV news photographer. Howard was impressed with Barton's devotion and love of the job, but the day he sent her out to cover a parade and had her lie in the street to get shots of feet was the day she realized she did not want to pursue a career in television camera work. Howard spent just eight months at the station before moving to Nashville, Tennessee, to the CBS affiliate.

Howard recalled that when she went to Nashville for her interview, Oprah Winfrey was at that station. She remembered sitting in her hotel room watching Winfrey do the weekend news at age 19. She thought, "This is a phenomenal woman." Winfrey was anchoring the news while still a student at Tennessee State. There was something about her voice and her commanding presence that set Winfrey apart from other anchors in Howard's eyes. Howard noted, "She was not white, blond or attractive by the standards television had set for an anchorwoman but there was something very attractive and powerful about her."[3]

Her Nashville experience would last two years. Howard served as education reporter while learning the basics of journalism. She won the School Bell Award for Best Education Series there. The station was progressive; the first in the nation to go live with microwave, giving Howard invaluable experience in live television reporting. She pictured herself in New York someday because that was the number one market; she did not know much about Philadelphia.

In 1977 Lisa Howard was in Nashville, Tennessee, the 33rd market in the nation, when a talent scout from Philadelphia came to town. He saw Howard on the air, called her at the station and said he thought the ABC affiliate would be interested in hiring her. The assistant news director then, Bob Feldman, said that he had seen thousands of tapes, but Lisa Howard "jumped off the screen."[4] He remembered that she was really unusual. Feldman recalled, "I first saw Lisa on January 9, 1978, interviewed her on January 16, 1978 and wanted to hire her." There was just one small issue, her name. There was already a news reporter in town by the name of Marc Howard so she could not be Lisa Howard because the viewers might get confused. Lisa would have to change her name. After much deliberation, she selected Thomas because it had special meaning; it was her mother's maiden name.

It came as a bit of a surprise to Philadelphians in 1978 when WPVI Channel 6, the news giant, hired a young black female as a news anchor. Lisa Thomas, then 24 years old, signed a contract on February 20, 1978. She was an instant success in Philadelphia, as was characterized in newspaper articles that addressed her on-camera presence and her ease with the audience.

Bob Feldman remembered exactly what captivated him. "Her eyes had it! They were very expressive. She was a delight, a real natural."[5] He noted that it was very important that Thomas, like all the other new anchors, be seen as a real journalist, not just an anchor.

Feldman recalled that Lisa was obviously a good reporter, showed terrific potential and looked very young because she was very young. "She dazzled us. It was a time of looking for people who are just good people. Part of the decision-making process was that she was a good person. It was better to hire a good person rather than one who was better at their job on day one."[6]

From the beginning of her WPVI days, Lisa Thomas captured the viewers. She was unmarried and received a lot of fan mail. The station had printed pictures for all their on-air personalities, and Lisa went through a lot of them. Her first story was at a carwash. Feldman remembered that story "because my wife was in the car with my kids and the reason we knew this was that she (Lisa) recognized my kids from a picture on my desk. . . . She walked over and introduced herself to my wife and kids."[7]

Lisa recalled that her relationship with Feldman was a unique one. He was constantly "on her" about her hair. Feldman was quick to substantiate his position:

What I said is that the most important thing in the way you look on the air is a lack of negatives. You do not want anything to detract from your communication between you and the viewer—a necklace, hair in your face (being blown in your face if you are out in the field). The women who had long hair, outside, the hair was always blowing. I would urge them to put so much hair spray on they had helmet hair. They had to Feldmanize their hair. I was very aggressive about keeping their hair intact.[8]

Thomas was considered a good reporter because she was able to personalize the story. She covered the royal wedding of Prince Charles to Princess Diana in London with producer Cheryl Fair. Feldman remembered that Thomas did a live shot from the royal wedding. "She had to climb up on something to do stand-up and security people were tugging at her dress, but she ignored it and kept reporting live."[9]

Thomas set the standards for showing that women, and in particular minority women, were equal to or even better than many of their counterparts who were white men. "She also shows that you can have a good life, a stable life, and a stable marriage and not give it all up because a career is the most important thing."[10]

When she came to Philadelphia, Thomas was not sure she would survive. She was hired as a news anchor and reporter without any previous anchor experience but admits station management obviously believed in her ability to do the job. She started on the noon newscast. When the station brought in new talent, they always "auditioned them" in a non-prime time slot like the noon newscast or a weekend newscast. They also worked in the field to develop recognition in the community. Then, they could move to other airtime shifts.

Fortunately, Lisa Thomas's first position was alongside Jim O'Brien, an established anchor, who took her under his wing. He was able to help her relax. In addition, station management hired Julia Wing, a voice coach from Temple University. Wing was also a respected professor of theater who worked with many professionals in the city and region. Thomas worked with Wing for six months to change her Appalachian speech pattern. Wing taught Thomas how to breathe from the diaphragm, to get rid of the twang, to talk normally and to stay relaxed. Thomas admitted that it was the best thing that happened to her. As she removed the stigma of an accent, Thomas relaxed and was better able to deliver the news. Her increase in comfort also was due in part to the support of the viewing audience. Her fan mail was evidence that the viewers had accepted Thomas.

On June 1, 1979, Channel 6 officials announced that the anchor team of Lisa Thomas and Chris Wagner would take over the noon newscast just prior to the Christmas holiday. This would mark the first time a regular news program in the city of Philadelphia was anchored by two women. Bob Feldman recalled, "If anyone could make it work, we were going from strength as far as the station [was concerned]."[11] After six months on the air, the local paper, the *Philadelphia Daily News,* reported that the dual anchor team had two times the audience of Channel 3 at noon.[12]

Just two weeks after the ratings announcement, it was announced that Lisa Thomas was engaged to Philadelphia physician William Laury. Seven months later, in July 1980, she married Dr. William Laury in Charleston, West Virginia. On-air she would be Lisa Thomas-Laury, and she agreed to share (via tape) part of the wedding with viewers on the WPVI public affairs program, *Visions,* which she hosted.

Thomas-Laury is a private person and this is evident in her relationships at the station as well as with viewers. Her colleagues Marc Howard and Jim Gardner recalled there was a big chemical fire and did not understand why Thomas-Laury wasn't covering the story, as she was their best reporter. Howard remembered that the news director called the two anchors into his office and said, "Lisa is pregnant and the doctor said she couldn't go near fires, especially chemical fires."[13] Thomas-Laury had asked her news director to keep the news quiet, but the situation seemed to warrant revealing the information.

Thomas-Laury is keenly aware that television news is a business where you come into people's homes and it is very intimate. She recounted an unnerving story in which a man who was waiting for her in the parking lot of WPVI-TV punched her in the face. She was leaving the building that night with one of her co-anchors and she recalled that she had never really thought of being in danger at her place of employment. But this experience changed things. Thomas-Laury admits she has to think about herself in relationship to the public. She is careful to keep her personal life private. If asked for an autograph in a public place she will generally consent. However, if someone approaches her in public while she is with her family, she will say, "I appreciate your loyalty but I am with my family now."[14]

Thomas-Laury has been a member of the WPVI-TV anchor team for more than 22 years. Her first news director, Alan Nesbitt, told her, "You know, you're going to get there one day, but you just need to look at that camera . . . pretend that the camera is a very special person and you are communicating with that person."[15] She knew what he meant and in fact, has been able to do what she had seen the other Lisa Howard do, build a bond with the audience. Lisa Thomas-Laury has become a symbol of good journalism and a representative for young women, especially young minority women.

In addition to her ability to communicate with the audience as individual people, Thomas has strong ethical standards and believes it is better not to show emotion. She also thinks it is important to be succinct and direct and as accurate as possible. Her colleagues say she arrived with poise and now "she has added experience and time to the poise . . . never lost that youthful exuberance—and [she] continues to be interested and excited by her work."[16]

Thomas notes that local journalism has changed dramatically during her career. She thinks that news today is more an entertainment business. It is still news, it is still informing the public, but the parameters are broader. Thomas-Laury used the morning newscast at WPVI as an example of a program where the anchors have fun with the news. Today it is a two-hour program. It was once a series of five-minute stories where the producer was the anchor, wrote the stories and even created his/her own rundown for the segment. The morning news has a bit more latitude, the anchors relax, joke with each other and seem to keep a light-hearted way about them. Another change Thomas-Laury has noticed is that news people today are freer as journalists to express themselves and even to react to stories or their feelings about a story. There is a very human side to what they do and the viewers see more three-dimensional people on screen. But she is upset when she sees some of the promotions of stories. Thomas-Laury said, "It can be extremely misleading the way stories can be promoted in a local newscast."[17] She also believes that coverage of a tragic story needs to respect those involved. For Lisa Thomas-Laury, a sound bite or a clip (a short piece of audio which might be the sound of a mother screaming out in grief) is probably not the best way to report news.

Her experience as a cameraperson and film editor early in her career (before there was videotape) has led to an appreciation for those with whom she works. She understands and appreciates how to explain to the cameraperson and/or editor what she is trying to create. Thomas-Laury continues to do a lot of her own writing.

In addition to coverage of the royal wedding (her favorite story), her other favorite story was Clinton's second inauguration, where she spoke to San Francisco mayor Willie Williams, Whoopi Goldberg, Johnny Cochran, John F. Kennedy, Jr., and Caroline Kennedy Schlossberg.

Lisa Thomas-Laury is a woman whose professionalism is immediately evident both in the field and on the air. What is most impressive is that her colleagues also praise it.

> The word that I think of is "class." She always handles herself with enormous class; she is dignified, at the same time very warm. She is an innate communicator. There are people who toil in this business for years trying to communicate. Lisa has this inherent ability to look people in the eye and communicate. I am not sure it can be learned. It is something that Lisa has and has always has since the day she arrived at Channel 6, to be involved in what she has to say.[18]

What is Thomas-Laury's legacy? Co-anchor Marc Howard believes that her mark on the industry is that "you can be a striking, stunning woman and you can be an intelligent, articulate newscaster. A lot of people think you can't. Lisa is leaving that as a roadmap or landmark for other people—that you can do both."[19] He says Lisa's sense of humor "is delightful. Her smile can make people feel more relaxed and more comfortable, and she can be entertainingly sarcastic but not bitingly sarcastic."[20]

She has managed to raise two sons while pursuing a demanding career. She receives high praise from co-workers: "She is intelligent; she is gracious, dignified, smart, competent. . . . I don't know that there is anyone who has ever gotten angry with Lisa. She has that quality that very few people have: there is nobody who doesn't like her, none who speak ill of her."[21]

Today, minority representation in television news is still not proportionate to the percentage of minority viewers nationwide and, in many cases, locally. In Philadelphia there are other African American women anchoring newscasts. The time may not be far off when a minority woman anchors a 6 p.m. and/or 11 p.m. newscast on one of the local affiliates in this fourth-largest market in the nation. But, Lisa Thomas-Laury seems content with her role at WPVI-TV and the viewers have shown great loyalty to her. Beyond a credible source for presenting the news, Thomas-Laury also represents the generation of women who have risen to the top in their fields with few compromises, demonstrating that you can be intelligent, a good writer, and a good communicator and be happy in your personal life. Longevity, consistency and being there day after day, month after month, year after year help to build a sense of trust with the viewers who rely on newscasters so much. Lisa Thomas-Laury has built that sense of trust for 22 years in Philadelphia and continues to strengthen the bond between newscaster and viewer.

Notes

1. Thomas-Laury, L. (2000, Sept. 18). Personal communication.
2. Thomas-Laury, 2000.
3. Thomas-Laury, 2000.
4. Feldman, B. (2000, Oct. 23). Personal communication.
5. Feldman, 2000.
6. Feldman, 2000.
7. Feldman, 2000.
8. Feldman, 2000.
9. Feldman, 2000.
10. Feldman, 2000.
11. Feldman, 2000.
12. "Local" *Philadelphia Daily News,* (1979, Dec 12). p. 39.
13. Howard, M. (2000, Oct. 23). Personal communication.
14. Thomas-Laury, 2000.
15. Thomas-Laury, 2000.
16. Gardner, J. (2000, Oct. 23). Personal communication.
17. Thomas-Laury, 2000.
18. Gardner, 2000.
19. Howard, 2000.
20. Howard, 2000.
21. Gardner, 2000.

Carole Kneeland. *(Courtesy of Mike Wenglar–KVUE TV)*

Chapter 10 _____ by John Mark Dempsey

Carole Kneeland
Lone Star Legacy

When the weekly *Austin Chronicle* published its "Best of Austin" in
1998 listing assorted superlatives, an item appeared in the Media sec-
tion titled "Best Legacy: Carole Kneeland."[1] While most people who
die at age 49 do not leave a legacy, Carole Kent Kneeland, news director and later vice president of news at KVUE-TV in Austin, Texas,
who died in January 1998, left behind a record of accomplishments in
TV news that most people of retirement age would be proud to claim.

Kneeland's experience as a Texas journalist comprised work in television, radio and newspapers. Before arriving at KVUE, Kneeland had
served for 12 years as the state capitol reporter for WFAA-TV in Dallas, a station that has won five DuPont-Columbia Awards. After graduating from the University of Washington, where she earned Phi Beta
Kappa recognition, Kneeland came to Texas in 1970 to work as a
newscaster for Houston radio station, KAUM-FM. She jumped from
radio to television at KPRC-TV in Houston in 1973. At first, she had
been turned down for television jobs because, she was told, "women's
voices were nagging and lacking in authority." Next she went to the
Corpus Christi-Caller Times before returning to television with WFAA.

She joined KVUE as news director in 1989 and immediately the
station claimed the Gannett chain's Television News Station of the Year
Award. In 1996, KVUE named her vice president of news.[2] Her husband of 15 years, *Austin American-Statesman* political editor Dave Mc-
Neely, said his late wife "strove to give people news they could use, not
titillation. . . . [Crime] reports had to be relevant and necessary."[3]
When Kneeland died in 1998 Linda Ellerbee called her "a world-class
journalist who toiled in local TV news, an arena that so many people
like to laugh at—at best. [She made] . . . local news more responsible,

eliminating gratuitous coverage of violence by installing guidelines on crime coverage. She also set standards for political advertising."[4]

Los Angeles Times columnist Howard Rosenberg met Carole in June 1996 when he went to Austin to do a story on KVUE's experiment of local newscasts going against the trend of covering gratuitous crime stories. He reported that under Carole's leadership the ABC affiliate established rigid criteria before it would air a crime story, noting "how rare it was for any station—but especially one that didn't need a gimmick because its newscasts already topped the ratings—to do something so daring, just on principle."[5] Two of the issues Kneeland focused on were violence in television news and truth in political advertising.

KVUE Crime Project

In January 1996, Kneeland and executive producer Cathy McFeaters unveiled a new policy for the coverage of crime news. They announced that KVUE would not report a crime story unless the answer was "yes" to one of the following questions: (1) Is there an immediate threat to public safety? (2) Is there a threat to children? (3) Do viewers need to take action? (4) Is there a significant community impact? (5) Is the story part of a crime prevention effort?[6] Under the policy, each crime story appearing on KVUE was accompanied by a graphic indicating which of the guidelines the story met. "If I'm going to get fired, it's going to be for doing something I really believe in," Kneeland said at the time.[7]

Part of Kneeland's impetus for putting the policy into effect was a concern that the overemphasis on crime news "gives people ideas about crimes they might commit."[8] Kneeland also said KVUE viewers had complained about television's obsession with crime news for several years.[9]

Almost immediately the new policy was put to the test. In the town of Elgin, about 30 miles east of Austin, a Saturday night altercation ended with three men being shot dead. The three other Austin television stations heavily reported the story, but not KVUE. KVUE sent a reporter to Elgin twice over two days to gather information and evaluate the story. Kneeland's decision was based on the fact that there was no immediate threat, no threat to children and no action to be taken.[10]

A few weekends later, KVUE reported on two violent crimes, after much consideration. In one, a University of Texas graduate student shot and killed his wife and four-year-old daughter at an apartment complex for married students and then killed himself. In another, a young man had been killed in a drive-by shooting. A suspect was in custody and there was no threat to the community. At first, the weekend staff made the judgment that the stories did not fit under the new guidelines. But they called Kneeland at home. "Carole told us to start digging on both, looking for larger issues," reporter Greg Groogan said. "She said, 'We cannot drop these stories. . . . We cannot use these guidelines as an excuse not to cover them. Our job is to gather facts and then decide whether to air.'"[11] Groogan's story on the murder/suicide focused on how the residents of the apartment complex responded to the tragedy and on counseling sessions intended to help them spot the signs of domestic abuse. Groogan said the extra effort required by the crime-story guidelines brought better context and perspective to the story.[12]

Joan Barrett, former executive producer at KVUE and currently the executive director of the San Antonio television consulting firm Broadcast Image Group, worked under Kneeland. She said, "When I was there, we used to laugh and call it the 'p' word because she would always say, 'Well, what's the perspective to that? What perspective can we bring to that crime story?' She forced us to step back on crime and not just do the 20-second VO [voice-over] or go cover the police news conference, but say, 'What's the perspective?'"[13]

Kneeland and executive producer McFeaters found it frustrating that many people believed KVUE had simply quit covering crime. KVUE reporters still raced to the crime scene and actually spent more time gathering facts about crimes to judge whether the story qualified under the new guidelines. One KVUE reporter, Bettie Cross, said reporters from other stations envied her because she had the chance to see if the coverage is valid.[14]

A salutary consequence of the crime policy was an improvement in other areas of coverage. Stories included "an explanation of how the flat-tax proposals would affect viewers; an analysis of why the cost of living had skyrocketed in Austin; [and] the story of a principal of an elementary school full of higher-income, successful students who decided to transfer to a low-income school . . . where she thought she might be able to make a greater difference."[15] Political columnist Molly Ivins said Kneeland "led the nation to rethink its definition of news."[16]

Kneeland's reputation and KVUE's approach to covering crime spread to the halls of academe. In a speech on credibility in American journalism to the American Society of Newspaper Editors, the chancellor of the University of California, Berkeley, Robert M. Berdahl, praised Kneeland and urged editors to give more thought to what he called the "framing" of a story. He applauded Kneeland's attention to story framing to avoid distortion.[17]

Response from viewers to KVUE's new policy on crime news was overwhelmingly favorable. Kneeland said the station received numerous calls, faxes, letters and e-mails, the greatest response in the station's history.[18] But not everyone agreed with Kneeland's policy. A local pastor wrote an *Austin American-Statesman* op-ed piece in which he said, "The reporting should not be sensationalized. Pictures may not always be appropriate. But the reality that people kill and are killed on a regular basis is newsworthy. We need to hear it."[19]

Kneeland's experiment also sparked an intense debate within the media over what constitutes ethical crime coverage. Other Austin stations were critical of the policy. One station attacked KVUE's crime-coverage guidelines in a broadcast editorial, accusing KVUE of improperly "filtering" news. "Is your newscast giving you all the news?" rival KEYE-TV asked in a not-so-subtle promo.[20] Others called it censorship.[21] The news director of KCOP-TV in Los Angeles, Steve Cohen, challenged the ethics of such an approach because it forces a journalist to be a super-gatekeeper instead of a gatekeeper. Cohen compared the KVUE policy to news suppression in the former Soviet Union.[22]

Other news directors maintained that doing it the old-fashioned way, using gut instinct was more appropriate.[23] Kneeland's former boss at WFAA-TV in Dallas, Marty Haag, admired Kneeland's integrity in implementing crime guidelines but wondered about their practicality. He called it intellectually stimulating but also acknowledged that such rules would tend to paint a news manager into a corner.[24]

Kneeland acknowledged that KVUE's approach to crime coverage was not an easy path to follow since it goes against competitive instincts. It required time for deliberation while the competition may be going on air with sketchy details and live reports from the scene of the crime.[25]

Truth, Justice and the American Way

Growing up in the 1950s and 1960s, girls had few role models in journalism to emulate. Kneeland told the 1996 graduating class of the University of Texas College of Communications that is was Lois Lane,

Superman's girlfriend, "who inspired me to go into journalism, she being one of the only female reporter role models when I was growing up. I've found over the years that Superman's credo—fighting for Truth, Justice and the American Way—has served me very well in this profession. It's a calling, like the ministry, medicine, teaching, parenting, public service."[26]

Kneeland believed that good broadcast journalism is essential to democracy and out of these ideals come "truth tests" for political advertisements. KVUE aired political commercials, but under Kneeland, KVUE news checked them for accuracy. Many other television stations and newspapers now do the same, but Kneeland was first to do it in television. Political columnist Molly Ivins wrote approvingly, "Because so much of the impact of political ads lies in clever use of video footage, seeing these ads analyzed on TV enables viewers to see how they are being manipulated more effectively than print analysis can."[27] The impact from this policy was strong and some politicians started writing the ads so they could pass the truth test.[28]

Kneeland's belief in the value of television news to democracy also led her to speak out on First Amendment and other "freedom of the press" issues. She testified for the Texas Association of Broadcasters before various lawmaker groups in Austin about open meetings laws, open records and the necessity for public boards to be open with recorded proceedings.[29] Kneeland also served on the Texas Association of Broadcasters' Open Government Task Force. KXAN-TV news director Bruce Whiteaker served with her on the task force and called her "a crusader for the public's right to know," always willing to drop everything in the office to go to the Capitol to address important issues.[30]

For her efforts on behalf of broadcasters under the Freedom of Information Act, the Texas Association of Broadcasters named her its Broadcaster of the Year in 1997.[31] The Texas Associated Press Broadcasters named their Freedom of Information Award after Kneeland before she died.[32] She served on the board of the Freedom of Information Foundation of Texas, which presented her with its James Madison Award in 1997.[33]

Carole Kneeland University

Kneeland was legendary as a mentor to young broadcast journalists. Haag, now senior vice president of news for the broadcast division of the Belo Corporation, said, "Once I was asked to name the best journalism schools in the country. Well, I said, one certainly has to include 'Carole Kneeland University' in the top five. That was not a flippant answer. I meant it. Few leaders have left such an indelible mark on young journalists."[34] Cinny Kennard says as an intern she learned from Kneeland how to log tapes, organize a system of archiving tapes, get interviews, and take notes at a press conference, which provided a very knowledgeable base for the newsroom.[35]

What Kneeland taught young journalists went beyond the nuts and bolts to standards and ethics. She believed you have to be meticulous with the knowledge because the profession has the capability of really hurting people if you take the wrong approach.[36] The Texas Association of Broadcasters director of programs, Michael Schneider, a former reporter at two of KVUE's rivals, said he marveled at Kneeland's capacity for coaching her staff, acknowledging that this happens in some quarters usually when someone's made a big mistake. Carole was effective in coaching before the development of a problem and this continued even after she had become ill.[37]

Kneeland as Manager

Kneeland's former employees praise her as much for her management style and stated expectations as for her skill as a journalist.[38] Carole is remembered for carefully reviewing and making program suggestions before she left for the day. Valerie Hyman of the Poynter Institute wrote that the newsroom "culture" Kneeland created valued "quality over speed, people over product, and democracy over monarchy in the newsroom. Kneeland established a philosophical underpinning for the newsroom that empowered staff with significant responsibility, enabling a news director to attend to the big picture."[39]

KVUE employees under Kneeland also had a direct say in whom their colleagues would be. Carole would create hiring committees, although she always made it clear it was ultimately her decision. It is a system now used in newsrooms all over the country.[40] Kneeland said her experiences as a reporter showed her how to manage. She felt that managers often were not in touch with field reporters and she added a grassroots out-in-the-field thinking to the newsroom.

In an effort to be more equitable, she scheduled holidays and vacations a year ahead so people would know when they would be off. With a seniority system that penalizes new people, senior employees might get off on both Thanksgiving and Christmas. With her revision, the senior people still got the first choice of days off, but they could work on Christmas if they had Thanksgiving off.

This helped to establish a culture in which information and ideas came from the ground up and were acted upon. She required that newsroom employees who were physically present attend the morning and afternoon editorial meetings. Everyone was expected to contribute, with Kneeland using the meetings as a coaching opportunity to reinforce the culture, to stimulate thinking, to show priorities in terms of coverage, and to encourage ethical decision-making.[41]

Kneeland's Character

Because of her influence, some staffers regarded Kneeland as almost a relative. Kennard, who regarded her as "a sister," noted that Kneeland's exceptional upbringing in the state of Washington laid the foundation for what she accomplished in life with an emphasis on hard work, education, and religion. She realized the importance of giving to your community, your profession, and your family. She operated without a lot of emotional baggage and was smart. "She was raised in a very functional home, so therefore, her mind was very clear. . . . She just didn't have all those demons that a lot of people walk around with."[42] Kneeland's husband credited her character as coming largely from her parents, Sanford and Lorrainne Kent, "though her mother said she came out of the womb bright-eyed and inquisitive. . . . They raised Carole to be optimistic, outgoing, trustworthy, self-reliant, resourceful, positive."[43]

The KVUE interim news director, John Miller, who worked with Kneeland at WFAA, sits in her old office and keeps her photo on what once was her desk. He credits her organization for part of her success. When members of WFAA's Dallas newsroom were coming to Austin for an event and Kneeland was the Capitol bureau chief, "she went around her office putting up Post-It notes. 'John sits here,' 'Doug [Fox] sits here,' 'Boxes go here.' And no one would dare say, 'Well, I'm not going to sit here.'"[44] KVUE Special Projects Producer Kathy Hadlock remembers once, as a practical joke, hiding Kneeland's daybook to upset the routine. "Her day was a complete waste."[45]

Linda Ellerbee, also a breast cancer survivor, took great encouragement from Kneeland's brave fight against cancer.[46] Ellerbee produced a network television program, *What Every Woman Should Know About Breast Cancer,* that featured Kneeland, among others. Kneeland wrote she was stunned when Ellerbee asked her to be profiled for the program. "You see, I have a tendency to forget about it. I still consider myself as never having had anything really bad happen to me. I have a great job and a great husband in a great city with lots of great music and canoeing and camping to be enjoyed. Then someone reminds me I had breast cancer."[47]

Kneeland's Influence Today

As of summer 2000, KVUE still employed Kneeland's crime reporting policy with only a minor modification. One of the original criteria of "threats against children" was changed to "crimes against children" and "immediate threat [to children]" was dropped as station decided that any crime against a child is a threat to all children. In all other ways, the guidelines are carried out in the same way they were under Kneeland, including use of a graphic designating which of the guidelines apply when a crime story is aired.

KVUE also continued to employ Kneeland's truth tests in its political coverage. When Colin Powell extolled Governor George W. Bush's record on education in Texas during the 2000 Republican National Convention, KVUE reported on each of those claims, pointing out areas of where Bush's record was exaggerated or where the story was not told in its entirety.[48] One of Kneeland's competitors and associates, Bruce Whiteaker, the news director of KXAN-TV in Austin, maintains that the KVUE crime project has not influenced his station's coverage of crime in any way. Rather, Whiteaker said Kneeland's lasting influence on the Austin television market has been to set a high standard of performance and professionalism. Also, because of the high standards she promoted, she enhanced the profile and performance of the entire industry in that capital city. "Austin has played a lot bigger than the 61st market. She brought the whole market up. It performs more like a top 30 market."[49]

Austin American-Statesman television critic Diane Holloway, says Austin has never been a market where sensationalistic crime coverage was prevalent. "Her long-term legacy [in crime coverage] may be that people [at other stations] talk about the crime stories they put on more than they did before. . . . Anything that makes people stop and think is a good thing, but I'm not sure KVUE's formulaic approach is the best way to make editorial decisions about crime or any other kind of coverage." Serious crime can have community impact, but Holloway believes Kneeland's greater contribution to be in political coverage: "The 'truth tests' . . . were extraordinarily consumer-oriented and very well done. A lot of people have tried to do their own versions. Just the fact that she was in Austin raised the bar. . . . I heard her speak several times, and just the way she talked, you wanted to race to the newsroom and become Edward R. Murrow. We were lucky to have her."[50]

Carole Kneeland Project

The Carole Kneeland Project for Responsible Television Journalism was organized by her friends after her death to extend her influence to developing young journalists. The project offers intensive leadership training in television news with an annual management workshop focusing on Carole's collaborative style based on ethics and high performance standards. The organization's website emphasizes the mission specifically in television news. Television journalists are eligible for a Kneeland Fellowship if they are newsroom managers or have at least five years' full-time experience in television news and wish to become a news director. The workshop includes sessions on coaching as a leadership tool; ethical decision-making; managing "up, down, and sideways"; and hiring and firing. By participating in the workshop, members develop a philosophy and the start on building a network of colleagues that serves as a professional support system.[51]

The first workshop took place in October 1998 and consisted of 18 young news people with a mission to become local news directors. The program has consequently grown in support. In 1999, Coca-Cola committed $150,000 over five years to the Kneeland Project. Other corporate contributors include American Airlines, Belo Corporation, Continental Airlines, Gannett, KVUE-TV and Southwest Airlines.[52] Most important, the Carole Kneeland Project has kept the spirit of a key news manager and a friend to Austin colleagues alive. Kennard says, "It was almost like Carole was in the room."[53]

In a commencement speech to graduates of the University of Texas College of Communications on December 8, 1996, Carole Kneeland told the soon-to-be alumni that journalists are servants of the people, an honor "we should not treat lightly. People depend on us for information. They act on information we give them. It's a responsibility of great importance and impact."[54] By virtue of the profession she chose, Kneeland's central concern—that everyone has a right to information and that everyone has a voice—is likely to ensure that her message will be heard for some time to come.

Notes

1. Best of Austin, 1998: Media. *Austin Chronicle* [On-line]. Available: http://www.auschron.com. Accessed July 18, 2000.
2. Barnes, A. (1990, Feb.). KVUE's Kneeland: Facing challenges. *Gannetteer,* p. 11.
3. McNeely, D. (1998, Feb. 1). Goodbye Angel. *Austin American-Statesman* [On-line]. Available: http://carolkneelandproject.com/ckp_dave.htm. Accessed July 18, 2000.
4. Ellerbee, L. (1998, June). We never outgrow our need for heroes. *New Choices, 38*(5), p. 10.
5. Rosenberg, H. (1996, June 25). Where crime does not play. *Los Angeles Times Calendar.* Personal papers of Joan M. Barrett.
6. Weiss, J. (1996, Dec. 22). Crime coverage arrested. *Dallas Morning News,* pp. 1-A.
7. Mennie, R. (1998, Jan. 6). Letter to Dave McNeely. Personal papers of Dave McNeely.
8. Weiss, 1998, p. 1-A.
9. Holley, J. (1996, May/June). Should the coverage fit the crime? *Columbia Journalism Review, 35*(1), p. 29.
10. Rosenberg, 1996; Holley, 1996, p. 28.
11. Holley, 1996, p. 32.
12. Holley, 1996.
13. Barrett, J. (2000, July 18). Personal communication.
14. Rosenberg, 1996.
15. Kneeland, C. (1999, Winter 1999/Spring 2000). A grueling standard to live by. *Nieman Reports, 53*(4), *54*(1), p. 74 (double issue).
16. Ivins, M. (1998). One helluva journalist. Carole Kneeland Project website [On-line]. Available: http://www.carolekneelandproject.com. Accessed July 17, 2000.
17. Berdahl, R. M. (1998, Oct. 8). A perspective on credibility in American journalism. Speech to American Society of Newspaper Editors [On-line]. Available: http://www. chance.berkley.edu. Accessed July 18, 2000.
18. Rosenberg, 1996.
19. Holley, 1996, p. 30.
20. Holley, 1996, p. 30.
21. Rosenberg, 1996.

22. Rosenberg, 1996.
23. Weiss, 1996, p. 8-A.
24. Haag, M. (2000, July 20). Personal communication.
25. Kneeland, Winter 1999-Spring 2000, p. 73.
26. Kneeland, C. (1996, Dec. 8). Graduation speech, The University of Texas. Personal papers of Dave McNeely.
27. Ivins, 1998.
28. Barrett, 2000.
29. Haag, 2000.
30. Whiteaker, B. (2000, Aug. 2). Personal communication.
31. Carole Kneeland, 1997 TAB Broadcaster of the Year. (1997). Awards program, Austin: Texas Association of Broadcasters. Personal papers of Dave McNeely.
32. McNeely, D. (1998, Apr. 18). Speech to Texas Associated Press Broadcasters. Personal papers of Dave McNeely.
33. Kneeland remembered for journalism, compassion. (1998, Jan. 29). Associated Press. Personal papers of Dave McNeely.
34. Ivins, 1998.
35. Kennard, C. (2000, July 24). Personal communication.
36. Haag, 2000.
37. Schneider, M. (2000, Aug. 1). Personal communication.
38. Barrett, 2000.
39. Hyman, V. (1998, Winter). Journalism loses a leader, but Kneeland's teaching lives on. *Poynter Report*, p. 1.
40. Barrett, 2000.
41. Kneeland remembered for journalism, 1998.
42. Kennard, 2000.
43. McNeely, 1998.
44. Miller, J. (2000, Aug.7). Personal communication.
45. Hadlock, K. (2000, Aug. 7). Personal communication.
46. Ellerbee, 1998, p. 10.
47. Kneeland, C. (1993, Nov.). First person. *Gannetteer*, pp. 24-25.
48. Hadlock, 2000.
49. Whiteaker, 2000.
50. Holloway, D. (2000, Aug. 14). Personal communication.
51. Carole Kneeland Project website [On-line]. Available: http://www.carolekneelandproject.com. Accessed August 18, 2000.
52. Carole Kneeland Project website, 2000.
53. Kennard, 2000.
54. Kneeland, 1996.

Other Sources

Carole Kneeland leaves a legacy of courage, compassion, and conscience. (1998, Winter). *Poynter Report*, pp. 6-9.
Rosenberg, H. (1998, Feb. 2). What if Murrow could comment? *Los Angeles Times* [On-line]. Available: http://latimes.com. Accessed July 18, 2000.

Carol Marin

Carol Marin
Chicago's Courageous Newscaster

Carol Marin grew up just outside Chicago, Illinois, in a largely blue-collar neighborhood. Although her parents did not have any formal education, they provided a foundation for her interest in news very early in her life. For as long as she can remember, the family received every newspaper that Chicago produced—at least four a day. Each paper was read religiously by her parents and later by the children.[1] Marin's mother was a Catholic Democrat and her father a Baptist Republican; these differing perspectives sparked intense conversations and debates. Her parents' addiction to news helped develop her interest in current affairs and politics. Marin's whole family spent a lot of time arguing and discussing the news and events they read about, which furthered her interest in news.[2]

Marin graduated from Palatine High School and the University of Illinois, Champaign-Urbana, with a major in English. Although she spent her first two years after college teaching high school English, her interest in the media and news never waned. In an interview with the *Chicago Sun-Times* in 1996, Marin identified Charles Kuralt, Richard Threlkel, and Michelle Clark as role models for her career as a reporter.[3]

Carol Marin began her broadcasting career as a morning talk show host for WBIR-TV in Knoxville, Tennessee, in 1972. In addition to hosting the talk show, she worked as a general assignment reporter and assistant news director. In 1976, she moved to WSM-TV in Nashville, Tennessee, to be the nightly news anchor and a general assignment reporter. Marin's investigative reporting on the Tennessee correctional system won several local television awards.

After two years with WSM-TV, Marin moved to Chicago to work for NBC-owned and -operated WMAQ-TV. Her career at WMAQ

121

began as a weekend anchor and reporter. By 1985, Marin was anchoring the 10 p.m. newscast. Marin added the 6 p.m. newscast in 1988 and stayed as news anchor for both newscasts until 1997.

Marin's reputation as a serious journalist began early in her career. Her 1989 documentary *Grief's Children* examined the long-term effects of violence on children. Marin earned a national Emmy award for this documentary. In 1990, Marin produced the documentary *Now I Lay Me Down to Sleep,* which examined the deaths of a Chicago woman's five children.

Marin has long been an advocate of television stations making a serious commitment to the journalistic integrity of their news programs. Her fight to maintain that integrity began in 1990. That year, WMAQ hired Chicago Bears' Steve McMichael as a commentator. Despite the boost in ratings McMichael produced, Marin argued that he did not belong on the news team. Marin believed that McMichael, who was known for verbally bashing women and gays, did not deserve access to the Chicago audience.[4]

In 1995 a more serious challenge to the integrity of local news began. WMAQ hired Lyle Banks as station manager. Interested in moving WMAQ's newscasts from second place in the local market, Banks began by hiring an industry consultant, Mark Antonitis, as vice president of news. Marin objected to Banks' move, arguing he should have hired a journalist for the position. Steve Johnson reported, "Carol Marin publicly expressed her disappointment with the choice of someone from a profession more tuned to market research than news values."[5]

Disagreements continued among Banks, Marin, and the WMAQ staff. Banks initiated a move to allow advertisers to partner with the station in community outreach programs. Using the slogan "Committed to Chicago," Banks lured advertisers to support station programs in exchange for on-air recognition by the news anchors and reporters. When that recognition included what Marin determined were advertiser-driven infomercials rather than news, Marin objected. Marin told Johnson, "When you start joining with advertisers to provide information it is an infomercial. That's a more serious and more insidious problem than any Jerry Springer appearance. The so-called community projects were in my judgment only cynically disguised commercial ventures."[6] Marin's refusal to read the news copy that linked news stories to certain advertisers led Banks to suspend her for three days.[7]

Marin's struggles with WMAQ-TV management continued. Banks wanted the news staff to increase the number of stories per broadcast from approximately 13 to 20 to 25. Banks' alteration meant the station's standard voice-over dropped from 30 seconds to 15 seconds, approximately three sentences. Johnson reported that newswriter Susan Kennedy objected because it lessened the amount of information included in a story. Kennedy questioned, "Is that worth it? I don't think so."[8] Marin expressed concern over the decline of the role of news anchors as journalists. The exaggerated reports of weather conditions, the "happy talk" phenomena between anchors, or the use of news programs to advertise entertainment programs were all representative of the decline of journalistic standards.[9]

In February 1997, NBC (the parent company of WMAQ) hired Joel Cheatwood as vice president of news for the network. Rumors surfaced that Banks and Cheatwood planned to offer Springer a spot for commentary on the 10 p.m. news. Despite Marin's and co-anchor Ron Magers's protests that Springer had no credibility as a serious journalist, Banks pursued Springer. Banks hoped to draw national attention to WMAQ and increase ratings to draw the station into first place in the Chicago market. Banks planned to have Springer on air in time for the May sweeps.

When Banks officially announced Springer's employment, Marin announced her resignation. Marin stated that WMAQ-TV hiring Springer was not her strongest concern about the decline of journalistic integrity in news, it was the one that provided an opportunity for action.[10] Despite a contract renewal on April 25, 1997, that extended her contract to the end of the year, the station opted to allow her resignation effective May 1. Co-anchor Ron Magers also negotiated an end to his contract but was required to stay with the station until May 21, the last day of the May sweeps period.[11] Marin made it quite clear that Jerry Springer was a symptom of a larger problem, the loss of credibility and integrity within her profession. She said, "This is not about Jerry Springer. It's about the focus and direction of news. Not just local television. And not just television, but print."[12]

Viewers rallied around Marin to express outrage. Over 3,000 calls were logged the day after Marin resigned.[13] Viewers also staged demonstrations outside NBC studios in Chicago. Noted author and Jesuit priest Andrew Greeley, S.J., a commentator at WMAQ, joined Marin in resigning from his position as a result of Springer's hiring.[14]

Marin was quoted in *People Weekly* as saying, "With Springer we've crossed a line. The commentary isn't important; it's the shock value of it."[15] According to Johnson, Banks defended the station's hiring as a move to bring the tradition of commentary back to local news. Banks later lamented that all the attention led viewers to believe the news program was converting to a tabloid format, rather than being serious broadcast journalism.[16]

Springer's first commentary for WMAQ was introduced by Alison Rosati, Marin's replacement.[17] Johnson noted that Rosati's introduction was, in essence, an apology to viewers. Ron Magers, Marin's former co-anchor, distanced himself by refusing to be shown in a camera shot with Springer.[18] Springer responded to the controversy by using his first commentary to attack Marin.[19] According to Johnson, Springer belabored Marin's resignation as an attempt to deny him his First Amendment rights.[20] WMAQ's invitation to viewers to respond to Springer's commentary resulted in almost 1,400 calls initially, over 1,300 in support of Carol Marin. Viewers continued to call in support for Marin over the next few days. Ratings for WMAQ continued to drop following Marin's departure. With Springer's first commentary, ratings continued to plummet.[21]

The protests and controversy associated with Springer's position led to his decision to resign five days after his first broadcast. Springer, in a note to Banks, cited the personal attacks he was enduring as not worth it.[22]

Carol Marin's position earned her commendation from the Society of Professional Journalists Ethics Committee. They wrote,

> The steady infusion of pure entertainment into the terrain of journalism troubles all conscientious journalists and threatens the credibility of dedicated professionals. While no one questioned that good journalism can be entertaining, the primacy of entertainment, especially when it masquerades as journalistic expertise, threatens our core values. We note that Carol Marin's station has every right to broadcast whatever commentators it wishes. And Jerry Springer has every right to expound his views. That does not lessen our view that Carol Marin has acted in the best interest of the profession in taking a stand against the confusion of journalism and entertainment. Carol Marin has championed the highest journalist ethics at a great personal cost. Many of us are not in the position to accept such a personal penalty in similar circumstances, so it is with even greater respect that we commend the courage of a journalist who stood up for her profession by relinquishing her job. It's the ultimate sacrifice for a reporter who values journalistic integrity.[23]

The Chicago Headline Club of the Society of Professional Journalists also honored Marin when they bestowed the Courage in Journalism Award to her.

Marin's resignation from WMAQ left the station in a distant second place behind ABC-owned WLS-TV.[24] Magers, Marin's former co-anchor, joined WLS as anchor of that station's 5 p.m. newscast the following March.

Marin remained in the Chicago area following her departure from WMAQ. In late 1997 Marin joined CBS-affiliated WBBM-TV in Chicago. Marin split her time being an investigative reporter and completing special projects for WBBM-TV, and CBS's short-lived program, *Public Eye.* While reporting for *Public Eye,* Marin provided follow-up to a story begun 17 years earlier. As an investigative reporter, Marin followed the life of Joel Sonnenberg, a young man who was a victim of a fiery car crash. In the concluding piece, Sonnenberg met the truck driver responsible for his accident. The story, titled "The Reckoning," earned Marin a George Foster Peabody Award. The honor cited her "commitment to ethics and integrity in local broadcast journalism."[25]

The hallmark of Marin's style as a newscaster is in-depth coverage of news and events that impact the lives of viewers rather than the soft news suggested by consultants at most stations.[26] For example, when considering whether to include a story or not, Marin goes beyond the surface and determines if there is a genuine issue that needs coverage. Often stories are selected for their appeal, ability to create a sense of disaster, or to tie into network programming.

In addition to reporting for WBBM, Marin was named a correspondent for CBS-News *60 Minutes II.* The weekly newsmagazine format was to be the same as the original *60 Minutes,* a tough television journalism show. Blowen wrote the *60 Minutes II* team, Carol Marin, Bob Simon, Charlie Rose, and Vicki Mabrey, work together on three major stories and one *60 Minutes* classic, a follow-up to a story previously aired on *60 Minutes.*[27]

Hank Price, vice president and general manager of the CBS-owned WBBM-TV in Chicago, spent six months trying to convince Marin to return to anchoring.[28] Feder reported, "When Marin quit Channel 5 in 1997 rather than front a newscast that engaged talk show host Jerry Springer as a commentator, she truly believed that she'd never go back to anchoring again."[29] WBBM-TV ranked third among the three local news programs in the Chicago market. Marin agreed to return if she was given journalistic control over the program. The assurance from NBC executives allowed Marin to create the news show she always dreamed of prompted Marin to return to the anchor desk. She said, "They convinced me we can do the kind of newscast I really want to do. They're promising me as much support as they can. That's an incredible opportunity."[30]

On February 7, 2000, Marin, a longtime Chicago favorite, debuted as sole anchor of the news program. Rather than follow current standards for local news, Marin chose to present the days' events in a serious format. Her journalistic style lent itself to in-depth reports, interviews with important people, and real discussion between herself and the reporters rather than the happy talk so pervasive in local news. Carl Gottlieb, former television news executive and deputy director for the Project for Excellence in Journalism, reported in an interview in the *Chicago Tribune,* "I think everyone will be watching. In focus groups, people tell us they are sick and tired of the 'happy talk' approach. Viewers aren't lying about that."[31]

Marin based her "experiment" with WBBM-TV's 10 p.m. news program in her belief that viewers wanted more than highlights, that they, in fact, were interested in learning the whole story. Marin's critics praised the high-quality writing, the different selection of stories.[32] Rather than adhere to a prescribed story count, Marin made decisions about stories based on their importance and relevance for viewers.

Price and WBBM staffers were elated with the initial ratings reports. Marin's first newscast placed WBBM-TV in second place among the three networks with a 10 rating and 16 share. Price said, "Getting a double-digit was a thrill. We haven't had that for a while."[33]

According to Johnson and Kirk, WBBM-TV was willing to experiment with the newscast because they perceived a "homogenization of local news, brought on by years of budget cuts and reliance on outside consultants.[34] In almost every city, most every newscast looks, more or less, the same, and many newsroom staffers are as aware of and troubled by the crust of cliches as the viewers."[35] Critics acclaimed Marin's efforts to return integrity to the news. Marin's news set was muted, with lower lights and less glamour than most of today's news sets.[36] Marin noted that there was not a set format for the program, rather the news staff would make a determination on a day-by-day basis, based on what was important. Even the time devoted to weather and sports would vary based on what events happened each day.

Marin's popularity with Chicago viewers was short-lived. Analyst Steve Johnson stated that viewer curiosity was a driving force in the early ratings.[37] Hank Price and other executives who strongly supported Marin accepted positions elsewhere during the summer of 2000. As WBBM-TV entered the July sweeps, ratings for the 10 p.m. newscast were 20 percent smaller than that of the news program that had aired previously.[38] Walt DeHaven, new vice president and general manager of WBBM said, "The newscast received overwhelming critical acclaim for its content, but the response from viewers told us that the style was one they could not easily become accustomed to."[39] Ratings continued to drop over successive months. By October 2000, executives at WBBM-TV made the decision to disband the program.[40]

In her typical classic style, Marin announced to viewers that she was leaving the program and thanked the management and her coworkers for the opportunity to present news as she believed it should be presented. She said, "For the last eight months I have been privileged to work in a newsroom filled with some of the best in the business. Our goal was to find good stories and tell them well. I am proud of the work we did, grateful for the chance to do it, and honored to have been part of the Channel 2 newsroom."[41]

With these words, Marin stepped down from a 27-year career in broadcasting local news. What critics billed as a noble experiment lost the ratings war. Walter Cronkite wrote the *New York Times* to express his dismay about the end of Marin's newscast. He wrote, it was "disheartening to those many of us in television journalism who had hoped that WBBM-TV's format would be successful and lead the way to a wide adoption of more serious and informative newscasts."[42]

Cronkite wasn't the only disappointed journalist. Steve Johnson, television critic for the *Chicago Tribune,* argued Marin did not have the time, resources, or management support to make the news program a success.[43] Television critic Robert Feder criticized WBBM-TV's management and their lack of commitment to developing the program format. He noted, "If there's one good thing that emerged from this whole crazy episode it's that it engaged the public in a dialogue. For the first time in my memory, viewers were actually talking about what local TV news should deliver, rather than just accepting what's been shoved at us. That's the enduring thing."[44] Cohen wrote, "We've just learned that Marin's last newscast was Monday, October 30. That's bad for Chicago viewers and bad for journalists everywhere."[45]

Awards and Honors

During more than 20 years in broadcasting, Marin has garnered numerous awards, honors, and commendations. These include 16 local
Emmy awards, one national Emmy award, and two Peabody Awards.
Marin also earned two Alfred I. DuPont-Columbia Awards and was
voted Best Reporter by the Associated Press and by United Press International for several years. Marin's documentary on the community of
Cicero won an Associated Press award in 1986.

The Chicago Journalism Hall of Fame inducted Marin in 1992.
In 1996, Marin received the Ethics in Journalism Award. The Chicago
Headline Club of the Society of Professional Journalists offered support for her commitment to journalism by awarding her the Courage
in Journalism Award. The Ethics Committee of the national organization of the Society of Professional Journalists also formally com-
mended her willingness to speak out about journalistic integrity. Marin
and former co-anchor Ron Magers won Best Newscast in Chicago
from Associated Press and United Press International seven times during their tenure with the 10 p.m. news. Marin has also earned a Herman Kogan Award (1993/1994) and five Peter Lisagor Awards.[46]

Marin remains with CBS 2 in Chicago fulfilling her contract with
60 Minutes II and adding duties as a correspondent for *60 Minutes*. In
addition, she does reports for the *CBS Evening News with Dan Rather*
and *48 Hours.*

Notes

1. Marin, C. (2001, Jan. 23). Personal communication.
2. Marin, 2001.
3. The scoop on Carol Marin. (1996, April 7). *Chicago Sun-Times,* p. 9.
4. Warren, J. (1990, Oct. 28). Offensive lines. *Chicago Tribune,* p. 52.
5. Johnson, S. (1997). How low can TV news go? *Columbia Journalism Review,* pp. 24-29.
6. Johnson, 1997, p. 27.
7. Johnson, 1997.
8. Johnson, 1997, p. 27.
9. Feder, R. (2000, Feb. 4). Back to you, Carol. *Chicago Sun-Times, Late Sports Final
   Edition,* p. 44.
10. Marin, 2001.
11. Johnson, 1997.
12. Pasternak, J., and Braxton, G. (1997, May 3). A line is drawn in TV newsroom.
    Los Angeles Times, pp. F1, F16.
13. This anchor's away: Two words—Jerry Springer—persuade newswoman.
    (1997, May 19). *People Weekly, 47,* p. 137.

14. Littleton, C. (1997, May 12). Springer drops WMAQ-TV commentary. *Broadcasting and Cable, 127,* pp. 32-33.

15. This anchor's away, 1997, p. 137.

16. Johnson, 1997.

17. Johnson, 1997.

18. Johnson, 1997.

19. Littleton, 1997.

20. Johnson, 1997.

21. Johnson, 1997.

22. Carter, B. (1997, May 9). Springer quits news show, citing attacks. *New York Times,* p. A22; Littleton, 1997.

23. Marin takes tough stand. (1997, Nov.). *The Quill, 85,* p. 13.

24. Johnson, 1997.

25. CBS News Biography: Carol Marin. (2000). [On-line]. Available: http://cbsnews.com/now/story/0,1597,26913-412,00.shtml Retrieved Jan. 10, 2001.

26. No frills news. (2000, May 24). *Online Newshour* [On-line]. http://www.pbs.org/newshour/bb/media/jan-june00/wbbm_5-24.html. Retrieved Jan. 10, 2001.

27. Blowen, M. (1999). *60 Minutes II* fills time with little substance. *Boston Globe,* p. E1.

28. Trigoboff, D. (2000, Mar. 13). Price right for WBBM-TV. *Broadcasting and Cable, 130,* p. 102.

29. Feder, 2000, p. 44

30. Borden, J. (2000, Jan. 10). Marin's mission: Save Channel 2: Can old-fashioned news win a race for news viewers? *Crain's Chicago Business,* p. 1.

31. Johnson, S., and Kirk, J. (2000, Feb. 6). With Carol Marin, Channel 2 shakeup newsworthy gamble. *Chicago Tribune,* p. 10.

32. Johnson, S. (2000, Oct. 31). Ratings game has no time or room for patience, risk. *Chicago Tribune,* p. A6.

33. Trigoboff, D. (2000, Feb. 14). Marin boosts WBBM-TV. *Broadcasting and Cable, 130,* p. 44.

34. Johnson and Kirk, 2000, p. 10.

35. Johnson and Kirk, 2000, p. 10.

36. Potter, D. (2000, June). A newscast featuring real news. *American Journalism Review,* p. 66.

37. Johnson, 2000.

38. Walker, J. (2000, Nov. 8). Station returns to "happy chat." *Jack O'Dwyer's Newsletter, 33,* p.3.

39. Johnson, 2000.

40. WBBM-TV News Release. (2000, Oct. 30). The 10 o'clock news with Carol Marin will be disbanded on Oct. 30 [On-line]. Available: http://biz.yahoo.com/prnews/001030/il-wbbm-tv.html Retrieved Jan. 10, 2001.

41. WBBM-TV News Release, 2000.

42. Hickey, N. (2001). Chicago experiment—Why it failed. *Columbia Journalism Review,* p. 15.

43. Johnson, 2000.

44. Hickey, 2001.

45. Cohen, D. (2000). Ratings threaten experiment in good journalism. *St. Louis Journalism Review, 30,* p. 25.

46. Carol Marin joins CBS to report for News 2 Chicago. (1997, July 14). *PR Newswire,* p. 1.

Other Sources

Erosion of values. (1998). *Columbia Journalism Review, 36,* pp. 44-47.

Donna Matson with a monkey that appeared in the Western Instructional Television series *Jungle Animals*

Donna Matson

Pioneer ETV Entrepreneur

Donna Matson of Los Angeles is a pioneer, an entrepreneur, an educator and an adventurer who has done more things than most people dream of doing. In the process she has affected the lives of thousands of children, usually one community at a time.

Donna Matson would never be accused of being shy. A tomboy and an adventurer from her youth, she became one of the first women to own their own production companies and one of the first women television directors and then developed a range of educational television programming that helped the children in many communities. Like many who laid the foundation for educational broadcasting, she did not plan to go in that direction.

Born in Southern California, her father was an entrepreneur who operated a trucking business in the 1920s and 1930s between Los Angeles and Phoenix, before roads had been built. Her mother, a farm girl from Illinois, was liberated long before the word applied to women, first by going away to college in Tennessee, then moving to Washington, D.C., to work for the weather bureau and finally to California as a newspaper reporter. Very athletic, Donna captained both her high school basketball and volleyball teams. She also was very active in scouting and served as a counselor while still quite young.

Donna was born in the Hollywood Presbyterian Hospital and now resides barely three miles away, but there are relatively few spots on the globe she hasn't visited, probably more than once. She was the first American woman to climb Kilimanjaro. She crossed the Jordanian desert on a camel, visited the mountain gorillas in Africa, filmed pygmies of the Ituri Forest, dived the Great Barrier Reef and wandered among the ruins at Angkor Wat. Yet, she is not some spoiled heiress.

She spent considerable time operating on a very tight budget. Hers is a story of what determination can do.

She fell in love with sailing early in her career, going to the University of California, Santa Barbara, so she could be near the ocean. Matson is not one to brag of her adventures, but one instance came close to being too adventuresome when she crewed on an ocean sailing ship in the Transpac race from Los Angeles to Hawaii. This was during the Cold War, and at one point they were followed by an unknown submarine that periodically raised periscope to watch them. A former Navy man aboard the racer was sure it was not American. That night, a major thump on the hull resulted in their rudder being broken off about 400 miles from Honolulu. Over the next two days, rudderless, they attempted to keep control but high winds and seas knocked the ship flat three times, in total darkness. The sails had to be cut loose to right it. Eventually they were spotted by the Coast Guard and towed to port. After this, things like dancing with Masai warriors perhaps seemed tame. However, this story is not about adventure but pioneering and accomplishment by hard work and determination.[1]

After acquiring B.A. and M.A. degrees in education and instructional television, she took a job as a teacher to acquire enough money to buy a ticket to Hawaii, where she became a teacher on a sugar cane plantation. On weekends she learned scuba diving, which is still one of her many loves. Returning to Los Angeles a year later, she applied for a teaching job in Morocco. Rejected because she had little experience, she said she'd hope for a last minute vacancy. The opportunity appeared when the call came the first week in September. Amid her excitement, her father pointed out a headline that showed there had been a massacre in Morocco in the battle for its independence from France. Still, she went, living in a tent for six months, and then spent a year traveling.[2]

After another stretch of teaching in California, she got an opportunity to teach in Lebanon at the American Community School. Before departing, she got a call from a top underwater photographer offering her a chance to dive for *National Geographic Magazine* in the Aegean Sea. He had seen an article that she had written for *Skin Diver* magazine. She would have to pay her way over, but once there, everything would be covered. Utilizing the money provided by the school in Beirut, she left early and spent the summer diving for Phoenician artifacts. Arriving to teach school, she found that while they paid your way over, you had to teach two years to get your way back paid, so, being short of funds, she stayed the two years.[3]

Returning home, she wanted to teach at a school near the small boat she had acquired. This led to a job in the Santa Ana schools, where she taught second grade for two years. One evening the board of education directed the superintendent to make major improvements in the system's instructional program. He returned with a plan to accomplish those goals by extensive use of televised lessons. At the time, Donna was conducting a lecture series in a nearby community on her travel adventures. In the audience was a school official who then recommended her to be a television teacher in the new operation. A supervisor visited her classroom, watched a while and asked her to audition. Donna said no, preferring to stay with her students. A week later he was back and talked her into giving it a try. The selection panel chose her. She was a bit taken back when she found she was to do four live science programs a week, two each for third and fourth grades. Her mandate was to do things the classroom teachers couldn't do. This led to a field trip series, with the programs done live and microwaved back. She headed for the ocean and did programs on the waves, fish, birds and plants of the sea and then, utilizing film, went to the desert and mountains for more programs.[4]

One of the problems every television teacher encountered was the lack of contact with the children during the lesson. "Trying to make a connection was a little difficult for me. But what I did was I took pictures of some of my students from my last class and taped them right on the camera around the lens and I looked right at them as I was talking to them." Ultimately, she did about 240 programs.[5]

In 1967, the summer after her racing adventure, she returned to Los Angeles and met a friend who had a television company called Western Video Industries (WVI). It had a production arm, the Hollywood Video Center, which was quite historic. Here Frank Sinatra had once produced his programs. Donna recalls going there as a teenager to watch, with a girlfriend who was a "swooner." The company was producing the *Steve Allen Show, Pat Boone Show* and other programs for ABC. The network had utilized all their facilities and needed to contract out some of the jobs. The friend told her that he had heard she had done some good television work and suggested she use some of their spare studio time to produce more programs for sale. She decided to give it a try.[6]

Donna was aware that the National Association of Educational Broadcasters would be meeting in Denver in a few weeks. She produced four pilots to show at the convention to see if there was any interest. She traveled the convention floor early, offering her tapes to all the exhibitors who were displaying equipment, so attendees saw her shows at many booths. She taught one of the pilots herself, and it promptly was the talk of the conference. School television programs tended to have rather sedate beginnings, but Donna began hers by emerging from the ocean in scuba gear. Word of the woman who began a school show by coming out of the ocean quickly spread through the hall and made everyone aware of her efforts.

Looking for a marketer, since she knew nothing of that side of the business, she talked with several distributors who offered a rather small share of the receipts to the producer. She went home to WVI and announced that she could see no profit in making school programs. Management responded that they wanted the prestige and the tax write-off. She should continue with the productions, and they would handle the distribution, since they already had such an operation.

Over the next three years she produced about 300 programs, working in the same studio that Sinatra had used. In 1970, the FCC changed the rules, requiring the networks to give up one hour of prime time each evening. Network production was cut back and suddenly things slowed at Western Video. Finances were tight and producer David Wolper offered to buy WVI, primarily for the production capabilities of the Center.[7]

Wolper didn't show much interest in Donna's instructional programs, although at the end, hers was the only division still making money. Drawing on a burst of courage, she went to their finance person and announced she wanted to buy the educational division of Western Video Industries. She made an offer that she felt was low, but it was accepted. She had 30 days to raise $500,000 in an era when women rarely were involved in deals of this magnitude, particularly an unmarried woman with gross savings of $7,500.[8] Further, she had no credit record, having been raised to save her money and pay cash for everything. Two friends from WVI interested in investing guaranteed some of the loan in exchange for stock. The first bank she approached turned her down, after stalling three weeks. Fortunately, Wells Fargo looked at her sales contracts and calculated they would take the risk. Additionally, the Wolper organization carried $100,000 of the debt for two years. She renamed her company Western Instructional Television (WITV).[9]

She set about producing more shows to establish herself with the market and tackle the debt she now was carrying. She soon encountered a problem with the veteran directors of commercial programs. They did not understand how she wanted educational programs to be shot. Their experience focused on three or four viewers seated in a living room. They tended to use too many wide shots, too brief close-ups, and too small lettering and tried to create action by frequent shot changes. Donna was a teacher and she knew her audience was 30 students, often young, seated in rows in a classroom. She wanted more closer shots held longer, so that the children could understand what they were seeing. Further, she wanted camera shots to move from left to right in the pattern of reading, as many young children have a tendency to look from right to left.[10]

This led to frustrations and disagreements until someone finally suggested she direct her own shows. However, it was soon pointed out that, in Hollywood, you had to be a member of the Directors Guild of America (DGA) to do any directing. She called for an application, but it never came, so she went to union headquarters and picked one up. One of the requirements was the signatures of three DGA members. She had two friends who were members and signed, and she maneuvered a third signature, so she became a member in 1968.[11]

She was the fourth woman member of the DGA. Her predecessors were Ida Lupino, Lucille Ball and Betty White (not the actress, the director of the soap opera *As The World Turns*). Donna recalls that her appearances at the annual union meetings were received coolly, but outside, members regularly approached her for work. She notes that women are still struggling today and the best way to direct, if you want to, is to have your own company.[12]

Still another hurdle she had to face arose when she took charge. Although Donna knew how she wanted the programs shot, she had no experience in doing it and so suffered the mutterings and snickers of the crew while she made mistakes and learned to direct. Some crewmembers resented having a woman director, particularly one who hadn't come up through the ranks and was just learning to put her ideas into actions. But she persevered, motivated in part by the massive debt hanging over her head.[13]

Donna put herself on a strict budget, paying herself only the salary she had once made as a teacher in the Santa Ana schools—$800 per month, no perks, no raises, no benefits. She worked 10 hours a day, seven days a week for seven years to pay off the loans. Not only did she pay off the debt, she was able to buy back the stock she had given up. The company was truly hers. However, she did not see this business as a route to riches. "I never had as a goal to make money. I had as a goal to teach what I felt were important values."[14] She tells of attending a Young Presidents Organization conference, held in Spain, where she heard about a study that showed a high percentage of the successful young leaders did not start out with the goal to make money. It was doing something they loved, something they believed in, something they thought would improve society or the quality of life. Still, after 10 years she realized that she was successful.

Although she was providing school programming nationally, she soon realized that what she actually had was many individual state and local markets, each with its own requirements and processes—a far cry from dealing with a national network. Some states, and even schools, where teachers were inadequately trained wanted "basic teaching" in which the television teacher essentially took over the class for that subject, presenting lessons that followed the textbook, page for page. Others, with either better circumstances or strong teacher unions, would consider only "supplemental programming" (which harked back to Donna's field trip programs at Santa Ana) presenting things the classroom teacher did not have the time, money or facilities to carry out. She set out walking a very thin line, trying to provide basic material that was enhanced enough with enriching experiences to appeal to all teachers. She began building a library of elementary textbooks and updated them regularly with new editions. Ultimately, she had nearly every one published. Hours were spent studying how the different publishers had sequenced the material, how much time was spent on each topic and which topics were covered. Out of this she synthesized the contents and order of her programs. She supplemented this with a teacher's guide that accompanied each of the series. In it she explained what she would be teaching and how she would teach it, and the guide included a review sheet and a quiz as well.[15]

William Meyers, former director of instructional television at Southern Illinois University recalls the value of her programs. "Her programs were geared right for the things that were necessary in the schools: science, language arts, music and art."[16] He also spoke highly of Matson's on-camera style and her willingness to travel to remote schools to meet thrilled teachers and students.

She attended regional meetings, showing her programs and seeking reactions. She soon learned that some agencies, in a program preview, would only watch the first three or four minutes and then decide if they wanted to see more of it. Programs that didn't impress quickly were pushed aside. This became one of Donna's guiding principles: Start fast. Dan Mihuta, an art teacher who did three series totaling 96 programs for WITV, recalls this requirement to get into the lesson quickly. When he got too "talky" at the start of an art program, Donna might burst out of the control room saying, "What are you doing, Mihuta? Trying to win a spot in a new movie?"[17]

Another annoyance she combated is the American tendency to throw in "filler" words such as "OK," "ya know," and "uh" into speech. She adopted a method of having an empty glass nearby that she tapped with a spoon every time one of the offending words was heard. Dan Mihuta recalls, "When she clinked that glass I could have killed her. But she drove these things out of my speech pattern. Now my delivery is much more continuous."[18]

Mihuta tells one story that says much about Donna. When visiting her on the West Coast, midwesterner Mihuta and his wife were soon on the sailboat and headed for Catalina Island. On the way back they encountered some heavy weather and Dan was trying to assist. He shouted to Donna, "Shall I pull on this rope?" Through the howling wind and the roaring sea, Donna shouted back, correcting him, "That's not a rope, it's a line."[19]

One of the problems Western Instructional Television encountered was that often the people making selections of programming originally had been high school teachers and had little knowledge of how elementary children learn. Donna commented, "They didn't have a clue about elementary teaching, what the vocabulary was, what the sense of humor was, what the attention span or the interest level was. We saw that with Mr. Rogers. Mr. Rogers came in and everybody laughed at it. The program people thought he was corny, but in my opinion its one of the finest children's programs that was ever done."[20]

Another headache became evident. Although companies like Encyclopedia Britannica, Coronet and Disney had been making and selling educational films for decades, Donna encountered a resistance from some who felt that it was inappropriate for a commercial agency to be producing instructional television materials, despite the fact she was a certificated teacher and educational supervisor. In reality, some who resisted her efforts were also producing programs at the local level and may have been trying to protect their turf.

But satisfactions came from the market as well. Barrow, Alaska, had a very simple system with only one recorder, the only television service for the whole region. They rented a variety of programs from Donna and later asked her to visit. For an adventurer, a trip to the northern edge of the continent was no problem, so she also planned to shoot film for another series she was currently doing while she was there. She discovered she was already well known to all the members of the community as they greeted her on the street. They had little else to watch but her programs. Meeting with local children who had seen her nature programs gave her some fascinating insights as they asked questions such as "What does a tree feel like?" and "What does a snake feel like?" She also got invited to go out in an umiak and spend the night on an ice flow for a whale hunt. Being a whale lover, she had mixed feelings but went and was relieved that no whales strayed close enough to be harpooned.[21]

Another satisfaction came from a California teacher who taught a class of students considered to be mentally retarded. The teacher reported that she was using Donna's programs and found that these children were understanding the television lessons and could pass tests on the material covered. She said that she had come to feel that half of the children put in her class basically suffered from an inability to read, but when they were provided with visual teaching, they got it.

One of the best known of Donna's television teachers was Julius Sumner Miller, a professor at UCLA who had been doing programs for Walt Disney as *Professor Wonderful* on *Why Is It So?*[22] He was preparing another series for that studio when Walt died, and succeeding management was not interested in his work. Donna had been soliciting ideas for teachers from among her friends and one happened to be aware of Miller's situation. Thus began a thrilling and occasionally stormy relationship as he transferred what he had been going to do for Disney to Western Instructional Television. He presented three series of 15 science demonstration programs for children up "to age 94."

The professor very much liked to do things his way. Actually he and Donna agreed on many techniques, such as keeping it simple and lots of close-ups. Miller often had been a guest on the *Steve Allen Show.* She tells of an occasion when another well-known host wanted Miller on his variety show. The professor agreed grudgingly but specified that he wanted no fancy set, which he viewed as a distraction. Everything should be simple. When he arrived, he found his wishes had been ignored and there was a giant set made of decorated shelves loaded with interestingly shaped glass bottles filled with colored liquids. Miller erupted, knocked over the set with a crash of broken bottles, rejected his substantial fee, and stormed out. Ultimately, he and Donna cooperated on four series that are in distribution to this day. He was noted for his enthusiasm and child-like interest. He also refused to prepare scripts or do a rehearsal. This got out of hand occasionally when, in the midst of a production, he would decide to repeat an experiment that had gone well, even though a repeat had not been planned. He seemed to have trouble accepting that television is a timed medium and that you had to finish when your allotted time was up. Being a director is not just giving orders. It is cajoling, coaxing and complimenting as well; these were more skills Donna learned. Also, as Miller was already well known, it gave WITV visibility more quickly than might have been expected.[23]

Ultimately, Donna produced and directed over 800 programs. She set out to make them ageless, to extend the life of her program assets as long as possible. That approach, the skill used in planning them and the careful selection and training of her television teachers has paid off far beyond what she might have imagined. Many programs are still widely used after 25 years. Her generous royalty policy to her teachers means that they are still benefiting long after they finished the work. The programs have been sold abroad to many countries, including Singapore, Hong Kong and South Africa. In South Africa they have a multi-lingual service, so in addition to English, her programs have been dubbed into Afrikaans and Zulu. She has commented that it's quite a surprise to watch yourself "speaking" Zulu, a language which has a variety of sounds not used in English.[24]

Educational television stations have evolved, and many do not do much instructional broadcasting today. Many programs are delivered to automated video recorders at 2 a.m. Western Instructional Television is no longer producing instructional programs, but the popularity of its library has kept Donna from retiring. Of course, retiring for her means time for another trip to Myanmar (Burma), a southeast Asian nation she loves, or a chance to explore newly discovered Mayan ruins in Central America, another of her favorite spots. An expert photographer and videographer, she has recorded her travels through much of her life. Additionally, she has approximately 45,000 slides of these adventures, each taken with a teacher's eye for explaining what was going on. Not only does she have 45,000 slides, but she also has them cataloged so that any one of them can be located within five minutes. This wealth of material has led her to propose two programs to the Discovery Channel. With Donna's skill and attention to detail, she may be entering a new career as a documentary producer.[25]

Donna has been involved in many other things as well. She has served on several boards, including the National Association of Educational Broadcasters, Hollywood YMCA, Children's Survival Fund and Columbia College. She is a member of many organizations, including the Academy of Television Arts and Sciences. An activist, she has been instrumental in the work of the Hollywood Chamber of Commerce and the Hollywood Coordinating Committee, which has been devoted to improving the image of that city. She is very generous; she has created a scholarship and quietly has helped many in her community who are in need.[26] She has found time to publish more than a dozen articles, many on her travels, and to receive a wall full of awards from organizations that appreciated her contributions.[27]

When asked to summarize her work Donna replied, "I really believe in entrepreneurship. I never applied for any funds or grants and for 30 years was able to just about break even. Every year I was able to do what I wanted to do, have a salary and a little for retirement. There was no big money in it. That's not why I went into it and that's why I had practically no competition . . . because it is not what you would call a profitable industry."[28] However, Donna Marie Matson has broken barriers for women and helped educate thousands of children throughout the country while living an adventuresome life that many would envy.

Notes

1. Stephenson, A. (2001, Jan. 19). Oral history interview with Donna Matson. Matson Project, Tape 1. The John Carroll University Media Archives, University Heights, Ohio.

2. Stephenson, 2001, Jan. 19.
3. Stephenson, 2001, Jan. 19.
4. Stephenson, 2001, Jan. 19.
5. Stephenson, 2001, Jan. 19.
6. Stephenson, A. (2001, Jan. 26). Oral history interview with Donna Matson. Matson Project, Tape 2. The John Carroll University Media Archives, University Heights, Ohio.
7. Stephenson, 2001, Jan. 26.
8. Western Instructional Television. (1980, Mar.). Biography of Donna Matson. Los Angeles, Calif.
9. Stephenson, 2001, Jan. 26.
10. Stephenson, 2001, Jan. 26.
11. Stephenson, 2001, Jan. 26.
12. Stephenson, 2001, Jan. 26.
13. Stephenson, 2001, Jan. 26.
14. Stephenson, 2001, Jan. 26.
15. Stephenson, A. (2001, Jan. 22). Recorded message from Donna Matson. Matson Project, Tape 3. The John Carroll University Media Archives, University Heights, Ohio.
16. Stephenson, A. (2001, Feb. 22). Oral history interview with William Meyers. Matson Project, Tape 5. The John Carroll University Media Archives, University Heights, Ohio.
17. Stephenson, A. (2001, Feb. 4). Oral history interview with Daniel Mihuta. Matson Project, Tape 4. The John Carroll University Media Archives, University Heights, Ohio.
18. Stephenson, 2001, Feb. 4.
19. Stephenson, 2001, Feb. 4.
20. Stephenson, 2001, Jan. 26.
21. Stephenson, 2001, Jan. 26.
22. Western Instructional Television. (nd). Program Catalog. Los Angeles, Calif.
23. Stephenson, 2001, Jan. 26.
24. Stephenson, 2001, Jan. 26.
25. Stephenson, 2001, Jan. 26.
26. NAEB Council on Instruction Outstanding Service Award. (1981, Nov.). National Association of Educational Broadcasters Press Release. Washington, D.C.
27. Western Instructional Television, 1980.
28. Stephenson, 2001, Feb. 4.

Other Sources

Avery, Matson and Ramsey elected to board. (1980, Jan.-Feb.). *Public Telecommunications Newsletter, 45(*1).
Donna Matson. (1982). *Who's Who of American Women* (12th ed). Chicago: Marquis Who's Who, Inc.
Kay, E. (Ed.). (1974-1975). Donna Matson. *The World Who's Who of Women, Vol. 2.* Cambridge, England: Melrose Press Limited.
Western Instructional Television. (1978). Biography of Donna Matson. Los Angeles, Calif.

Charlotte Peters with sidekicks Stan Kann and George Abel during a skit on her show. *(Courtesy of the Western Historical Manuscripts Collection, University of Missouri, St. Louis)*

Charlotte Peters

One of a Kind

The outstanding qualities that distinguished Charlotte Peters as a popular television pioneer in St. Louis will long be remembered. She left her mark on a developing industry but also on a city attuned to her talents.[1] The challenges Peters' faced as a young person herself were far from funny. Her mother died when Charlotte was just eight years old. Charlotte and her older sister, Vivian, went to work at an early age. Their father, Charles G. Wiedemann, covered sporting events for the national press. After her mother died, her father remarried. Charlotte and her sister were sent to live with their father's sister. Charlotte held many different jobs and quickly learned how to effectively interact with the public. She discovered her outgoing personality was well suited for the field of entertainment. She was encouraged to perform as a singer by winning an amateur radio contest at the age of 17 even though she could not read music.

Vivian, Charlotte's older sister, competed in beauty contests in the Midwest and frequently won. She was named Miss St. Louis and could have easily pursued a modeling career. Vivian wed and the connection provided Charlotte an introduction to a cousin, her future husband Bill Peters.[2] Although Charlotte had shown an early interest in show business, she married and dedicated herself fully to her family. This status as something of a starstruck housewife and mother with an eighth-grade education and no formal training would stand in contrast to her accomplishments. It enhanced the underlying respect and admiration of her from viewers who were so much like her.

Peters was selected for her first television position by Russ Severin, founder of the *To the Ladies* program on KSD-TV. Severin developed a large number of programs and selected talent from a wide range of aspiring artists. When he started a daily afternoon program geared specifically toward housewives, it occurred to him that someone with the same background might attract a large following.

True to form, his recruitment of Peters offered viewers someone with whom they could identify—and laugh. In addition, the hundred women who trooped daily to that program were completely won over by someone they perceived as being like themselves in terms of concerns for the welfare of their families. Peters frequently discussed her family, especially her husband, and credited him with having lots of patience. A running joke was that he was earmarked for sainthood because of a willingness to tolerate the celebrity status that she had achieved.

In the vernacular of broadcasting for well over a decade at the start of television, Charlotte Peters "owned" the St. Louis scene. As the premier performer on the only television station in town, she controlled the airwaves in terms of bolstering community activities. She hosted *To the Ladies* at noon on KSD-TV, then the program became her namesake, *The Charlotte Peters Show*. Later she would move over to ABC-affiliated KTVI-TV; but starting out, KSD had special significance because that station had important status in the community.[3]

KSD-TV was the first television station owned by Pulitzer Publishing, owners of the *St. Louis Post-Dispatch*. The station followed on the success of KSD radio, also a Pulitzer property. Stations used staff from the newspaper for collateral coverage, including city government and sports. The fledgling television station set the standard for what would follow. KSD-TV went on the air February 8, 1947, and was developed by Pulitzer's ad director, George Burbach, who later became general manager. He had seen television demonstrated a decade before in England and carried on a campaign to introduce the medium to St. Louis. The station tied itself to cultural and civic institutions, covering events such as the Veiled Prophet Ball, a society gala that highlighted debutantes, daughters of prominent business leaders.

By June 12 of the inaugural year, the station developed a mobile unit to cover the U.S. Golf Association's 47th Open Championship played at the St. Louis Country Club. Later, when Senator Estes Kefauver conducted Crime Subcommittee hearings, KSD-TV was an active participant.[4] The station's news director, Frank Eschen, was even called upon to testify about the influence of television on hearings.

Newspapers speculated on influence, estimating that local drinking establishments had invested in the purchase of TV sets with the idea of attracting patrons to view the hearings.[5]

Earlier, Frank Eschen had traveled with the archbishop of St. Louis, John Glennon, and reported on his installation as a cardinal directly from the Vatican. When Glennon died on his way back to the United States during a stopover in his birthplace, Ireland, Eschen reported it, an important story given St. Louis' large Catholic population.[6] This type of coverage reinforced KSD's role as integral to the community. Peters fit nicely into this niche. It would suffice to say that hosting a daily TV program, she was ahead of her time. She prided herself on being open-minded, candid—willing to share views at odds with the norm.[7]

She pushed the envelope on occasions to openly and honestly discuss subjects considered taboo, such as the challenges faced by working women and the respect accorded public workers such as police officers, firemen and schoolteachers. She always made the case effectively, using humor to poke fun at conventions. She hosted community groups. After participating in some display associated with responsibilities, she might comment on sacrifices made for their work. As a result, she had many friends among organizations. She would host Irish policemen on St. Patrick's Day. She covered a fire adjacent to the studios and talked to firemen on the scene about demands of their jobs.[8]

Behind the scenes, she worked for various charities. She often made frequent reference to her religious faith and proudly pointed to the impact her program had on the lives of viewers, especially housewives. In newspaper interviews and community talks she would often comment on the role her faith had played in addressing challenges she faced as a wife, mother and television performer. She had an eighth-grade education but frequently incorporated educational features into her program. If she took a trip, she would discuss the important historic and artistic sights, illustrated with photos. She invited civic leaders to the program to discuss development. She was recognized as an advocate and spokesperson.[9]

There has been considerable speculation on the amount of preparation that went into the program. The show was usually not scripted but had a topical outline. Performances could be tricky because ordinarily there was no formal rehearsal. On one occasion, Peters hung from a trapeze in studio rafters singing while dressed in a space helmet and red flannel outfit. She insisted that too much practice might destroy spontaneity. Just before going on the air, however, staff would engage in a run-through. As the program developed, less time was devoted to slapstick antics and more public affairs material was offered.

The staff of the program included talented organist Stan Kann, reporter John Roedel and host George Abel. Stan Kann went on to make many appearances on the network, including the popular *Tonight Show*. John Roedel continued as a reporter and anchorman with the station. George Abel appeared on the late afternoon children's program *The Wranglers' Club* with Harry Gibbs. Singer Marty Bronson often participated in the program. This was consistent with the station's history of having supported extensive music programming before the teen-dominated '60s era. KSD-TV sponsored the *Laclede Little Symphony* as early as 1950, featuring performers from the St. Louis symphony. Conductors from that prominent symphony, such as Harry Farbman and Vladimir Golshmann, followed in the footsteps of the NBC network's maestro Arturo Toscanini.

The station broadcast a *Muny Preview* program and imported a Chicago disc jockey, Dan Sorkin, for a series. Magician Ernie Heldman complemented TV staples of children's and quiz shows. There were sports features with Buddy Blattner and Dizzy Dean, former Cardinal baseball stars who were among professional athletes able to easily make the transition to broadcasting. By the middle 1950s, Marlin Perkins had caught on, first with *Zoo Parade* and then Mutual of Omaha's *Wild Kingdom*. Perkins and his wife, Carol, were frequent guests of Charlotte Peters. Housewives delighted in hearing the tales of life in the wild from Carol Perkins.

Peters had a broad canvas to draw upon for ideas. This most popular local program boasted a technical staff of 10, and sponsorship by major grocery chains furnished guests with premiums for visits: groceries, dry goods, cleaning products and cosmetics. Peters would focus on an item and sales would go up. If a guest was in town on behalf of a sponsor, Peters saw to it that products were displayed and their importance discussed.

She would invite her audience to engage in competitions and had tangible rewards for good behavior. These included singing or dancing exhibitions, quiz or trivia contests. Peters also loved to dress in costume. A skit would accompany every holiday. She and her crew would appear in complementary costumes. On Thanksgiving, she would dress as a turkey. The Halloween audience could expect her appearance as a wicked witch. Later, public appearances might reinforce behavior. When sidekick Stan Kann appeared in concert at the Fox theatre, he accompanied a horror film. As he rose from the orchestra pit, Peters was lying in a casket on top of the organ in a witch's costume. Kann had been instructed to knock a few times when he wanted her to jump out. He knocked repeatedly. She opened the casket and yelled: "Am I supposed to come out now?"[10]

She might portray a mermaid singing "Tiny Bubbles" while bubbles floated over monitors. All outrageous conventions of early television were spoofed. She might don a wig and mimic Elvis Presley. Like Lucille Ball, Peters appeared before a live audience as comic but, unlike those involved with a scripted program, she would sing and dance as a seasoned vaudevillian. To keep her audience on its toes, she would sometimes invite representatives from male-dominated professions to test her audience's knowledge on how they conducted their work.

Police and firefighters were favorites. She would assist them by supporting a common cause. She might scale a ladder in firefighter gear or provide information regarding a missing person or fugitive from justice. Inventing content for a new medium meant improvisation. Peters was often at her best when filling time. The fact that suburbs consisted of many municipalities offered chances to have geographic representation and also elicit laughter aimed at those who might possess an inflated opinion, all accomplished with humor and without any rancor.

She often mocked conventions of society as when she spoofed network television stars (such as Donna Reed or Harriet Nelson) portraying housewives in formal attire or mimicked Loretta Young's elaborate televised entrance in a fancy dress. Peters would make the same type entrance accompanied by orchestra music, then fall on her face. She sometimes invited her audience to partake in the comedy by offering a reward for anyone who would put their pride on the line in front of the TV cameras.[11]

Peters might stage a trivia contest or cooking competition with contestants unaware that an ingredient had been replaced. Pie fights and water balloons could be put to good use. Sometimes staff would move outside of the studio and even outside the station's coverage area to engage in a stunt that would create hilarious conditions. When a circus or parade came to town she would sometimes broadcast from those locations. On other occasions, she would emanate from the State Fair in Sedalia, Missouri. The station once reportedly received 40,000 entries in response to a contest in the late 1950s.[12] She attracted a great deal of attention in 1962 when she embarked on a diet program in a successful effort to lose 30 pounds.

Because of production challenges, Peters would sometimes be heard making demands in tones uncharacteristic of network celebrities who left the production details to others. The staff of *To the Ladies* viewed the uproar as characteristic of a talented performer under the pressure of having to fulfill many complicated tasks at once. She enjoyed mocking the types of celebrities who took themselves too seriously. Since she entertained so many Hollywood performers on her program, her talent was recognized well beyond the confines of the Midwest. She once received a letter from Paramount Film Studios inviting her to Hollywood to complete a screen test for the movies. She said she not only would not go to tinsel town but would frame the invitation and hang it over her washing machine.

In spite of her comic demeanor, Peters was a most demanding taskmaster who insisted that her staff adhere to high standards and demands for perfection for her program. Personal displays of temperament became known but she was sensitive to effects. While interviewing a potential staff member to serve as assistant, she said: "I will be your worst enemy if you take this job. When I act like I'm demented don't pay any attention to me because later I'll apologize to you."[13]

In her first six years on the show, Peters left many staff members in her wake. They either found her pace too fast or perhaps she found theirs too slow. In some cases staff sought even bigger challenges on the West Coast or at the network. Alumni of Peters' program commented on how much they had learned under her tutelage. This was due to the fact that her program was one of three "live" variety shows airing then, great training for nationally produced live shows.[14]

The *To the Ladies* program lasted nearly eight years on KSD-TV and for most of that time Charlotte Peters was in charge of decision-making even as she functioned in front of the camera. Her co-producer at that time, Charles Sherwood, was a relaxed counterbalance because of his casual approach to the demands of a daily program. Sherwood replaced Mason Morfit, son of national television veteran Garry Moore, who established firm credentials following in his father's footsteps. Paul Campbell directed the program and, later on, Fred Komma directed Peters at KTVI-TV.

Peters' day typically began around 10 a.m. She would review the schedule with her staff and briefly rehearse songs she might perform with an accompanist. The program aired live from 12:05 to 1 p.m. The staff would meet with Peters to discuss plans for the next show. Sometimes she stayed as late as 7 p.m. reviewing files or notes in preparation for an important studio guest.

When she and her family went on vacation, Peters would photograph her exploits and share them with viewers when she returned to town. After a visit to Miami, Florida, she displayed pictures of herself skin diving, swimming, fishing and being a guest at a luau in which she pretended to be tortured in some fashion.

Charlotte and her family happened to be vacationing in Greece when she ran into Tippi Hedren, featured in the Alfred Hitchcock film *The Birds*. They were also visiting the Alps when *Sound of Music* was shot on location. Peters had photos taken with some of the stars and the production staff. Peters would use these opportunities to encourage visits when movie actors or comedians came to town to perform at the "muny" opera in Forest Park. Peter's program was considered a key to promoting their performances. She developed close ties with some major entertainment figures and tried to create memorable moments for viewers. When Bob Hope appeared on her program, she teamed him up to interview a popular entrepreneur known as "Sam the Watermelon Man." She would sometimes focus on the hidden talents of her guests. When prominent actor George Raft—who frequently played a Hollywood tough guy—came to town, Peters kidded him to lighten up that persona.

Most national performers in town for theatre or book promotion stopped by to visit. Comedian Jonathan Winters said it was one of the "fastest-moving" shows he had ever seen. In a typical scenario when Eartha Kitt appeared at the American Theatre in the play *The Owl and the Pussycat*, members of that troupe visited and discussed production details and road show experiences. Major motion picture actors and singers of that early era, such as Perry Como and Andy Williams, commented on the quality of the show and the vitality of the staff. This was a subtle way to compliment Peters on her level of dedication and commitment.

Nationally known guests would often suggest how well her program compared to network productions. Charlotte was encouraged to consider such assignments but always discouraged that thinking, because it would obviously mean a move from her home. Ironically, once, toward the end of her career, Peters did appear on national television. She was in a kinescope excerpt from her program consisting of a very uncharacteristic condemnation of a national news program.

CBS filmed a documentary on teen life, *Sixteen in Webster Groves*.[15] The production showed youngsters in Webster Groves, a middle-class suburb of St. Louis that was the longtime home of Peters. It reflected behavioral norms and values for the entire nation. The students were presented as obsessed with grades, gaining admittance to prestigious colleges, and acquiring high-paying jobs to continue an affluent lifestyle.[16] The result of the original documentary was an outcry from the community that the film was not an accurate reflection of local teenagers. Many cried foul and indicated that they had been misrepresented as shallow and overly materialistic.[17] There were also allegations of staging and careless editing. The characterization of the community as obsessed with material goods was challenged. CBS went back to Webster Groves and filmed a follow-up in which the original participants reviewed the original program.

This follow-up permitted students and parents to clarify their positions and air grievances about the picture that had been painted. Since some of them had taken a firm stand on issues such as student independence, this gave a chance to show concerns and made for much less harsh and judgmental views than those represented in the original program.[18]

In a concluding segment of the follow-up, correspondent Charles Kuralt reviewed the controversy and showed Charlotte Peters' reaction. He introduced the country to a segment of commentary from her program, then airing over KTVI-TV. She interviewed local journalists and civic leaders, including the police chief, about program flaws. As a longtime resident, Peters vehemently objected to the thesis of the film.[19]

Participants in Peter's program enumerated oversights, including failure to show religious lives of teens. After Peter's was shown forcefully stating her position, Kuralt said no one could accuse CBS of not having stimulated the audience. Beyond national impact, Peter's appearance was unique since it was the first time a network returned for a follow-up and her appearance came from another TV source.[20] Many viewers felt that this was an admission that elements of the program were unrepresentative, that something had gone wrong. The follow-up program was unique in the sense that Peters was critical of a program that had aired on CBS while her own affiliations included ABC's KTVI and NBC's KSD-TV.

After eight years, Peters left KSD in the fall of 1964 and joined KTVI. Her parting from KSD-TV produced unusual results. The departure was front-page news.[21] Her transfer of loyalty was marked by a public footnote when her former station refused to release special scripted musical material. It was clear that this material was bought, paid for and fully owned by that station, but it appeared as petty after her many years of service. Later press accounts focused on the fact that mail addressed to *The Charlotte Peters Show* was held and sifted by her former station. This was proper according to officials from the U.S. Postal Service, but it had not been anticipated and appeared unusual in light of her extended service.[22]

Her new station tried to bargain briefly for the services of another employee. In the aftermath of the dispute, those who had written to Peters were advised to resend their letters to her new station. In one newspaper, the report on disagreement appeared adjacent to an invitation to viewers: Call a telephone number and "have a chat with Charlotte Peters."[23] Just before her departure from KSD-TV, it was announced that KTVI's public affairs director, Bruce Hayward, would leave that station to join *The Charlotte Peters Show.* Hayward replaced George Abel, who was leaving. Within a month, singer Marty Bronson would become central to a program KSD-TV retitled *The Noon Show.* Peters moved to her new assignment.[24]

In spite of her popularity and length of service, Peter's departure may have been less a surprise than one might have expected. One aspect of Peter's switch focused on the fact that she did not have a contract at KSD. This was not unusual for early TV, but a KTVI contract gave security. At the time, KTVI had been purchased by Newhouse Broadcasting. She was the third person to join that station within a two-week period in September and October 1964. Pat Fontaine, a weathercaster with the *Today* program and also CBS's KMOX-TV, left to join KTVI, as did newsman Spencer Allen, a veteran of CBS.[25]

News reports concerning Peter's move to KTVI focused on the fact that few people in St. Louis anticipated that she would seek a new affiliation. One critic said that rumor of departure had circulated but many wondered whether Peters would have the gumption to make a switch after such long ties. He added: "That is not meant, of course, as any questioning of Charlotte's show biz guts—she is well equipped with that commodity." Perhaps she would stay regardless of concerns.[26]

The move produced speculation on how KSD would recover. Some suggested they push the idea that a new staff of "handsome men" would do better with female audiences. The rationale was that during the early "pre-Oprah" era, male hosts such as Merv Griffin and Mike Douglas dominated daytime talk shows. Perhaps speculation about audience makeup had validity. Peters had been the center of the KSD program and staff deferred to her. KTVI's group was newer, perhaps not as open to direction.

Peters did exit that station in July 1970. It was reported that her "usual outspokenness" had cost her.[27] This departure came in conjunction with use of Forest Park. She condemned a planned concert, urging viewers to contact the mayor or board of aldermen to prevent a "Yippie ruckus."[28]

In the aftermath, station management maintained that cancellation of Peters' program was a business decision. The station gave decline in audience as the rationale. Peters provided local press with details, saying she was informed of her status after completion of a program. She explained the timing as a means to avoid controversy over her departure. She said station bosses also explained that although they were going to replace her in August, knowing what an outspoken person she was, they were merely protecting her from something she may say on air.

In spite of controversy, she performed so well she had become an icon. There was talk of her starting another program. While it never materialized, she continued making appearances. Near the close of her career, Downtown St. Louis, Inc., selected Peters as Outstanding Working Woman in Communications. This occurred when Leonor K. Sullivan, a member of Congress, was also honored for national contributions. By the time the National Academy of Television Arts and Sciences honored Peters with a Silver Circle Award, she had been gone for a decade but her influential presence was still strongly felt.[29]

For anyone visiting the St. Louis area, Peters is commemorated at Charlotte's Rib Western Barbecue, a restaurant owned by her daughter, Patricia Peters Schwarz, and her husband. Peter's photo in cowgirl regalia sans "Annie Got Her Gun" greets patrons as they enter.[30] Her Silver Circle Award from the National Academy of Television Arts and Sciences is on display as further testament to a broadcaster who inspired her community. It also reflects an understanding of the integral relationship between viewers, broadcasters, and their communities.

Notes

1. Hannon, R.E. (1962, Jan. 28). Putting together the "Charlotte Peters Show." *St. Louis Post-Dispatch*, pp. 2-3.
2. Keasler, J. (1956, May 20). Away from the frying pan into TV. *St. Louis Post-Dispatch Everyday Magazine*, p 2.
3. Murray, M.D. (1987, Feb. 8). KSD-TV 40th Anniversary TV supplement, *St. Louis Post-Dispatch*, p. TV-8.
4. Blair, W.M. (1951, Feb. 25). "Outraged" over video, Carroll defies senators. *New York Times*, p. 1.
5. Murray, M.D. (1985, July). Keith Gunther: Audiences were in his hands. *St. Louis Journalism Review*, p.14.
6. Murray, M.D. (1987, Jan.). Frank Eschen gave for 20 years. *St. Louis Journalism Review*, p. 8.
7. Runyan, M. (1958, July 20). Being a lady isn't her line: 40,000 letters a month for Charlotte, *Miami Herald*, p. B-14.
8. Roedel, J. (1985). Personal communication.
9. Hunter, F. (1966, Feb. 13). Charlotte Peters. *St. Louis Globe Democrat Sunday Magazine*, pp. 4-5.
10. Berger, J. (1988, Dec. 30). Kann offers praise of Charlotte Peters. *St. Louis Post-Dispatch*, p. D-1.
11. Olson, C. (1989, Jan. 11). A tribute to Charlotte Peters. *St. Louis Post-Dispatch, You Magazine*, p. 6.
12. Runyan, 1958.
13. Goellner, G. (1961, Jan. 20). Charlotte Peters discloses her secret of success. *St. Louis Review*, p. 1.
14. Murray, M.D. (1997). Pulitzer's prize. In Murray, M.D., and Godfrey, D.G. (eds.), *Television in America* (pp. 309-330). Ames: Iowa State University Press.
15. Corrigan, P. (1966, Mar. 4). Webster Groves: Are teens still clad in diapers? *St. Louis Globe Democrat*, p. 1-B.
16. Murray, M.D. (1994). *Political Performers*. N.Y.: Praeger.
17. Corrigan, P. (1966, Apr. 12). Webster once more in spotlight. *St. Louis Globe Democrat*, p. 10-D.
18. Start, C. (1975). *Webster Groves*. Webster Groves, Mo.: City of Webster Groves, p. 231.
19. Corrigan, P. (1992, July 6). Class of '67: Image still rankles. *St. Louis Post-Dispatch*, p. 3-D.
20. Levins, H. (1989, Mar. 6). Film still drives 'em crazy after all these years. *St. Louis Post-Dispatch*, p. D-2.
21. Rahn, P. (1970, July 11-12). KTVI fires Charlotte Peters suddenly after Friday's show. *St. Louis Globe Democrat*, p. 1.
22. Rahn, P. (1964, Sept. 9). Local TV's personality pot still boiling. *St. Louis Globe-Democrat*, p. C-10.
23. Lowry, C. (1964, Sept. 11). Few big successes likely in new shows. *St. Louis Post-Dispatch*, p. D-8.

24. Rahn, P. (1964, Aug. 31). They'll be some changes made: Flurry of activity. *St. Louis Globe-Democrat,* p. A-13.
25. Terry, D. (1964, Sept. 25) Marty Bronson: He just likes to sing. *St. Louis Post-Dispatch,* p. D-2.
26. Rahn, Sept. 1964, p. C-10.
27. Rahn, 1970.
28. Rahn, 1970.
29. Murray, M.D. (1986, Feb.). KSD veteran John Roedel retires. *St. Louis Journalism Review,* p. 23.
30. Berger, 1988.

Other Sources

Anything goes on Charlotte Peters' shows. (1956, April 28-May 4) *TV Guide,* p. A-37.
Charlotte Peters, St. Louis pioneer on TV, dies. (1988, Dec. 30). *St. Louis Post-Dispatch,* p. A-3.
Charlotte's world. (1954, Mar. 16-31). *Key Magazine,* pp. 34-35.
Corrigan, P. (1989, Mar. 7). Personal communication.
Crime inquiry attracts crowds like World Series. (1951, Feb. 24). *St. Louis Globe Democrat,* p.1.
Have a chat with Charlotte Peters. Call MI7-9210. (1964, Sept. 11). *St. Louis Globe Democrat,* advertisement, p. A-8.
Hernon, P. (1986, July 7). Class of '66 remembers. *St. Louis Post Dispatch,* p. A-1.
KSD-TV covers fire. (1962, Aug. 27). *Broadcasting.*
Peters, C. (1964, May). This is St. Louis. *McCalls,* p. 24.
Schoyan, W.O. (1958, Nov. 2-8) Charlotte Peters builds show on whim. *St. Louis Post-Dispatch, TV Magazine,* pp. 6-7.
Webster Groves Revisited. (1966, Apr. 8). *CBS News* national broadcast.
Woman TV producer, KSD's Betty Barnett, also a director, is one of few women in such jobs. (nd). KSD-TV, St. Louis, Mo., illustrated station publication.

Wanda Ramey and Ronald Reagan on the KPIX news set circa 1966

Wanda Ramey

KPIX's Girl on the Beat

Wanda Ramey is an American television pioneer. She was the first woman news anchor in the western United States and the second woman news anchor on local television in America. Ramey holds the distinction of being the co-host of the first local television noon newscast in America. She is also one of the most honored women from the early years of local television news.

Wanda Ramey was born in Terre Haute, Indiana, the daughter of Hiram and May Ramey. She attended both high school and college there. After graduating from high school in 1941, she attended Indiana State Teacher's College, now Indiana State University. She graduated in 1945. "I majored in speech, radio and the emerging television industry. I worked at the local radio station and at the college radio station where we did everything, announced, wrote and so on. At the local radio station, WBOW, On the Banks of the Wabash, we had a program called the *Story Princess of the Music Box* and I would introduce this and then have various people tell stories."[1]

After graduation and her on-air stint as the Story Princess, Ramey moved to Oakland, California, where her father had been transferred by American Express. After living there for a while, she moved to Los Angeles and took a job at a recording studio. She then accepted employment in the movie theater division of Warner Brothers. After some time there she found a job in broadcasting at a radio station in San Luis Obispo. "I loved that station; it was KPIK, Pick of the Listening. I was on the air and set up interviews and such. I then came back up to the San Francisco Bay Area and worked at a number of stations."[2]

Before her pioneering news work at KPIX, Ramey was employed in myriad broadcast positions in the Bay Area. In 1947, her first job was interviewing celebrities at the Hearst Ranch near Pleasanton, about 30 miles east of San Francisco, for KSFO, a popular San Francisco AM radio station. On Sundays she hosted a program series called *The Woman Behind the Man* and interviewed the wives of well-known men. Another series she hosted during this period was *You Count on Your County.* For this program she interviewed officials of the various Bay Area counties about "how they got started and what they were doing and things of that sort."[3] Another Bay Area radio station that she did on-air work for was KROW (later, KABL) in Oakland.

In a history written by the Bay Area Broadcast Legends group some of her pre-KPIX exploits were described: "Wanda Ramey joined the staff of KWBR-radio in Oakland as the program director's secretary in 1948. There was no program director, so Wanda filled in at secretary's pay. It was only a year or so before she moved to KROW and began an illustrious on-the-air career which led her to KGO-TV where she hosted a mid-day show."[4]

Few women were on the air in the early days of broadcasting. Ramey tells a story of Vince Francis, general manager at KGO-TV, who told her women didn't do a good job as newscasters. That was the way he informed her that she was fired.[5] Wanda was out of work for months before she took a job on KCBS radio in San Francisco.

According to Beth Ashley, "At 24 she was hired as anchor of a short-lived mid-day news and interview show on Channel 7 [KGO-TV]." The show, broadcast in 1952, was called *Midday with Wanda* and was the result of her assisting with a program hosted by Les Malloy at KGO.[6] "We did a number of shows from the Sutro Mansion [where the Sutro broadcast tower and transmission facilities are presently located]. It was a great place to go because . . . you'd get in the car and start up into the fog and it was a very mysterious feeling . . . that the place was like Wuthering Heights and I gave that item to somebody and got credit for having started it and I'm sure I didn't."[7]

After her dismissal from KGO-TV she took a job at KCBS radio doing on-air interviewing work as "Jane Todd." One of her programs was called *Meet Me at Mannings,* which featured interviews with the wives of well-known Bay Area and national celebrities. While at KCBS she also worked with Dave McEllhatton doing interviews at KCBS's studios in San Francisco's legendary Palace Hotel. In 1957, while she was at KCBS, she interviewed and was hired for a newscaster position at San Francisco's first television station, KPIX, Channel 5.[8] "I got to

KPIX through an interview for a woman newscaster. And there were people who came from all over the country, from New York, from Chicago. This was an innovation to have a woman as a straight-out newscaster. And I was chosen, . . .and it just seemed like the normal thing to me, that that was what I was supposed to do. And it was great, and I loved doing that."[9]

KPIX was soon to make history creating something quite original. According to Dave McEllhatton in a KPIX news feature on the station's history, Ray Hubbard, an innovative programmer created "*The Noon News.* There had never before been a half hour of midday news. The anchors were John Weston, 'Channel 5's Guy on the Go,' and Wanda Ramey, 'Channel 5's Gal on the Go.' Wanda was one of the first women news anchors in the country and talented enough to survive the title they hung on her."[10] That may not be entirely accurate. In a videotape of one of the early *Noon News* broadcasts, the program ends with a superimposition over Wanda Ramey of "Girl on the Beat" as Ramey closes by saying, "Wanda Ramey, Woman on the Beat."[11]

Within the year, KPIX "promoted" Ramey from "girl" to "woman." The spoken introduction to the *Noon News* became, "Now, live from San Francisco, it's the Channel 5 *Noon News,* all the news from all the world, with exclusive features from your man and woman on the beat, Wanda Ramey and John Weston."[12]

Local television's first noon newscast, *Noon News,* was broadcast on KPIX on Monday, February 16, 1959. Without newspaper fanfare, it appeared that day in the "TV Today" listing of the *San Francisco Chronicle* as "*Noon News,* New show, Wanda Ramey, John Weston."[13] Within six months the *Noon News* on KPIX had become the highest rated 30- minute newscast in the Bay Area.[14]

One reason the *Noon News* became the top rated half-hour news show in six months was that viewers found Channel 5 news exciting with Ramey's style of broadcasting. She put on a workman's helmet and from a construction elevator beamed out a KPIX special on the progress of the newest, tallest building in San Francisco. She rode with the S Squad at midnight to give KPIX *Noon News* viewers the lowdown on San Francisco Detail Police. Ramey brought her viewers face to face with one of their new neighbors, a bearded beatnik recently moved to North Beach from Greenwich Village. She wanted to find out just what makes a beatnik tick.

Ramey has many fond memories of the early days of co-anchoring the *Noon News.* She enjoys describing those pioneering times and paints a rather vivid picture that helps provide a feeling of what the *Noon News* must have been like to view and to participate in, "The *Noon News* was my main thing, always with John Weston. . . . I remember what fun it was to go in and pull news; you felt really great. Pull the news off the wire, tear it off, that was always fun."[15]

Ramey always had an interview and did one or two stories in the top part of the newscast. Her co-anchor, John Weston, always did the hard-hitting news stories. Since sometimes guests would not show, Ramey always had a taped interview ready. She used a few notes and cue cards but never used a TelePrompTer.

She was popular with the audience and received a lot of mail. Once a viewer named a dahlia after her. Her habit was to answer the first letter but not the second to avoid encouraging unwanted attention. Although she never had a stalker, she was careful.

By the time Ramey began anchoring the *Noon News,* the commercial value of newscasts and their anchors had been long obvious. According to Ramey, there was always profit potential in the news.[16] Right at the beginning of the *Noon News* in 1959 she began to participate in some of the commercials broadcast within the program. Ramey remembers doing commercials for Supphose stockings and wearing them but that was stopped soon after the program began to prevent newscasters from being associated too closely with a product.

One of Ramey's most vivid memories was the day President Kennedy was assassinated: "We were just about ready to go on the air, and all of a sudden our producer came up and he said, 'My God, the President's been shot.' Well, of course everything changed. We were close to airtime. We got some local people in a hurry to get down there who had known the president and somebody to discuss what the impact might be on this."[17]

In 1963 Ramey was featured in an article titled "From Fashion Shows to Fires, Wanda Ramey Is KPIX's Woman-on-the-Beat." She is described as "calm and reserved" and "petite and mild-mannered, . . . one of the few women in broadcasting who successfully manages to polish the rough corners off the hard news." The article notes that she was chosen because she is flexible as a newswoman and can cover a wide variety of stories and is adept at interviewing "colorful celebrities and outstanding political figures."[18]

Throughout her career in journalism and broadcasting, Ramey seems most happy with her interviewing. She has interviewed well over

1,200 important and well-known personalities, including Ronald Reagan, Carl Sandburg, John Kennedy, Caryl Chessman, Hubert Humphrey, Richard Nixon, Lyndon Johnson, Martin Luther King, Jr., and astronaut James McDevitt. She interviewed her mother once on Mother's Day. "But of all these interviews, Wanda still remembers one of her first as the most memorable: Eleanor Roosevelt, the woman who was Wanda's own inspiration and role model growing up."[19] Her reflections on that part of her life are consistently positive, provide insight into her own character, and are even, at times, touching: "It's the only job in the world I ever wanted and the most fulfilling thing anybody could do, to get a chance to keep up with what's going on and to meet all those wonderful people. I tried to count 'em up once, how many people I had interviewed, thousands that I'd been able to touch their life and they mine for a few minutes at a time; it's been great."[20] Part of her success may be because she considers television an intimate medium. She believes that as a communicator you talk to one person, not thousands.[21]

In 1959 when Ramey was promoted to the position of news anchor on KPIX, she became a source of pride for KPIX. She also provided the station with some notable firsts. According to the station, she was the first woman anchor in the western United States and the second woman anchor in the country.[22] Another source has stated, "Barbara Walters, Diane Sawyer, Jane Pauley and countless other women in broadcast news have Terre Haute native Wanda Ramey to thank for their rise to journalistic stardom. Ramey was the first female television news anchor."[23] Her nomination to the Marin County (California) Women's Hall of Fame (c1992) notes, "In 1959 Wanda Ramey made history in the broadcasting industry when she became the first female television news anchor in the country, co-hosting the *Noon News* on Channel 5, San Francisco. She has been recognized in both radio and television as a genuine pioneer in broadcasting, paving the way for the many women who today have an easier entree into an industry that has been dominated by men."[24]

In 1958 Ramey married Richard ("Dick") Queirolo, a sheet-metal contractor. He developed an interest in filmmaking and video, was hired as a stringer by KPIX and often accompanied his wife on assignments as well as co-producing feature stories with her for the *Noon News*. When they began a family, Ramey continued to work. Wanda and Dick's child, Kristie Louise, was born in 1962. "It was good to be on the air at noon because we had a marvelous housekeeper who would come about nine o'clock in the morning and she would stay until I got home, usually around two or two thirty."[25] Ramey remained with KPIX until 1967.

On New Year's Eve in 1960, Wanda and Dick visited San Quentin Prison to film a story on prison life. "This led to a continuous relationship with the prison and its inmates which resulted in the prison's own prison-run closed-circuit TV station [SQTV]."[26]

Over the years she and her husband have taught television journalism as well as film and television production skills to a large number of prison inmates. He helps the prisoners learn the particulars of cameras, while she fills them in on the details of narration and coordination. "Hopefully, they will be able to go into another business when they get out, one that is meaningful and creative for living."[27]

In 1965 Ramey's student inmates thanked and honored her by naming her an "Honorary Inmate." That same year, as part of a film workshop taught by Ramey and her husband, a group of inmates produced a sports documentary. During the summer of 1966 a documentary on emergency farm labor was shot on location in the San Joaquin Valley by a small and select group of their students.

As a result of Wanda Ramey and her husband's early community service commitment at San Quentin, a group of about 50 of their trainees produced a telefilm, *The Cage*. It was broadcast on Wednesday, February 15, 1967, at 10 p.m. on KQED, Channel 9, San Francisco's pioneering educational television station. According to *San Francisco Examiner* columnist Dwight Newton, "It is . . . a grim, sometimes gripping, semi-real, semi-fanciful half-hour drama of four convicts captive in a barren, bunkless, chairless, concrete cell. . . . [It] is by no means a slick, professional production. Much of the equipment was begged or borrowed."[28]

The prison allowed the telefilm to be produced because of the potential therapeutic value to the participants and of the possibility of obtaining funds to acquire equipment for the prison's film workshop.[29] Ramey and her husband's work with the inmates at San Quentin Prison continued into the 1990s.

After leaving KPIX, Ramey went to KQED, San Francisco's public broadcasting television station, to work on a national series called *The Public Broadcasting Laboratory*. Then she was asked to do Voice of America. "That was good. You pick up on local stories and feed them by telephone to New York. 'This is Wanda Ramey with the Voice of America in San Francisco' was the end cue."[30] She was the Bay Area correspondent for the Voice of America for well over 10 years. According to Ramey, whatever was an important local story was welcome. During the late 1960s she also worked as a hard-news reporter on KGO-TV's *Newsbeat* nightly newscast.

Since retiring from television and radio in the 1970s, she has continued to stay active in media. She has produced a number of videos for the Buck Center for Research in Aging. She has co-written a history of the Tamalpais retirement community, where she and her husband reside. She has participated on the Board of the American Federation of Television and Radio Artists (AFTRA) and is active with Broadcast Legends, an informal group of media pioneers.[31] She has also worked with her husband on various media projects for his production company, Q-Rolo Film and Video Productions, as well as continuing with him on their San Quentin prison volunteer work.

For her more than 40-year career in television and other media Wanda Ramey has been honored with many awards and much recognition of her significant achievements. In 1958 she received the Emmy Award for Television Journalism from the Northern California Chapter of the National Academy of Television Arts and Sciences. In 1965 she was the first reporter and first woman to be named "Honorary Inmate" by the prisoners of San Quentin Prison. In 1968 she was honored with the Alumni Distinguished Service Award from Indiana State University in recognition of notable achievement reflecting honor and distinction on her alma mater. In 1982 she received a Commendation by the City and County of San Francisco Board of Supervisors "on the auspicious occasion of her being honored by the Golden Gate Chapter, American Women in Television, Inc., for her outstanding contributions to broadcasting."[32] In 1982 San Francisco Mayor Diane Feinstein issued a proclamation commending Wanda Ramey "for her dedication and invaluable contributions to the broadcasting industry and . . . on her truly impressive and distinguished achievements."[33] Other awards include the American Women in Radio and Television, Golden Gate Chapter, Outstanding Achievement in Broadcasting Award (1982); the Woman of Achievement Award from Women in Communications (1986); the Silver Circle Award from the National Academy of Television Arts and Sciences, Northern California Chapter, "in honor of your contribution as a Northern California television pioneer" (1989); and a Special Honor from the Society for Professional Journalists (1990). She also served the community in various roles. She was the first female president of the San Francisco Bay Area Chapter of AFTRA, the first female member of the Press Club of San Francisco, and an active member in AWRT (American Women in Radio and Television), the National Academy of Television Arts and Sciences, and Women in Communications, Inc. (WICI).

Wanda Ramey is well respected and loved for her spirit, friendship, helpfulness and positive outlook. Her longtime friend, and the godmother of Wanda's daughter, comedienne Phyllis Diller perhaps expressed the feelings of many when she said at the 1986 WICI luncheon honoring Ramey:

> Having Wanda for a friend is like having a million dollars in your checking account. Wanda has been my closest personal friend for more than three decades. She is a *remarkable* woman. Dear Wanda Ramey was one of the few people who gave me *total* support at the beginning of my career when it was "iffy." She's a trailblazer in broadcasting; a loyal wife and a wonderful mother. She's as soft and quiet as a rose petal. . . .[34]

Ramey has a number of insights concerning television journalism and her career, both as a pioneer television journalist and as a skilled communicator. She says she never felt discriminated against because she was a woman. She also did not accept barriers that someone else may have placed in her way. "I was just going to do this . . . without thinking about the fact that there might be somebody to say, 'Why are you here? What are you doing in the news field and not doing recipes or child care items?'" Ramey also considers the news to be more shocking than in the past. She describes the news in the "olden days" as "kind and gentle."[35]

Wanda Ramey is one of the many pioneering women in American local television. While many had somewhat parallel career paths, they all had their own unique place in the development of television. For Ramey, it was a positive and fulfilling career. "The most important recognition was being selected and getting the job to be the first woman. That was very special, always has been. The first woman to do hard news and not being relegated to home hints and recipes, and it was natural for me not to do them but to do the hard news."[36]

Notes

1. Ramey, W. (2000, Sept. 22). Oral history interview conducted by Steven C. Runyon. Transcribed audio recording. Personal papers of S.C. Runyon, University of San Francisco.

2. Ramey, 2000.
3. Ramey, 2000.
4. Broadcast Legends History. (c.1992). Nomination of Wanda Ramey for the Marin County Women's Hall of Fame. Personal papers of Wanda Ramey.
5. Broadcast Legends, c.1992.
6. Ashley, B. (c.1988). First anchorwoman steams ahead. *Marin Independent Journal.* Newspaper clipping. Personal papers of Wanda Ramey.
7. Ramey, 2000.
8. Runyon, S.C. (1997). San Francisco's first television station: KPIX. In M.D. Murray and D.G. Godfrey (eds.), *Television in America* (pp. 353-366). Ames: Iowa State University Press.
9. Ramey, 2000.
10. McEllhatton, D. (c.1994, Dec.). KPIX-5 History. Draft of news script. KPIX Public Relations Department files, San Francisco.
11. *Noon News.* (c.1959-1960). Compilation of early *Noon News* broadcasts [Videotape]. Personal papers of Wanda Ramey.
12. *Noon News,* c.1959-1960.
13. TV today. (1959, Feb. 16). *San Francisco Chronicle,* p. 32.
14. Westinghouse Broadcasting Company, Inc. print ad. (c.1959-1960). Newspaper clipping. Personal papers of Wanda Ramey.
15. Ramey, 2000.
16. Ramey, 2000.
17. Ramey, 2000.
18. From fashion shows to fires, Wanda Ramey is KPIX's woman-on-the-beat. (1963). Newspaper clipping. Personal papers of Wanda Ramey.
19. Broadcast Legends, c.1992.
20. Broadcast Legends, c.1992.
21. Ramey, 2000.
22. KPIX 40th anniversary list of station firsts. (c.1988, Dec.). KPIX Public Relations Department files, San Francisco.
23. Wabash Valley profiles, a series of tributes to hometown people and events that have shaped our history. (1996, Feb. 29). *Terre Haute Tribune-Star,* p. A2.
24. Broadcast Legends, c.1992.
25. Ramey, 2000.
26. Broadcast Legends, c.1992.
27. Eberle, R. (1969). Honorary inmate KGO-TV's Wanda Ramey helps convicts. *CaptraNews,* p. 5. Newspaper clipping. Personal papers of Wanda Ramey.
28. Newton, D. (1967, Feb. 14). San Quentin *Cage* on 9. *San Francisco Examiner,* p. 23.
29. Newton, 1967.
30. Ramey, 2000.
31. Ashley, c.1988.
32. Commendation. (1982, June 22). City and County of San Francisco Board of Supervisors. Personal papers of Wanda Ramey.
33. Feinstein, D. (1982, June 22). Proclamation. Personal papers of Wanda Ramey.
34. Diller, P. (1986, June 29). Message from Phyllis Diller (read at WICI luncheon for Wanda). Personal papers of Wanda Ramey.
35. Ramey, 2000.
36. Ramey, 2000.

Marciarose Shestack with Vice President Hubert Humphrey in his office in Washington, D.C. It was the day of President Lyndon Johnson's surgery when Humphrey was, as he put it, "acting President."

Marciarose Shestack

A Broadcaster Who Happens to Be a Woman

Marciarose Shestack was the first American woman to anchor prime-time news in a major market, that of fourth-ranked Philadelphia. She prefers to be called a broadcaster who happens to be a woman rather than a "woman broadcaster" because the latter highlights the gender of the person rather than the job. Despite some resistance from people who didn't think a woman was credible enough to do the news, she did the job with great success, earning large audiences and numerous awards. Awards include a McCall's Golden Mike Award for Outstanding Woman Broadcaster in the United States and the DuPont Award for Outstanding Broadcasting. She has been an anchorwoman, a talk show host, documentary producer and narrator, reporter, theater critic, and arts editor.

Marciarose Shestack is referred to simply as Marciarose. Throughout her broadcasting career she was known only by her first name after her station decided her full name was unpronounceable. Her unusual name became something of a trademark, most evident in her column "Marciarose" for *The Philadelphia Inquirer* and *The Marciarose Show* on KYW-TV.

Marciarose developed her interest in news through several early experiences. She did her undergraduate work at Northwestern University, then earned a master's with honors at Louisiana State University, both in communications and in theater. Her ambition at the time was to be an actress. During the 1950s she completed all her coursework for a Ph.D. in political science at the University of Pennsylvania, where she was a Fels Scholar. A "serendipitous" start on *College Press Conference,* ABC's program featuring a panel of college students, meant that she didn't finish her degree. TV became her great love, and she didn't need a Ph.D. to do what she was doing.[1]

The Shestacks were new to Philadelphia and had a mentor and friend who was dating a woman producing *College Press Conference*. The friend suggested putting Marciarose on the panel as a political science student. She appeared once before the summer break, then in the fall of 1954 became the assistant producer. The producer put her on air one night, and then the next, and again the next week, and after a month Marciarose was the show's regular panelist. She took charge of booking the other rotating panelists, students from all over the country, as well as the guests, who were senators, cabinet members, ambassadors, business leaders. Like *Meet the Press,* the panel grilled their high-profile guests on current issues. Marciarose met Larry Spivak, host of *Meet the Press* one day at a cocktail party. "They say you're just as mean as I am," he told her, adding, "but you're prettier."[2]

College Press Conference originally aired from Philadelphia and later from Washington, D.C. Coming home on the train from a Washington assignment, the show's producer commented that she knew Marciarose no longer really wanted to be an actress. Marciarose nodded. "You may not know why," the producer said, "but I do. Acting is playing at life, and what we do, the news, is life itself."[3] *College Press Conference* was a fortuitous introduction to that life. This led to her being asked to serve as radio and TV coordinator for Adlai Stevenson's 1956 presidential campaign, an experience that helped develop her political thinking and heightened her interest in both politics and political reporting.

Philadelphia's Channel 3 took note of her work on *College Press Conference* and in 1957 asked her to join their team. She would spend the next 18 years there as a talk show host, producer, anchor, and arts editor. She also became an active and well-known part of Philadelphia's community life.

Marciarose describes her first two shows as "the fight show" and "the egghead show."[4] The fight show was *Speak Up,* a weekly news talk show Marciarose began producing and moderating in 1958 in which guests would debate current issues. The egghead show was *Concept,* an educational public affairs series that started in 1957 as a studio show and moved three years later to an on-location documentary film format.

Speak Up looked at a range of issues in the news and brought people from opposing sides together in debate. Even if issues weren't resolved, they were at least brought to the attention of the city. This aspect of being a journalist and public figure was, and continues to be, important to Marciarose: "If you have the potential to make a difference, you should use it; as Robert Kennedy said, it's incumbent on everyone to try. If you also succeed, it's a wonderful feeling."[5] Marciarose continued to do *Speak Up* for about eight years.

Concept was an intellectual, educational, and public-service program that was interesting, creative and very popular. The idea for the show arose one day in the late 1950s as Marciarose was having lunch at the faculty club of the University of Pennsylvania. A public relations director approached her about doing a program for the University that would promote the school and its resources. Marciarose was not interested in working for the University but the conversation sparked the idea of an educational show taking advantage of the vast resources a university has to offer. Fortunately, she was asked by the station if she could develop a program with educational content to help the station meet FCC requirements for a certain amount of educational programming.[6]

The show began as a studio show with only Marciarose as producer and talent. It aired live on Sunday afternoons. Marciarose describes the show's beginnings as "a sophisticated show and tell." She would bring professors into the studio to discuss their field of interest. In 1960 Marciarose talked the station into changing to a weekly half-hour documentary format, which Channel 3 placed in the Tuesday 7 p.m. time slot, an indication of the faith the station had in Marciarose. She agreed to produce one show a week "not knowing that it couldn't be done once a week." The result was 16- to 18-hour days and one very popular show. Initially the staff was Marciarose as producer, writer, and talent; a director; and a film crew shared with the news department. After a year the show's budget was expanded and a writer was added to the small staff, making the team able to take on more ambitious projects and expand their university affiliations beyond the University of Pennsylvania. They worked with over 30 universities, medical schools, hospitals, and other institutions involved in higher learning.[7]

Concept was billed as "weekly explorations into the world of ideas," with the aims of demonstrating the wide range of university interests, activities, and ideas and how these institutions interact with the world around them in trying to combat social problems.[8] In the spring of 1963 Marciarose and her crew traveled to Guatemala to explore the Mayan ruins of Tikal and Chichicastenango under excavation by a University of Pennsylvania archaeological team. *Concept* also did a three-part series, *The Homeless Man,* looking at both life on the streets and an experimental hostel trying to help Philadelphia's homeless men get back on their feet. At this time the issue of homelessness hadn't yet reached the level of national awareness it has today.

Marciarose frequently covered medicine, because of its potential for high drama.[9] They filmed open heart and brain surgery. In a program titled *The Birth of Tommy Rohlfing,* Marciarose and her crew followed a mother preparing for natural childbirth through the stages of her pregnancy, during checkups with her doctor, and into the delivery room. It was the first time a birth had been filmed for U.S. television audiences and was a very moving experience for the *Concept* team. Marciarose recalls running back to the studio after Tommy was born, shouting, "We had a boy! We had a boy!"[10]

Forty years later the airwaves are filled with much more shocking topics than childbirth and the homeless and other topics *Concept* explored, but in the early 1960s it was on the cutting edge. Marciarose credits WRCV with being open-minded and willing to take that risk, and trusting her judgment rather than questioning her choice of topics. Bill Leonard, another documentary program producer, asked Marciarose how she was able to do her programs. Every time he asked program manager Neal Van Ells, the answer was "no." Marciarose responded: "I never ask."[11]

In 1963, *McCall's* presented Marciarose with their Golden Mike Award for the Outstanding Woman Broadcaster in the United States. "The station that had been letting us go our own way suddenly took notice, and began actively promoting the show." WRCV and Marciarose were also honored with the Philadelphia County Medical Society's Benjamin Rush Medical Award for their "outstanding contributions to the health of the community," the first time the award had been given to a broadcaster.[12]

Marciarose describes the face of Philadelphia television when she started out in the late 1950s as "a man's world. There were no prominent professional female role models. The only woman on the evening newscast was the . . .'weathergirl,' invariably young and pretty; there were some women during the day doing children's programming."[13] Being part of the news team had become one of Marciarose's goals. "I was interested in news, and wanted to do news, and didn't see why a woman couldn't do news." She went to the general manager to tell him she wanted to do the news and he replied, "A woman will do news over my dead body. A woman is not an authority figure, and women do not have good voices."[14]

In 1965 Channel 3 (now KYW) wanted to start a daily noon news program. They interviewed and auditioned actresses, models, and other celebrities from New York and Los Angeles for the co-anchor positions but chose Marciarose because of her strength in the market. As her co-anchor, KYW brought in Tom Snyder, the well-known talk show host. *Eyewitness News at Noon* immediately preceded *The Mike Douglas Show*, a popular nationally syndicated talk and entertainment show originating in Philadelphia.

Marciarose and Snyder made a powerful team. She recalls that the noon news held a 52 percent market share for that time slot. They built up great ratings but also serious news credibility. Marciarose's daily five-minute live interview segment, which she did in addition to her co-anchor duties, often dealt with politics or international relations, and the local papers monitored her interviews closely, often using them as the source for a story the following day.

In the midst of this success, Snyder and Marciarose were called into a meeting with station heads. They were told: "You're doing the best news show we have. It's better in quality than the 6 or 11 p.m. newscasts." Marciarose remembers herself and her co-anchor beaming with pride, until the other shoe dropped: "Now don't do it any more."[15]

The show wasn't attracting the demographics the station was looking for. Men were watching; the station wanted to attract advertisers targeting women ages 18 to 39. Marciarose went out and bought every women's magazine she could find, spread them out on the floor in front of her, looked them over and noticed a pattern of topics: medicine, childcare, money management, health, cooking, fashion. Snyder and Marciarose felt it was important to maintain the integrity of the news and continued their hard-news lead stories. But they introduced softer pieces into the mix, and it worked. "We didn't lose the male demographic, but we got the female demographic, and our ratings soared." It was a valuable lesson in the importance of the marketplace.[16]

Marciarose and Snyder also wrote much of the news they read. Marciarose soon realized it's very hard to be completely objective. No matter what your personal views are, a reporter needs to be scrupulously fair. When you have 30 seconds to tell a story, "it's very easy to give a wrong impression by omission," something she always kept in mind and fought against in her newswriting.[17]

At the same time that she was co-anchoring at noon, Marciarose was also reporting for the 6 p.m. news and doing theatre and movie reviews for the 11 p.m. news. Her theatre reviews were reflective of Marciarose's belief in her audience. She wanted to expand the horizons of her viewers and make ideas accessible rather than elitist. An assignment editor told her she was crazy to try to put arts in a newscast, but he gave her a chance even though he thought the audience wasn't intellectual enough to get it. Marciarose would film an arts story, then accompany the footage with fun music and nonpompous copy, trying to shatter the idea that the arts are inaccessible. Years later, she had a program manager who took issue with the topics she presented, saying he wanted to be "broadcasting to truck drivers." Marciarose trusted her audience as much as they trusted her, broke through the myth that theatre, politics, and so-called intellectual topics are only for an elite segment of the population. Her ratings proved her success.

In 1966 Marciarose had been co-anchoring the noon news for about a year when she and her husband decided to have a baby. She was asked to stay on the air as long as she could. The station turned this situation into a ratings coup. Marciarose would do a segment on pregnancy every day on the noon news. She conducted interviews with doctors, talked about books, even discussed breastfeeding and, in one particularly daring episode, showed photographs by a Swedish photographer of a fetus developing in the womb. Although this does not seem controversial today, in the mid-1960s this was daring enough that the station's phones began to ring as soon as the segment ended. One caller accused Marciarose of "blasphemy" and told her God would punish her by taking her baby away, but the segment sent noon news ratings "through the roof."[18]

Jennifer Shestack was born amidst a flurry of publicity. The station took out a full-page newspaper ad saying, "KYW is having a baby." There was a contest to guess the baby's name, photographers at the hospital, presents from Marciarose's audience. To this day, Marciarose says, people still ask about "the baby," who recently got married.[19]

Marciarose's noon news co-anchor, Tom Snyder, had also been KYW's 7 p.m. anchorman. When he left in 1971, the station's program manager was willing to "run against the tide" and put her in the 7 p.m. co-anchor's chair, the first time a woman had anchored primetime in a top-five market in the United States. By this time she had spent about 14 years on local television and viewers were being asked to accept into their living rooms at dinnertime a trusted, respected, well-known member of their community. Marciarose recalls her excitement was not in being the first woman in that position but in consistently beating Walter Cronkite and the *CBS News* in that time period. "Now that," she says, "was an ego boost."[20]

Marciarose had little awareness at the time of being a "groundbreaker" for women in television despite the fact that she did encounter resistance. The "men's club" was used to doing things their own way, and there was both industrywide resistance to a woman in a position of prominence, as well as resistance from individual men. She recalls making much less money than her male colleagues; when it appeared, during the 1960s, that her annual income would soon top $50,000, "the general manager blanched," even though men's salaries already topped that amount.[21]

Through the early part of her career there were no laws requiring equal opportunity or equal pay—and even passage of such laws, such as the EEOC Equal Pay Act of 1963, didn't immediately make a difference. There were so few jobs in television that women had to focus on competing for space, equal pay being a later battle.[22] There was the added problem for women of being, as Marciarose says, "a slave to your hair." No matter how smart, talented, and trustworthy you were, if you were female and on TV, you had to look good.[23]

Many of the problems she faced as a successful woman in television weren't necessarily an inherent part of the business but were social attitudes that would only fade with time. She worked well with her camera crews but in non-work-related conversations, these men would make it clear that they would never allow their wives to do the things Marciarose did, such as work freely with men and travel independently.[24]

Her relationships with women were also affected by the fact that she was a successful and high-profile professional.

> I had initial problems with women, who also weren't happy with my being part of the workforce. They for the most part were home having babies. . . . At parties I would invariably be talking to the men, because they were interested in the things I was interested in—politics, current events—and it was the men who I'd be calling for interviews. I felt uncomfortable with most of the women. But then we had a baby and I discovered what a great leveler toilet training could be.[25]

Her son Jonathan was born in 1959. When he was little, Marciarose would sometimes have to set up a playpen in her office; it was a time when "support systems weren't really there" for working mothers.[26]

Marciarose appeared on the 7 p.m. news for one year until the station decided to change format and cancel the show. Her next few projects gave her a chance to delve more deeply into topics and get to know some very interesting guests. From 1972 to 1974 she hosted *The Marciarose Show,* a daily one-hour talk show on KYW with both a studio audience and call-ins.

"Through interviews, people become part of your life forever," she says. "You learn so much—especially when someone trusts you enough to open up in a way they had no intention of doing at the start."[27] Sylvia Plath's mother talked about her relationship with her daughter. Jimmy Carter revealed to her his primary-election strategy when he was running for president. Maya Angelou became a close friend after their interview. Marciarose believes listening makes it possible for you to ask the right questions. With an evasive politician she would be "aggressive and insistent"—and, she says, that style is not always accepted in a woman interviewer. "When people see that in a man, they say, 'boy, was he good'—but with a woman, they say, 'boy, was she pushy.'"[28]

In 1973 Marciarose had the extraordinary experience of being one of 14 professional American women to visit the People's Republic of China just after President Nixon began to open talks with the Chinese. The only journalists to visit China since relations had been reestablished were those who had accompanied Nixon on his trip. KYW didn't really want Marciarose gone for a month. But she went and filed reports by telephone whenever possible.

It was "mind-boggling," Marciarose says, to visit China in those days. After a quarter-century of no official relations, "it was another world, a world we knew nothing about." Her American colleagues included educators, economists, and other high-level professional women, including Margaret MacNamara, wife of Defense Secretary Robert MacNamara. The goal was to match them for an exchange with their professional counterparts in China. There were no women broadcasters in China then, but Marciarose was able to visit a television station. She also met with the wife of the Chinese premier, Madame Chou-en-Lai, for a three-and-a-half hour interview. After her return, she not only broadcast special reports on KYW but also was invited by NBC's *Today* show to do a special segment on the trip.[29]

Shortly thereafter, Marciarose began writing a column, "Marciarose," for *The Philadelphia Inquirer.* She wrote from 1974 to 1978 on in-depth interviews with local, national, and international figures. Her newspaper column is relevant to her broadcasting career for several reasons. First, she was hired because she was a popular TV personality and because of a well-known ability to introduce someone to an audience through her interviews. More importantly, it demonstrated that Marciarose came to mean something special to the city of Philadelphia. When her column ended in 1978, she received a lovely compliment in the form of a protest letter to the newspaper, saying, "Don't take away Marciarose, she's my window on the world." [30]

In 1975 Marciarose left Philadelphia to anchor her own 90-minute news/talk magazine show, *Sunday*, for NBC's flagship station in New York, WNBC. She took over the show when the show's male host left and of the four people auditioned for the spot, she was the only woman. The format of *Sunday* was a winning combination of its host's many interests: one "hard-news" guest interview, such as Jimmy Carter, plus five or six more guests, often from the worlds of art and politics; a live entertainment segment; and a mini-documentary feature. She also appeared on WNBC's 5 and 6 p.m. newscasts and hosted and narrated the documentary series *New York Illustrated*. Throughout the late 1970s and the 1980s Marciarose worked as a freelance television journalist, including for PBS, where she hosted such specials as *Iran at the Crossroads* and *Conflict on Campus: The Changing American Woman*.

Another of Marciarose's significant contributions to local television is that she understood the responsibility involved in being a high-profile member of the community and used her status to make a difference. She has always taken a very active role in the community, even more since she began freelancing, taking up interests she couldn't pursue while on the air in the interest of political neutrality and fairness. She was appointed by President Carter to the Judicial Nominating Commission for the Third Circuit U.S. Court of Appeals; she has served on the boards of directors of such organizations as Planned Parenthood, International House, the World Affairs Council, the Moore College of Art, and The Mayor's Task Force to Restore City Hall. She is the only non-architect member of the Philadelphia chapter of the American Institute of Architects and in 1990 was presented with the chapter's Distinguished Service Award for her public service work. She is a frequent lecturer and moderator, having addressed, among many other audiences, college classes on their graduation day and new U.S. citizens at a naturalization ceremony.

Decades after intense involvement in a difficult business, she remains enthusiastic but understands the pitfalls and figures out how to step around them. When Marciarose addressed an audience consisting largely of young women studying journalism at the American University in Cairo in May 2000, she told them that women in broadcasting have come a long way but there's still a way to go. She's proud of the letters she's received from both men and women saying how good it was to see a woman in a position of authority, someone whom they could trust, and, having been through it all, she's happy to help young people, especially women, who are just starting out.

Marciarose was a very visible part of a generation of newswomen who began to change public perceptions of women's credibility, seriousness, intellectual ability, and news sense. The significance of Marciarose in terms of the story of women in broadcasting is that she demonstrated that women could succeed, and in doing so made it easier for women who came after her.

This is why, despite the resistance she faced professionally and personally, it was never enough to hold her back. Being first is something to be proud of, and she's happy if she made it easier for women who came after her, but she had more substantial things to focus on. And this is why today's young broadcasters and not just those who happen to be women have a mentor in Marciarose.

Notes

1. Shestack, M. (2000, Sept. 12). Personal communication.
2. Shestack, 2000, Sept. 12.
3. Shestack, M. (2000, Aug. 20). Personal communication.
4. Shestack, 2000, Aug. 20.
5. Shestack, 2000, Sept. 12.
6. Shestack, 2000, Aug. 20.
7. *Concept.* (nd). WRCV-TV news release. Personal papers of Marciarose Shestack.
8. *Concept,* nd.
9. Shestack, M. (2000, May 17). Personal communication.
10. Shestack, 2000, Aug. 20.
11. Shestack, 2000, Aug. 20.
12. WRCV-TV and *Concept* producer-hostess Marciarose receive dual Rush Awards from Philadelphia County Medical Society. (1964, Jan. 14). WRCV-TV news release. Personal papers of Marciarose Shestack.
13. Shestack, 2000, Aug. 20.
14. Shestack, 2000, May 17.
15. Shestack, 2000, Aug. 20.

16. Shestack, 2000, Aug. 20.
17. Shestack, M. (2000, Sept. 13). Personal communication.
18. Shestack, 2000, Sept. 13.
19. Shestack, 2000, Sept. 13.
20. Shestack, 2000, Aug. 20.
21. Shestack, M. (2001, Jan. 14). Personal communication.
22. Shestack, 2001, Jan. 14.
23. Shestack, 2000, Aug. 20.
24. Shestack, 2000, Aug. 20.
25. Shestack, 2000, Aug. 20.
26. Shestack, 2000, Sept. 13.
27. Shestack, 2000, Sept. 13.
28. Shestack, 2000, Sept. 13.
29. Shestack, 2000, Sept. 13.
30. Shestack, 2000, Aug. 20.

Other Sources

Concept documentary on WRCV-TV Tuesday traces childbirth from early pregnancy to delivery. (1963, Sept. 18). WRCV-TV news release. Personal papers of Marciarose Shestack.

Hostel for skid row residents to be documented by *Concept* Tuesday, Jan. 21, 7-7:30 p.m. (1964, Jan. 14). WRCV-TV news release. Personal papers of Marciarose Shestack.

The new American marriage. (1976, Oct. 25). *New York Magazine,* 46.

Shestack, M. (1980, Oct. 29). Welcome to new citizens. Speech presented at the naturalization ceremonies before Judge Norma L. Shapiro. Personal papers of Marciarose Shestack.

Shestack, M. (2000, May 17). American women in TV journalism: Past, present and future. Speech given at the American University in Cairo, Egypt.

Tom Snyder, Marciarose, and Dick Goddard to team up for 30 minutes of news at noon beginning August 23 on KWY-TV3. (1965, Aug. 5). KWY-TV 3 news release. Personal papers of Marciarose Shestack.

Gayle Sierens

Gayle Sierens

Keepin' On

"Touchdown, Herman Heard!"

It's unlikely that many people remember that particular call from the broadcast booth during a game between the Seattle Seahawks and the Kansas City Chiefs two days after Christmas 1987. Herman Heard probably doesn't even remember it. But that call and the rest of the play-by-play call from that game televised to about 15 percent of the country went down in sportscasting history. It was on that day that Gayle Sierens, then 33, became the first woman to do network television play-by-play of a National Football League game.[1]

Sierens took a decidedly laid-back approach to the history-making event. In the week leading up to the game, she was in the midst of a national media blitz during which reporters asked every question imaginable about how she felt. Sierens noted that if she bombed, it just showed that she couldn't do play-by-play and she would happily return to the anchor desk at WFLA-TV in Tampa (the *news* anchor desk) and continue reporting about events of importance in her hometown.[2]

She didn't bomb, and the head of NBC Sports then, Michael Weisman, committed to having Sierens do more NFL games the next year. But several things transpired to change those plans. Sierens had her first baby in July 1988 and the baby was definitely her first priority. She had already committed to be in a friend's wedding on one 1988 broadcast date Weisman had in mind, and station management at WFLA didn't think she should do the Bucs-Dolphins games from Tampa Stadium that year. At the time, Sierens said that because she did sports at the station for nine years before the management asked her to anchor the news, station managers wanted to make sure local

179

viewers knew her first commitment was to news. She honored their request not to announce a game that would be seen in her market.[3] Then, Weisman was replaced at the top at NBC Sports. The new regime didn't share Weisman's interest in doing things out of the ordinary. (Remember, Weisman was the one who came up with the concept of the announcerless football game.) So that day late in 1987 was the first and only time a woman has done NFL play-by-play.[4]

Her place in broadcast history earned Sierens the distinction of being the answer to a trivia question on a popular network trivia show in April 2000. Regis Philbin had a check for $500,000 waiting for the contestant if the guest could tell the host the answer to the question. Despite having only two possible answers remaining, the player had to give up. He just wasn't sure who was the first woman to do NFL play-by-play.[5]

Though Sierens is more widely known for her foray into NFL football announcing, she has made her career in local news. It isn't often anyone in local news manages to hang on for more than 20 years at the same station. But Sierens has done more than hang on. She has been one of the most popular anchors in the market for years and normally ranks at the top in viewer polls. Co-anchor Bob Hite occasionally knocks Sierens out of the top spot, but according to WFLA News Director Dan Bradley, even when that happens, "viewers see her as the strength of the team."[6] WFLA's 6 p.m. report has been the news ratings winner in the Tampa–St. Petersburg market for years,[7] which is due in no small part to the staying power of Sierens and Hite.

The two have worked side by side on the anchor desk since 1985. He says she's been like a sister to him all these years. Their "chemistry" gives viewers the sense that they like and respect each other and both say that assessment is true. But even real siblings have spats. During one disagreement in the late 1980s, Sierens told Hite that he could just go back to anchoring by himself, and the station could go back to being number two in the news ratings, as it was before Sierens joined Hite on the anchor desk. Sierens and Hite don't disagree often, though, and Hite says when they do squabble, "We don't go away mad, we just go away and everything is okay by the next morning."[8]

Hite and others know Sierens has never had any qualms about standing up for herself and can do so regardless of whom the "opponent" is. She called the head of CBS Sports to task for being critical of one of her practice broadcasts leading up the NFL game she announced. Though Sierens says she's not the "I-am-woman, hear-me-roar type," her spunk is part of what got her to where she is and what has kept her there.

She started displaying that spunk at an early age. One has to be confident, and perhaps even headstrong, when all the neighborhood kids call you "Froggy." Even as a child, she had a gravelly voice. She sounded like the character on *The Little Rascals,* and when she began leading cheers at Tampa Catholic High School, her voice became even raspier. As an adult, Sierens has often been mistaken for a man by phone callers, and many people say she sounds as though she's always battling a cold,[9] but the throaty voice is one of her trademarks.[10] Sierens has often heard people compare her voice to that of actresses Demi Moore and Angie Harmon, who plays on NBC's *Law & Order.* Sierens says her voice is similar to theirs in that it is deep, raspy, and somewhat guttural. She says many times she's been out in public, perhaps right after a workout to pick up something at the store, and wasn't as dressed or made-up as she would be on the air. But as soon as she says something, someone will say, "You're Gayle Sierens. I'd recognize that voice anywhere."[11]

Vocal cord surgery relieved some of the strain Sierens had put on her voice for years, and she now does a regimen of exercises to help her reduce the strain caused by what speech pathologists says were a number of bad habits and voice abuse. She also has to avoid tobacco smoke, caffeine, and alcohol, all of which tend to dry out the vocal cords.[12] Still, many people recognize her voice before they recognize her face. She says that if what a newsperson says is significant, viewers will overlook a minor regional accent and other things about an anchor's voice that might otherwise be distracting.

Sieren's interest in sports was something else that came early in life. She says she's always been something of a tomboy, and her slim, muscular frame suggests that she has a continuing interest in staying fit. In addition to cheering at Tampa Catholic, she played softball and volleyball and swam in high school.[13]

Gayle's father was killed while working on an elevator when she was just six, and it was just her, her mother, and her grandmother for most of Gayle's growing-up years. Her mom, Betty, was 29 when Gayle's dad was killed; then and at many other times in Betty's life, she has faced adversity and managed to triumph. Gayle says her mom is and has been her role model throughout her life. "She's a stellar human being. She taught me to think outside the box."[14] Betty's interest in sports probably played a role in why Gayle had an interest in athletics despite not having a male figure in the house. Her mother is an avid baseball and football fan. In Gayle's formative years, Betty was especially fond of the New York Jets and Joe Namath. (Namath's good looks probably had nothing to do with that, but Betty has been known to comment on how cute soccer players' legs are.)

Gayle originally intended to study math at Florida State University in Tallahassee, but she landed a job at the campus television station (WFSU) that allowed her to become proficient at numerous positions in the newsroom, including sports reporting. That led to a job doing weekend sports at WFLA in January 1977, less than a month after her December graduation. Milt Spencer hired Sierens,[15] but he wasn't the first sports director in the market to hire a woman to do sports. Sierens replaced another woman as weekend sports anchor at Channel 8. Pam Jones left the station to take a public relations job with the New York Yankees. Another station in the market also had a woman doing sports at the time, but Sierens became one of fewer than half a dozen women on the air at her station when she was hired. She says the thinking by news management at the time appeared to be, "If you can find one [a woman] who can do the job, hire her."[16]

Sierens covered sports in Tampa for nearly eight years and won an Emmy for a feature story about a barefoot water skier who became a champion at the sport despite major injuries he suffered in an auto accident. Doctors said he'd never walk again. Gayle is especially proud of that Emmy because in addition to doing the reporting, she also edited the piece.

Sierens also remembers a piece that didn't win an award but did help set her apart. During baseball spring training the year after the Pittsburgh Pirates won the World Series, she did a feature story about superstar Willie Stargell, whose bat played a big role in Pittsburgh's success during that era. Sierens asked Stargell such questions as "What's your favorite color?" and "If you were a tree, what kind of tree would you be?" She says it would have been the most embarrassing moment of her life if Stargell has said, "What kind of goofy questions are you asking?" but he didn't. He seemed to welcome talking about something other than his batting average for a change.[17]

She continued to try to do more with sports than just show highlights and give scores, and her abilities and approach attracted the notice of other media outlets. She was offered a job at what was then a fledgling cable sports network, ESPN, but the position ESPN managers were hoping to create for her never materialized. Then in 1985, news director Bud Faulder approached Sierens about switching to news from sports. He needed a woman on the anchor desk and Sierens was already one of the most popular personalities in the market. Audience surveys and focus groups conducted by station management suggested that viewers would accept the move, and Gayle left sports behind, professionally at least. In 1987 (the same year as her play-by-play debut), she married Mike Martin, a former University of Kentucky linebacker, assuring that sports will always be a part of Sierens' life in one way or another.

Sierens says the transition to news wasn't immediately successful. "My first appearance on news as an anchor was at 6:00 p.m. I was frightful. I was the grimmest. Like the reaper. I acted like I had a gun in my back."[18] But Gayle learned that though news is more serious and has a different feel and tone than sports, it isn't deadly serious all of the time. She made the adjustment and learned to be herself. Co-anchor Hite said, "A good journalist is a good journalist, whether it's covering sports or news. I think the viewers were so fond of her that they accepted her without question."[19]

Like Hite, most of Sierens' peers were confident that she could make a smooth transition from sports to news. But some were skeptical that she had what it took, so Sierens felt she needed to prove herself. That wasn't an easy task. As a sports anchor, the worst news she delivered was that someone's favorite team had lost a game. Suddenly, she was faced with delivering news about crime and violence. But Sierens' sports background came in handy. She was used to ad-libbing, and that became an asset when the electronic prompter stopped working or when she did live reports.

Though she didn't make very much money when she started working at WFLA, Sierens says she's never experienced a "glass ceiling." Female anchors make as much or more than their male counterparts in the Tampa market.

Whatever her station pays her, it seems to be a good investment. If she were to leave for some reason, thousands of viewers might decide to watch a different station. Sierens was offered the opportunity to work for another station in the market, and says she almost took it. Because of the noncompete clause in her contract with WFLA, she wouldn't be allowed to go on air at the other station for a year. Management at that station seemed willing to "pay me to sit on the beach for a year,"[20] but ultimately the station at which she has spent her entire professional career won the bidding war and Gayle remained part of the WFLA team. In 1997, she celebrated her 20th year with Channel 8. That a competitor would be willing to go to such lengths to get her says something about her popularity in the market. It seems that Tampa loves Sierens. It certainly is unusual in such a transient business in which many people are looking to move on to larger markets, and a business in which judgements of one's abilities are very subjective, for anyone to last for more than 20 years in an on-air position in the same market.

Sierens attributes it all to being a hometown girl. She grew up in Tampa, began her career there and doesn't plan to leave. Her viewers know they're getting "the real deal," not some "glamour girl" who got a job because of her looks rather than her journalistic skills. Bradley says, "She works hard not to be full of herself," as he thinks often happens with news anchors.[21] Hite says, "She's the most unlikely anchor in the country. Most female anchors definitely aren't tomboys."[22] Viewers also know that Sierens truly cares about the Tampa area. She doesn't act emotional when she's not, or passionate when she's not. "In the immortal words of Popeye, 'I am what I am and that's all that I am.'"[23] What happens in Tampa affects her, her future and her children's future. Because of that, she says, she respects news and her job of letting the audience know what's going on humbles her. Hite says because of her empathy for people, "she's an excellent journalist—a superb storyteller."[24]

Dan Bradley, who started working at WLFA two years after Sierens, says her strength is that she has both passion and compassion. She cares deeply about the newscast, about the people she works with, and about the people she covers. Bradley says Sierens hasn't yet reached the level achieved by another female anchor in the state, Anne Bishop, who worked at WPLG in Miami, but "she's certainly on path to become almost [as] lionized by the local viewers" as Bishop was.[25] Bishop anchored and reported in Miami for 25 years and was revered by colleagues and viewers alike. Bradley says Sierens has a lot of career ahead of her, and she certainly could reach the same level of viewer loyalty Bishop achieved in her years in Miami (Bishop died in 1997). Sierens says she's "flattered to be mentioned in the same breath as Anne Bishop" when it comes to her professional achievements.[26]

Bradley says that like Bishop, Sierens isn't a threatening personality, as many anchors are, but instead is more like a neighbor. Sierens says she doesn't fit the anchorwoman mold in a lot of ways. She thinks her girl-next-door looks and straightforward approach to reporting the news give viewers a sense that they can trust her, that she's "one of them." She's been able to connect with the audience, and that has led to a long and fruitful career. A benefit of not being a glamour queen is not having to fight against the perception that a woman can't be both beautiful and smart. She counsels lots of young women who have just entered or are trying to get into broadcast journalism, telling them, "Don't take no for an answer. Be solid at your career. But most importantly, know what your station expects of you." Most of the young women she counsels, she says, are beautiful. She tells them the biggest obstacle they'll face is their beauty. If they happen to be blonde, "Ooh, boy, that's a big-time stereotype they'll have to overcome."[27]

Sierens never faced that particular stereotype. She certainly doesn't fit into the goofy anchor image described in Don Henley's 1982 song "Dirty Laundry"—a bubble-headed bleached blonde who comes on at five and tells about a plane crash with a gleam in her eye. Sierens defies that image in two ways. She has reddish hair, not blonde, but more importantly, she "feels" the news rather than just reading words off the prompter and worrying only about looking and sounding good. When the news is serious, her approach is serious; when it's funny, she has fun. And when it's news about "real people," Sierens is there to tell their stories.

It's an approach that has served her well. In addition to her sports Emmy, Sierens also has one for news. She loves the story that earned her the news Emmy. The subject was a woman who spent 40 years as an educator. Even after the woman retired, she kept coming back to help at the school. She loved the children and made sure that those who needed school supplies or new shoes got them. Sierens thinks it's no coincidence that both of her Emmy Award–winning reports were "people stories"—one about a young man who overcame adversity and the other about a woman willing to help others in need.

Sierens is proud of her awards, her accomplishments, and her staying power. She's covered some big stories, such as the *Challenger* explosion. She met the Pope and went to President Bill Clinton's first inauguration. She covered civil unrest in South Korea prior to the Seoul Olympics. "I was reporting with a gas mask on," she says. "It's every journalist's dream to be assigned to the big story."[28] But what means most to her is having a great newscast day in and day out, one that "kicks butt," one in which she and her colleagues have presented the news fairly and accurately.

One would think that's what most stations want. Sierens thinks that her station is a leader in that area. Sometimes stations that are third or fourth in the ratings use gimmicky approaches trying to attract viewers, but Sierens says that WFLA covers news "with good, sound news judgment based in journalism. . . .I work at a station where we set the bar for excellence. We definitely take the high road in our approach to news. I'm always proud of the news that we present."[29]

The tools used to present the news change continually and Sierens has seen a lot of technological changes during her years in television news. When she started at WFLA in 1978, she'd have to leave at half-time of a pro soccer game (which she was shooting herself using a Bolex camera) in order to get the film back to the station and processed in time to have some highlights on the 11 p.m. news. She has witnessed the transition to video from film in the late 1970s and the introduction of live reporting from beyond the station using microwave technology in the early 1980s. Sierens was able to report live from Italy and South Korea using satellite technology in 1987.

In her years in the business, coverage has gone from including things that happened close by and up to a few hours before a given newscast to instantaneous coverage of events from anywhere on the globe.[30] But perhaps the biggest change Sierens has witnessed is one that, as of this writing, is in its infancy. Media convergence could change the face of journalism and Sierens is working in a newsroom that is blazing the trail. WFLA, the *Tampa Tribune* and Tampa Bay Online are all housed in the same state-of-the-art facility. All three share news-gathering capabilities and even collaborate on stories. She says it feels very strange to tell viewers to look to the morning paper for more details about a particular story when she spent her career trying to beat the newspaper on stories. But, she adds, online journalism gives her and her colleagues the opportunity to reach far more people than was ever possible before. "People today want news on demand" and it changes the way things are covered. "By the time I retire, TV news won't even resemble the business I entered."[31] So far, the "girl next door" is faring well in the world of media convergence.

There's no doubt that Gayle Sierens' job is important to her, but there's also no doubt that it's not what's most important to her. She is and always has been a family person. She now has three children, and because she wants to excel as a journalist and as a wife and mother, "Monday through Friday is relentless."[32] Her husband's business,

Mike's Pies, keeps him on the road. When Mike is away, everything falls to her and, as has always been the case, her mom. Sierens says it's a huge challenge to juggle everything in her life, especially because her kids are "high maintenance. None of my kids goes on cruise control."

For her, sleep is overrated and she's learned to do with less of it than many people need to function effectively. She gets home near midnight and often reads her children's books and homework assignments so she can talk with them before they leave for school the next morning. Sierens accepts her life and doesn't complain, but says that by Friday, she's a bit grumpy. To get over that grouchiness, she works out, takes piano lessons, gardens, and tries to read, but often falls asleep after reading just a few pages. She loves to spend time with her friends and manages to eat breakfast with a core group once a week as well as have group workout sessions.

Sierens is passionate about the things she believes in and won't sit back and wait for things to get done. One scribe wrote of Sierens that when she talks about what we can all do to solve the aching problems in society, "there's a sense of urgency in her voice you don't usually hear when she's delivering the news."[33] Sierens thinks everyone should get involved in community efforts, and she certainly practices what she preaches. She considers it a privilege to host the local children's hospital telethon each year, and often cries when she talks about the children who are helped there. Sierens thinks viewers understand and share in her emotions, "You're not human if this [stories about sick children] doesn't touch you."[34] She serves on the board of the Boys and Girls Club, she's the Honorary Chair of the Big Brother Big Sister Bowl for Kids' Sake, and emcees the Salvation Army Christmas kickoff and a handful of other events.[35] She also finds time to do charity videos and be involved at church and her children's school.

Some people marvel at her ability to take on so much, but Gayle says it's natural to her. "I think it takes a lot to fill me up. God has blessed me with so many gifts and I feel like I should use them. I don't relax. I just always have to feel full. I get a lot of pleasure out of being involved, whether it's with my children, their school or anything else."[36]

Sierens hopes that little girls don't say, "I want to be just like Gayle Sierens when I grow up." But she does hope that through her, they're able to see that a woman can have a career, a family, and personal time. Sierens wants girls to look at her and say, "Who's stopping me from going out and finding out what opportunities are out there for me?"[37]

Then it's up to them to seize the opportunity, as Sierens did. Some call it stick-to-itiveness. More than a dozen years ago, a *St. Petersburg Times* reporter wrote that the ability to "keep on keeping on" is the attribute that has most guided Sierens' career. "Such steadfastness requires a solid center. If there is anything a woman with a career should be blessed with, more than looks or brains, fortune or health, this is probably it. And Sierens was almost certainly so blessed."[38]

Notes

1. Stewart, L. (1987, Dec. 28). Sierens' call from booth wins top marks. *Los Angeles Times,* Sports, p. 3.
2. Sierens, G. (2000, Oct. 14). Personal communication.
3. Fischer, R. (1988, Aug. 23). Sierens will join NBC's NFL show during Olympics. *St. Petersburg Times,* Sports, p. 1C.
4. Canepa, N. (1993, Mar. 14). It's about time a woman got a PA job: Now, how about a play-by-play gig? *The San Diego Union-Tribune,* Sports, p. C-2.
5. Belcher, W. (2000, Apr. 10). Of v-chips and would-be millionaires. *The Tampa Tribune,* Baylife, p. 3; Davis, P. (2000, Apr. 8). "Gayle Sierens" answer worth no trivial sum. *St. Petersburg Times,* City and State, p. 2B.
6. Bradley, D. (2000, Nov. 21). Personal communication.
7. Belcher, W. (1996, Mar. 4). Bob and Gayle lead WFLA to ratings victory. *Tampa Tribune,* Baylife, p. 6.
8. Hite, B. (2000, Nov. 2). Personal communication.
9. Barrs, J. (1996, May 18). A few familiar voices: Her friends called her "Froggy." *The Tampa Tribune,* Baylife, p. 1.
10. Froelich, J.D. (1988, Mar. 14). The news on Gayle Sierens: Olympics are out. *St. Petersburg Times,* Floridian, p. 1D.
11. Sierens, 2000.
12. Yant, M. (1995, Aug. 17). Sierens will have surgery on ailing voice. *St. Petersburg Times,* Tampa Bay and State, p. 2B.
13. Belcher, W. (1997, Jan. 20). Score one for Gayle: Popular news anchor Gayle Sierens marks her 20th year at WFLA, Channel 8. *Tampa Tribune,* Baylife, p. 1.
14. Sierens, 2000.
15. McEwen, T. (1998, Apr. 17). Air Force. *Tampa Tribune,* Sports Extra, p. 5.
16. Sierens, 2000.
17. Sierens, 2000.
18. Sierens, 2000.
19. Belcher, 1997, p.1.
20. Sierens, 2000.
21. Bradley, D. (2000, Nov. 21). Personal communication.
22. Hite, 2000.
23. Sierens, 2000.
24. Hite, 2000.
25. Bradley, 2000.
26. Sierens, 2000.

27. Sierens, 2000.
28. Sierens, 2000.
29. Sierens, 2000.
30. Tuggle, C.A., Carr, F., and Huffman, S. (2000). *Broadcast News Handbook: Writing, Reporting, and Producing.* New York: McGraw-Hill.
31. Sierens, 2000.
32. Sierens, 2000.
33. Stevenson, J. (1994, Apr. 13). Ch. 8 tries to make a difference. *St. Petersburg Times,* Tampa Bay and State, p. 6B.
34. Sierens, 2000.
35. WFLA (2000). [On-line]. Available: wfla.com.
36. Sierens, 2000.
37. Sierens, 2000.
38. Melone, M.J. (1988, Jan. 31). Calling her own shots: Gayle Sierens doesn't let criticism diminish her goals. *St. Petersburg Times,* Tampa, p. 1.

Laurel Vlock interviewing Bartlett Giamatti, president of Yale University, for *Dialogue. (Courtesy of Linda S. Kantor, New Haven, Connecticut)*

Laurel Vlock
To Be Is to Do

Laurel Fox Vlock was a television producer and host of many television programs, including the longest-running television series in Connecticut, founder of the first television station to be owned and operated by women, and founder of the Holocaust Survivors Film Project, Inc. She was born August 5, 1926, in New Haven, Connecticut, the first of two daughters of John J. and Rose Greenberg Fox. She died as a result of a car accident on July 7, 2000, leaving her mother, husband Jay, three children and nine grandchildren.

Laurel grew up in New Haven in a family that was very active and supportive of their community, especially the Jewish community. Laurel's father, John Fox, ran the Fox Steel Company, and her mother, Rose, was a sculptor. Rose was most proud of two terra cotta busts that she produced: one of Golda Meir, Israeli prime minister, and another of Myriam Mendilow, a teacher and founder of "Life Line for the Old" in Israel. Both women would be very influential for Laurel. One of her proudest memories was of a visit with Golda Meir, who made tea for Laurel in her home in Israel; Laurel in turn entertained Meir's children when they were studying at Yale University. Myriam Mendilow directed and motivated many people to help others. Since Mendilow's death, many in the United States raise monies for "Myriam's Dream" to fund projects for the elderly poor and follow Mendilow's motto "To be is to do." Laurel would be a stellar example of that motto.

Laurel attended the public schools in New Haven and, following in her father's footsteps, attended Cornell University. She graduated in 1948 with a B.A. in psychology. She also met Jay Vlock at Cornell and married him in 1948; they moved to New York City. She received a master's in education from Queens College in 1952 and worked as a substitute teacher. In the early 1950s, the Vlocks moved to the New Haven area and started their family.

Laurel was an active volunteer and very concerned about her community. New Haven was the third largest city in Connecticut and had many of the problems of northeastern cities—a collapsing industrial base and whites fleeing to the suburbs, while the inner city was being revamped by urban renewal. Racial unrest was simmering, and Laurel met with others discussing what they could possibly do to give the disenfranchised a voice, to help the community work together. Laurel thought if more voices could be heard, then ways would be found to improve the community. She was going to use the media. The first place that was interested in her proposal to host an interview program was the radio station of the Yale Broadcasting Corporation. She hosted *Your Community Speaks* on WYBC each week from 1963 to 1966. Although not everyone was receptive to her ideas—some were openly hostile—after some time, the program was recognized as a showcase for the community.

One of her listeners was a director at the local commercial television station, Channel 8, WNHC-TV (later known as WTNH-TV). As a way to provide community programming, the television station asked three religious organizations to serve as co-producers of a weekly half-hour series that aired Sunday mornings and was repeated in an early morning time slot during the week. For the Catholics, the Archdiocese of Hartford produced a weekly mass and a children's program; for the Protestants, the Council of Churches produced *Eighth Day;* and for the Jewish, the Anti-Defamation League (ADL) produced an interview program, *Jewish News and Views.*

In 1966 Bill Harris, Channel 8's director, asked Laurel to tryout as host of this program. Laurel was successful, but she would only agree to serve as host if the name was changed. *Jewish News and Views* was a title that implied it was only attempting to speak to the Jewish community, while she wanted a program that would be perceived as a means to build bridges of understanding across all groups within the community. They decided to call it *Dialogue,* which later became *Dialogue with Laurel Vlock.* It aired weekly on television from 1966 until 1992 on Channel 8, then moved to WHAI, Channel 43, in Bridgeport from 1993 to 1996. The final move was to WBNE, Channel 59, where it aired on a monthly basis until her death in 2000.

At Channel 8, *Dialogue* was taped in the evening after the evening news and completed before the late news. Often she would attempt to produce two programs an evening. The studio crew welcomed working with her and knew what was needed before she arrived. People who were interviewed by her always commented on how interested she was in them as a person and how she was able to project her fascination with the topic. She had done her research, prepared her questions and also prepared her interviewees for the program. She always made it clear that there may be tough questions that have to be asked, not just the ones that will highlight the positive aspects.[1]

Laurel had made the move from a weekly show on radio to one on television with seeming ease, but she also moved among competing stations and networks freely. She produced a monthly program for Channel 8's major competitor, Channel 3. Channel 3, WTIC, later known as WFSB, had studios in Hartford and a director who gave Laurel her first real experience producing film documentaries. She was the producer and host for the documentary series *About People* from 1969 to 1973.

In 1969 she also started producing documentaries for Public Broadcasting, including *Strat,* a film about a student's life at Choate, a private school in Wallingford, Connecticut. This film won numerous awards, including the Chris Award from the Columbus Film Festival, the Silver Hugo from the Chicago International Film Festival, and Dateline America Award. Her work on *Dialogue* for Channel 8 won her the Public Relations Award for best television program in 1973, 1974 and 1978. Her work at Channel 3 in Hartford won her the Public Affairs Award in 1973 for the documentary *You Learn to Adjust* on Hartford's elderly and in 1974 for the documentary *The History of the Jews of Hartford.* A documentary on the contributions of immigrants to America, *They Came to America,* for Channel 3 in 1982 won a New England Emmy Award in 1983 for best informative special.

Her guests included authors, politicians, educators, professionals, community workers—usually people with a national reputation or a major influence within the state. There were a few times that the half-hour was dedicated to a film that Laurel produced based on a particular issue. One example was a documentary about drip irrigation that Israel was pioneering; another was on the Holocaust.

In 1981 Laurel and three other people started the Jewish Television Institute. They produced programs in a New York City studio for distribution across the country on 30 cable television systems. Her program was entitled *Jewish Spectrum,* which she co-hosted with David

Schoenbrun, a former CBS correspondent.[2] One of her most famous guests for that series was Hillary Clinton in 1992.

Her most serious television work resulted from a discussion with one of her guests from *Dialogue*. One evening after the taping had stopped, the guest complimented Laurel on the compassion she exhibited during the interview and asked if she could tell Laurel a story that she didn't want to tell but felt obligated to do so. Laurel agreed and set up another interview time. Laurel listened. She listened for four and one-half hours about the woman's experience surviving the Holocaust, about Auschwitz and afterwards.

Laurel was moved and distraught; there were so many other survivors who needed to tell their stories. She later said, "Everybody talks about the unspeakable, but it is speakable, and when it is spoken, it has a force that isn't found anywhere else."[3] After many sleepless nights, Laurel contacted a psychiatrist and Holocaust survivor, Dr. Dori Laub, to help her interview. They formed the New Haven–based Holocaust Survivors Film Project to collect the interviews before another generation passed away, but there were many obstacles. First they had to convince the people—people who had kept their stories secret for decades—who thought no one was interested and who were frightened of listening to their stories themselves. And they would need money for archiving and taping. Laurel also wanted to be sure to videotape the interviews, to record the "demeanor evidence." It would make a great difference watching a person recall their memories if they were crying instead of showing no emotion.

Laurel first used her own resources to videotape Holocaust survivors. She traveled to Illinois, Florida, Massachusetts, New York, Israel, and Europe. For WNEW-TV, the metromedia station in New York City, she produced a documentary called *Forever Yesterday*, which won a regional Emmy. In June 1981 Laurel covered the world gathering of Holocaust survivors in Jerusalem for PBS. She and Dr. Laub raised more monies from the community, the Revson Foundation, and then Fortunoff, so that more interviews could be taped and kept. The president of Yale University, Bartlett Giamatti, thought that Yale was the right place for the collection. By 1985 there were 700 videotaped testimonies in the Fortunoff Archive of Holocaust Testimonies at Yale University.

In 1977 Laurel attended the National Women's Year Conference in Houston, Texas, for a production for PBS. She was "inspired by the impact of the women's movement,"[4] impressed with the power that they could have, and determined that there was a need for women to "become part of the economic mainstream."[5] When a communications lawyer spoke at the conference about possibilities women could have in the field of communications, she was listening intently.

The lawyer mentioned that a television station in Connecticut had recently gone off the air and the Federal Communications Commission was committed to encouraging minority ownership of broadcasting, then suggested women take that opportunity. At the time, the only woman-owned television station was the station in Austin, Texas, owned by Lady Bird Johnson.

Laurel was captivated by the possibility of women owning and operating a television station. Although all of her work in television up to this point had been done on an unpaid volunteer basis, this station was to be run as a business. It was not to be just another charitable or eleemosynary project, a term she loved to use probably because so much of society at the time thought that that, and only that, was what women were interested in. Laurel knew broadcasting was a business, one in which she had been involved in over the past decade. She wanted women to be able to run the business and do it so that it worked on building community. If women were the owners they would have an influence on the content, but the station would not be geared to women only. It would address women's needs, but also those of the larger community. It would do more programming for children and for the whole local community. If the women were the ultimate ones in control of the station, that station would be different. Later they would call themselves a nontraditional entrepreneurship.

Laurel returned from Houston, ready to convince other women of the possibilities available with Channel 43. She called together a group of 10 women from a variety of fields and asked them to each contribute $5,000 to form Bridgeways Communications, Inc. The very title speaks to the goals of the station, a means to link the community and work together. Bridgeways Communications, Inc. was incorporated, in the state of Connecticut on May 17, 1978, with 11 investors, to apply for the license and construction permit from the Federal Communications Commission to operate Channel 43. Joining Laurel Vlock as investors were 10 women from Connecticut. Some of the women readily joined in Laurel's hopes and dreams but others took more time. Geraldine Johnson noted that Laurel really had to convince her that she was needed. It was the programming plans for incorporating education issues and Laurel's persistence that persuaded her.[6]

Many thought the channel would never get on the air because the women would fractionalize; they were wrong. The group remained a committed group throughout their history from 1978 until the sale of the station in 1996. Others saw the station as a golden calf, an investment that would pay off handsomely and quickly; they were wrong. Although those investors who stayed in the whole 18 years did make a profit, it was not a quick or easy gain.

The UHF station Channel 43's city of license was Bridgeport, 60 miles from New York City and the largest city in Connecticut. Bridgeport had a daily metropolitan newspaper and a number of radio stations but no television station. There was a cable system with 7,000 subscribers, but that system carried very little local programming. The other television stations in Connecticut rarely covered the area because it was usually included in the New York market. For television viewers, there was no sense of the community of Bridgeport. When students were asked to identify their mayor, they would identify the mayor of New York City rather than that of Bridgeport. Bridgeways hoped to build community by providing local television.

It seemed a natural outgrowth of Laurel's beginning in broadcasting. She had started in radio, providing local programming for New Haven, and liked to think she was building bridges between Yale University and New Haven. Now she would provide a commercially viable outlet for Bridgeport and a showcase for the community.

But there were obstacles. They applied for the license in 1979 and suddenly found they were competing for the license with Francis D'Addario, a Bridgeport businessman. But after much concern, "D'Addario decided to withdraw his application after questions were raised about his qualifications for a broadcast license."[7] The FCC approved Bridgeways application in 1980, but then they found that their tower could not be sited within the city limits lest it interfere with Channel 50 of Little Falls, New Jersey. The nearby community of Trumbull had an existing transmission tower but it was owned by their erstwhile competitor, D'Addario, and they couldn't come to an agreement.

Bridgeways received an extension from the FCC in 1982 and continued looking for a tower site. In neighboring Shelton, the community accused Bridgeways of trying to violate the "essentially rural nature of the region."[8] The Bridgeport newspaper even editorialized that they were not serious about serving Bridgeport if they were trying to wreck another community with their transmission tower, and urged them to place the tower in Bridgeport.[9] Finally they were able to double up on Seymour Valley Cable Vision's tower. Bridgeways arranged to build a tower taller than the cable system needed for a free permanent position on it.

Next they looked for network affiliation, but all the networks were currently affiliated with existing stations and none wanted to change. More money was always needed, and as much as they wanted to have only women investors, it was difficult getting women to feel confident investing on their own. And the male banking institutions balked. As investor Jean Cherry, who is black, was quoted as saying, "It was the same kind of patronizing that blacks get. The people wanted to know, 'What are your qualifications?' 'What is your expertise?' But their attitudes changed after we assured them that when it came to the management of the station, the employees could be male, female or Martian—as long as they had hard business sense."[10]

Channel 43 went on the air on Monday, September 28, 1987, as an affiliate of America's Value Network, a home shopping format. Bridgeways saw it as a temporary measure to earn revenues for other programming while keeping its FCC license.[11] By this time, Laurel's son, Michael Vlock, had become president. He noted that since so much time had been taken up getting a transmitter and the local cable system was now providing community programming, Channel 43 should start an alternative programming service for the Jewish community, which would then make the station desirable for the cable systems in the tri-state region of New York, New Jersey and Connecticut. They changed the station's call letters from WBCT to WHAI-TV; *Hai* means life in Hebrew.

Many investors backed out of the Jewish programming concept and the station was finally sold to Value-Vision International, Inc., which then sold it to Paxson Communications Corporation in March 1996. In the meantime, Bridgeways had been working to get the station carried on cable systems in the tri-state region under the "must-carry" stipulations. Time-Warner had promised to carry it and reneged on its promise. Bridgeways sued Time-Warner, and Time-Warner finally settled out of court.

Laurel was the public affairs director for the station and produced a weekly program. She had brought *Dialogue* from Channel 8 to Channel 43, but there was no studio and she had to search for one.

She asked various local universities if she could use their studio to tape a half-hour interview show that would air on WHAI, volunteering to pay some fee for the usage. Most universities turned her down, responding that their facilities were available only for their students. However, Paul Falcone, director of media services at the University of New Haven (UNH), responded positively to Laurel's request. He had just started producing programs with various organizations such as the state Tourist Bureau.

It was the beginning of a very fruitful relationship. Laurel would come to the UNH studios prepared to tape an interview. UNH students were the camera crew and Paul Falcone directed the taping. She produced about 28 programs a year while school was in session. The programs were aired on Bridgeways, WHAI, Channel 43, from 1993 to 1996. Then she took the programs back to Channel 8 for a year. She was not happy with her time slot and did not like having her shows interrupted with commercials. So she arranged to purchase time from the new independent station in New Haven, WBNE, Channel 59.

Gail Brekke, general manager of WBNE at the time, recalls meeting Laurel in 1996 and thinking she was in the path of a fireball. Laurel was passionate about the issues she was covering, had an insatiable curiosity and was undaunted by the opinions of others or by other obstacles. Brekke was glad to be able to provide Laurel's community-oriented programming at a very reasonable cost. Laurel raised the monies for underwriting the production and time purchase.[12]

The last four years of the programming Laurel produced tended to be more extensive productions but fewer in number. The topics ranged from privacy and medical records, to a genetic engineering laboratory in Maine, to a home for people with AIDS, to a new community arts center. Laurel would set up interviews and location shooting for a secondary source of film and Paul Falcone would take a few students and shoot with her on location. Laurel, whom many noted had an extraordinary capacity for work, transcribed all the interviews and planned the editing based on the transcripts. They then shot an in-studio interview, introduction, transitions and conclusion. Laurel took the finished tape to WBNE, Channel 59, and to CTV, the public access channel for New Haven.

Laurel was a very busy executive producer of these programs and she selected only those topics she determined were significant and not otherwise covered by television. Many of the topics came from her conversations with others or from her reading. Paul Falcone remembers times when she had to work at convincing people that they wanted to be the subject of one of her programs.[13] She would make a demo tape from her previous programs, but each demo tape was made especially for that person, based on their interests and objectives. Very few turned her offer down.

Once selected, the person/organization would be introduced to the whole production process. She would work with them in determining what the objectives of the program would be and what uses it would have beyond the initial airing on WBNE, and she would help them raise the money to produce the show. For example, she worked with Dr. Elizabeth Brett in adapting the topic of managed health care to privacy and medical records and then found ways to ensure funding from the American Psychological Association so that the program would be distributed to stations all over the country. Laurel showed Ann West, founding director of the Tabor Community Arts Center, how to have the show aired on the appropriate cable television access centers. For the program *Connecticut Voices for Children,* Laurel had produced a guide to public access television in Connecticut that indicated the contact person for each access channel and the requirements or needs of each channel.

Laurel had long been a teacher, or a mentor. She was always concerned with everyone she worked with, passionate for the subject and compassionate with those around her. In the last few years of her life she was supporting the studios of the University of New Haven so it could be a studio to be used by others in the community. The university honored her with a honorary doctorate in 1998 and selected her for their board of trustees. Her whole life had been one of working toward improving the community through television. Her communities were many, from her local New Haven to the state of Connecticut to the Jewish community, working for women to have an influence, to the whole world seeing the horrors of the Holocaust lest it happen again.

In a column in a local newspaper that was written after her death, Patricia McCann Vissepo recalled Laurel's possession of an "insatiable curiosity . . . tempered by a sharp intellect"; . . . "a devotion to the Jewish community . . . that allowed her to embrace other cultures and people."[14] Vissepo recalled the screening of a documentary that Laurel had produced about a school project with mostly African American and Hispanic children. The children flocked around her, filled with pride. "More than simply documenting a project, she had validated the children's sense of self-worth."[15] In another tribute, Sherry Haller said of Laurel: "There never was a woman with a stronger sense of self who was so selfless."[16]

Notes

1. Falcone, P. (2000, Oct. 11). Personal communication.
2. Laurel Vlock due on national Jewish Cable TV progam. *CT Jewish Ledger.* (1981, May 7). p. 5.
3. Pace, E. (2000, July 12). Laurel F. Vlock, 74, filmmaker who started Holocaust archive. *The New York Times,* p. B9.
4. Klemesrud, J. (1979, June 12). Women attempt to get own TV station. *The New York Times,* p. C14.
5. Schwartz, T. (1980, Nov. 11). 10 Connecticut women licensed for new Bridgeport TV station. *The New York Times,* p. 15.
6. Johnson, G. (2000, Oct. 16). Personal communication.
7. Schwartz, 1980, p. 15.
8. Meyers, J. (1982, Jan. 16). 11 area women remain hopeful about bringing station to town. *Bridgeport Post,* p. 17.
9. TV tower in city? (1982, Jan. 23). *Bridgeport Telegram,* p. 6.
10. Klemesrud, 1979, p. C14.
11. Singer, K. (1988, Aug. 20). WBCT to aim shows at Jewish audience. *Bridgeport Post,* p. 22.
12. Brekke, G. (2000, Oct. 2). Personal communication.
13. Falcone, 2000.
14. Vissepo, P.M. (2000, July 27). Laurel Vlock gave lasting gift of love. *New Haven Register* [On-line]. Available: http://www.NewHavenRegister.com. (Paragraphs 5, 8).
15. Vissepo, 2000, (paragraph 12).
16. Haller, S. (July, 2000). Letter in memory of Laurel Vlock. *Connecticut Jewish Ledger* [On-line]. Available: http://www.ctjewishledger.com.

Other Sources

Brekke, G. (2000, Oct. 2). Personal communication.
Brett, E. (2000, Nov. 6). Personal communication.
Brozan, N. (1993, Jan. 16). Chronicle. *The New York Times,* p. 22.
Cavanaugh, J. (1987, Nov. 15). Station makes a quiet debut. *The New York Times,* p. 12.
Cole, S. (1981, May 10). Bridgeways leaders confident of Bridgeport TV outlet in '82. *Sunday Bridgeport Post,* p. AA-6.
Ellison, W. (2000, Oct. 4). Personal communication.
Falcone, P. (2000, Oct. 11). Personal communication.
Group plans TV station for Jewish audience. (1988, Sept. 6). *The New York Times,* p. 22.
Henry, D. (1980, Nov. 16). TV outlet, licensed, still faces hurdles. *The New York Times,* Sec. 11, p.1.
Izzo, C. (1982, Nov. 6). Valley cable gets OK for higher tower. *Telegram-Bridgeport Post,* p. 6.

Johnson, G. (2000, Oct. 16). Personal communication.

Kantor, L. (2000, Nov. 13). Personal communication.

Local TV station woos shoppers. (1987, Sept. 9). *Bridgeport Post,* p. 11.

Malinconico, F. (1979, July 24). Company of area women seeking television license. *The (New Haven) Register: Nutmegger West,* p. 4.

Mann, W. (2000, Oct. 11). Personal communication.

McGoldrick, M. (1979, Oct. 9). Feminist firm seeks license to buy Bridgeport TV station. *Greenwich Time,* p. 17.

Oates, S. (1985, July 14). Yale archive saves Holocaust tapes. *The New York Times,* Sec. 11CN, p. 20.

TV sale completed. (1996, Mar. 1). *Connecticut Post.*

TV station gets 6 months. (1982, June 25). *Bridgeport Post,* p. 37.

Vlock, J. (2000, Oct. 4). Personal communication.

Wasserman, H. (2000, Oct. 16). Personal communication.

Webber, M. and Webber, R. (2000, Oct. 11). Personal communication.

Women licensed: To call the shots. (1980, Nov. 16). *The New York Times,* Sec 4, p. 7.

Yale to get videotaped interviews with Holocaust survivors. (1981, Dec. 13). *The New York Times,* Sec. 1, p. 62.

Alice Weston with director *(standing)* and Ralph Besse, CEO of Cleveland Electric Illuminating Co. *(Courtesy of John Carroll University Media Archives, University Heights, Ohio)*

Alice Weston

Cleveland's "First Lady of Television"

Television began its remarkable development after World War II. During this early period, the television freeze (1948–1952) resulted in a limited number of stations on the air. However, during this time, Cleveland saw the activation of three major television stations. Television in Cleveland began in December 1947 with the sign-on of WEWS, Channel 5. In 1948, WXEL, Channel 9 (later Channel 8), started service and in 1949, WKYC, Channel 4 (which became Channel 3), began to broadcast. During the late 1940s and early 1950s, Cleveland was a top-10 market and was expected to be a major contributor to national television programming.

The contributions of women in the Cleveland market, especially those hired by WEWS, Channel 5, within the first months of operation, tell an important story of the work of women in the development of the television industry. Dorothy Fuldheim (*see* Chap. 5) was one of the first women in the country to broadcast news and opinions; Betty Cope was the first woman director; and Alice Weston was the first host of a women's program in Cleveland. Their combined work in television continued into the 1990s and all continued to work in the Cleveland market throughout their professional careers. The contributions of Alice Weston are documented in this chapter.

Alice Weston was one of the most popular and famous local television hosts. Described by co-worker John Fitzgerald as "an absolute fixture in this market; one of the pioneers,"[1] Weston started her Cleveland television career with WEWS in 1948 when she was near the age of 40, actually doing a show before she ever saw television. She remained on the air until 1997, ending her career as a seniors' reporter at WKYC-TV, Channel 3.

Weston used an informal, conversational style of performance that was done totally ad-lib. Educated as a journalist who also studied language and speech performance, she had overcome a speech impediment as a child and loved to talk, especially in an improvised manner. She worked as a newspaper reporter prior to coming to television. Her experience and education were important aspects of her ability to develop a television style. She traveled and interviewed the important figures of the day. At press conferences and on press trips she often was the only woman. She has been compared to Barbara Walters in her ability to interview and maintain a personal touch with people. Her connection to the audience was an important aspect of success over such a long time. She knew and liked her viewers and devoted much time to community groups. She was also fortunate to be in Cleveland in 1947 and to be hired by the first general manager of WEWS-TV, James Hanrahan, who believed in providing opportunities for women.

Finding a Career

Alice Bater Schowalter Weston grew up in Holland, Michigan, as one of six children. Her father was born in the Netherlands and met her mother when he immigrated to Michigan. He was very sensitive about his accent and insisted that all the children learn to speak well. As a child, Weston had a lisp, and with the help of surgery and her father (who enjoyed public speaking and insisted that she never use notes because they would be a hurdle), it was corrected. Her interest in journalism began in high school when she volunteered to write for the school newspaper. She won two small scholarships from Northwestern: one in journalism and the other in drama. Unfortunately, a bad financial situation at home meant that she had to stay at home, so she decided to attend Hope College and began to work for the local newspaper. When her older sister finished college, Weston was able to complete her degree in journalism at Michigan State. In her senior year she competed in the Speech Contest, won and became the first woman to represent Michigan State in a Big Ten competition. She placed second in the contest held at the University of Iowa.

Weston's father was opposed to a career in journalism for her, but when she was offered a job at the *Detroit Free Press,* she moved to Detroit. While at the *Free Press,* she covered the 1933 World's Fair in

Chicago and men's fashion. After about 18 months, she was offered a job by the *Detroit News* to host a morning radio program. She knew nothing about radio and was sent to Ann Arbor for two weeks of vocal training. The show was called *Tonight's Radio Dinner,* which featured menus and recipes that were published the next day in the newspaper. Her first program tested Weston's ability to ad-lib, a strength that she used throughout her career. As she was about to go on the air, a jealous colleague grabbed the script and she had to ad-lib the entire first show with a few recipe cards. Ty Cobb, the baseball player, was her sponsor and urged her to go on. He held her shoulders during the full 30 minutes of the program, which she was able to complete.[2] The program became very successful. At the *News,* she eventually became the women's editor—the youngest editor in the country.

In Detroit she met Arthur Schowalter and married him in 1936. They moved to Elyria, Ohio, a suburb on the far west side of Cleveland, but for about a year she continued to commute to Detroit two days a week for special assignments. After her children were born, she spent the next eight years raising her family.

Eventually, she enrolled in a writing course at the Cleveland Playhouse and, as a result, met people from an ad agency. They were impressed with her writing skills and hired her for half a day a week to write the radio program *Armchair Planning.* After a while, they asked her to audition for a television show. Weston was not really interested since she had never seen television and hated having her picture taken. However, they told her that if she didn't audition, she could no longer write for them. This was a primary concern for Weston. Her husband had become quite ill and money was needed; she had twin daughters to support. For her audition she was to demonstrate a cooking show and do an interview. The person who she interviewed was Betty Cope, playing the role of Mary Margaret McBride. Cope tested her ability when she only provided "yes" or "no" answers. Weston said she couldn't be related to the famous radio hostess because of her one-word responses. She was hired on the spot. Cope became the director of her programs at WEWS.

The management at WEWS was not happy with her married name, Schowalter. WEWS thought that name was not appropriate for television. She wanted to use the name Alice Holland, after her hometown, Holland, Michigan, but station management insisted that Weston sounded right for the station.

The First Television Programs

On Valentine's Day 1948, about six weeks after WEWS signed on, Alice Weston became the first woman to have her own television show in Cleveland. *Distaff* (the word for women's work) was an hour-long magazine show aimed at women; it included cooking food, answering questions and showing the proper way to serve food. Weston described the program: "Back then cooking was the only creative thing in house-keeping. . . . When women were feeling lonely, they were challenged to get up and *do* something."[3] Within the first year, this show evolved into three live half-hour television shows, broadcast about 30 minutes apart Monday through Friday: *The Alice Weston Show, Kitchen Clinic,* and *Alice Weston at Home.* Later an additional 15-minute program, *Family Fare,* was added. These shows were not scripted; they were done live and were ad-libbed. No recordings exist. She was paid $75 per week for all the shows. When she received a raise, it was 25 cents per commercial. She couldn't afford to purchase a television set until she had been working for three months.

In addition to her programs, Weston did all the commercials live and ad-libbed. The ad agencies were not in tune with television yet and wired her a fact sheet with instructions to do what she pleased. Since she had no copy, she really had to know the product.[4] There were mishaps during live commercials, including cutting herself demonstrating a knife. She thought she hid the fact very well (on black-and-white television blood was not so obvious) and continued with the commercial. However, her helper, Ophelia, ran in front of the camera and said, "Dear Lord, please let Miss Alice's finger stop bleed-ing."[5] On another commercial, Ophelia opened a can that exploded into Weston's face. Other mishaps included ashtrays falling from the ceiling. Lighting men had fallen asleep on the catwalk high above the commercial table and knocked over the ashtrays, which fell and broke the nonbreakable dishes that Weston was demonstrating on air. A light once exploded and injured her eye.[6]

The programs were very successful and after about 18 months, one of the sponsors, Frigidaire, asked the station to limit the program to one-half hour so they could syndicate it on the Ohio Network, a group of five Ohio television stations. The station refused, so the spon-sors took her and the program to a competing station, WXEL-TV.

The Move to WXEL-TV

In 1950, Weston moved to WXEL-TV, Channel 9 (now WJW-TV, Channel 8), to host a half-hour Ohio Network cooking show for Frigidaire. In addition, she also hosted a daily interview show called *All for You*. She received a salary increase to $250, almost four times what she was earning at WEWS.

WXEL built her a special kitchen for the 30-minute cooking show, *The Alice Weston Show*, which was syndicated to five Ohio cities. She also had a new assistant, Leona Guerin. Unlike today's regimented schedule, in the early days there was time to visit with the audience since there was not much concern if the program was three or four minutes over. Weston recalled, "In those days if you got a sponsor, you just went some more."[7] The show was a great success. Each month Frigidaire published recipes and began contests for Frigidaire appliances. The mail response was overwhelming. The viewers loved the informality and became close to the crew, often writing to them of "their dreams and needs."[8]

In the early days Weston remembered there was a team spirit because all worked together, which developed a family rapport. The owner of the station, Herb Mayer, made everyone feel like family and would bring back souvenirs from trips for all of the members of the station. To maintain this family spirit, Weston would put extra talent fees in a kitty and divide them with the rest of the crew, explaining they were just as important as on-air talent.[9] Announce copy for *Nite Owl Theater* on Thanksgiving night 1954 included this "thank you" to Alice Weston for planning a Thanksgiving dinner for the crew: "It's people like you, always with a good thought for people like us that makes us thankful."[10] This caring attitude and the time to visit made the audience feel close to the talent as this letter from Weston's scrapbook indicates: "I feel I really know you, since I have been listening and watching you every day since I was married."[11]

Another aspect of her show was community involvement. One segment of her programs, "You and Your World," looked at people, customs, and foods of different countries. "The idea was to acquaint us with other nations to promote understanding and world peace."[12] The U.S. State Department of Information photographed her show on India in 1955 to send to India on exhibit. "To show what the U.S. is doing towards understanding and world peace. It showed what TV can do for this purpose."[13]

Sometimes her concern was very personal. She once arranged for an abusive husband to have therapy and showed up at a doctor's request to encourage a patient to have surgery.[14]

The Ohio Network show ran for seven and one-half years and then she stayed for another year doing interview shows. One day she was called into the manager's office and told her services were no longer needed because he didn't particularly like women's voices on air.[15] When the news got out, two burly cameramen went to his office and threatened to beat him up. Her next job took her to Pittsburgh, although she continued to live in Elyria, Ohio.

The Move to WIIC-TV, Pittsburgh

During the time between television jobs, Weston worked for the Cleveland Safety Council and the Lamb Council. Ed Herp, her director at WXEL, called her one day and asked her to come to an audition in Pittsburgh at WIIC. They were auditioning for an audience show and had five men and four women apply and wanted to have one more woman in the talent pool. He assured her they were not going to hire from outside of Pittsburgh. She decided to go as a favor to Herp and two weeks later she was offered the job.

In 1959 Weston went to WIIC-TV in Pittsburgh as host and producer of a one-hour interview program, *Luncheon at the Ones*. The program was described as "a fun-filled hour of music, interviews, fashions, and surprises designed to suit every viewer."[16] The show was done live in front of a studio audience of about 200 people. She was the host for almost nine years. She described it as the happiest time of her career.[17] She never used notes and feels that this helped her guests feel more comfortable. Her program was a little different than today's interview shows. The interviews were done on a podium and the audience was recognized but did not participate. She did all the interviews, arranged for the guests and did the mail; she had no behind-the-scenes staff. She also did extensive research prior to interviewing a guest. "Otherwise the show is padded; it doesn't go anywhere."[18]

Her warm and open personality allowed her to make friends with many of the celebrities she interviewed. "The best part of the job has always been the people."[19] Phyllis Diller, Nanette Fabray and Paul Anka are among her favorites. Interviews with celebrities included Princess Grace of Monaco, Kirk Douglas, Natalie Wood, Johnny Carson and Yul Brenner. Weston found that celebrities were often lonely and needed friendship, but she always thought of them as people, not as a career move. She discussed raising twins with Jimmy Stewart, the loss of a spouse with Nanette Fabray and the difficulty of waiting for scripts to be written with Yul Brenner. This ability to touch people at the human level contributed to her many long friendships with celebrities.

Her personal style of interviewing is associated today with Barbara Walters, yet Alice Weston used this style from her early days in television. Weston once reported that this style was seen by some in her business as a shortcoming. "When I put people on the spot, I try to do it nicely." She wanted to be herself and remain a lady.[20]

Weston began her television career doing a typical women's show, but as she gained experience, and as both the managers and the public began to accept women in a variety of roles, she broadened her work. She began to interview politicians, including President Nixon, King Saud, Congresswomen Frances Bolton, Secretary of Labor Arthur Goldberg and First Ladies Rosalynn Carter, Pat Nixon and Lady Bird Johnson. Her most rewarding political interview was with David Ben Gurion, former premier of Israel. In her biography she recalls the meeting. On a press trip to Israel, she had obtained a letter of introduction. Although Ben Gurion was not granting interviews, Weston was fortunate enough to obtain a meeting. She was told no notes, no pictures, no tape and to bring no one with her. According to her recollections, they had a lively discussion and eventually he asked her to consider coming to Israel to teach. He ended the interview by saying, "May God bless you and keep you well."[21]

Her work also included press trips to France, Rome, Corsica, Greece, Israel, and the Dominican Republic. Often she was the only female among the reporters, although she may not have realized this until boarding the plane. Before departing for the Dominican Republic to cover the Latin World's Fair, all the reporters were to assemble in New York. When she arrived, she was asked to join the group for a picture, but she wanted to wait for the other women. It was then she was told she was the only female traveling with 48 men. Although she had the opportunity to move to the national level, she preferred to stay close to family and friends.

Leaving and Returning to Television

Weston's program in Pittsburgh ended when the network (NBC) demanded the time slot from the station. She went to New York, where she was vice president of Jean Loach Public Relations Company. While there, she had assignments in Rome and Athens. However, after one year her husband became ill again and could not travel. So she returned to Elyria, attended Kent State University, and received her master's in journalism. At the same time, she continued to do public relations work for composer Peggy Coolidge. This gave her a chance to visit Tokyo and Hong Kong.

In 1967, while at Kent State, her former program director from Channel 8, WJW-TV, Ted Baze, called her and asked her help in setting up a new UHF television station licensed to the city of Lorain to be called WUAB-TV, Channel 43. Lorain is a sister city to Elyria, where Weston had lived most of her life, and this relationship was a tremendous asset for the new television station operation. The people in Elyria trusted Alice because she was a longtime resident and was active on many community boards. She decided to join the station for "just six months to get it started"[22] but remained for over 20 years. An advisory council was set up, and she gave talks to groups to explain how the station would benefit the community. With Weston's help, a good relationship with the citizens of Lorain was established and the station received its license, despite the fact the studios would be located in Parma, Ohio, some 40 miles away in a suburb of Cleveland. Weston eventually became the public affairs director and also hosted *Lorain Conversation.* She did two other programs, *Coffee Shop* and *43 a.m.,* with Linn Sheldon, another popular Cleveland broadcast pioneer. She also did four one-hour documentaries a year and special salutes to cities.

During this time, she interviewed Rosalynn Carter, and it is memorable for a couple of reasons. She once again demonstrated her "the-show-must-go-on" spirit as she had earlier in her career. She had a badly bruised and blackened eye from an accident involving a car door. Makeup could not hide the injury. She did the interview and when it was over Mrs. Carter said she hoped her eye would get better. Mrs. Carter came to Lorain to honor the volunteers who had saved the Palace Theater. Weston met Mrs. Carter in Springfield, Ohio, and came back with her on a plane to Cleveland Hopkins Airport. She interviewed her twice: once on the plane and once at the theater. Weston sent her copies of the interviews and waited for a response. Six weeks later, she received a letter from the White House with a bill for $450. It seems this was part of the Carters' economic policy and she was expected to pay for the plane ride.

In August 1988, at the age of 77, Weston decided to retire from WUAB-TV as public affairs director. However, she continued to work part time for five more years with a weekly segment for the *Ten O'clock News* on senior citizens' issues called "Senior Forum." Then, in 1994 she decided to retire for good. However, two days later a Cleveland television station, WKYC-TV, Channel 3, called and asked her to continue her senior reporting with them. Her first reaction was "Why would you want a woman 83 years old doing a show?"[23]

In September 1994, Weston joined WKYC-TV Channel 3 as a seniors' reporter. The program was called *Senior Report* and aired Friday's on the noon news. She had been in broadcasting for 45 years. During this time, Weston now had worked for all of the original VHF Cleveland television stations and had helped in establishing one of the first UHF stations. WKYC-TV gave her the opportunity to continue to do something significant. She accepted the offer because she felt that "It is vital to get information out to seniors. . . . I hope my stories will not only inform seniors and address their needs and issues, but tell them how to have fun as well."[24] Three years later, in 1997, she retired from WKYC-TV. This wonderful and long career was not without its rewards.

Honors

In 1949, Cleveland voted Weston "First Lady of Television." She received the top local award for her show *Alice Weston at Home* in 1952 and won Best Women's Show in Cleveland in 1956 and second place in the public service Golden Quill Award in Pittsburgh in 1962. In 1964 she won another Golden Quill Award for best women's show in Pittsburgh. Also in 1964, she won the McCall's Golden Mike Award for service to families for her series *The Lonely Sickness,* a report on women alcoholics. That same year she also received a national honor from Alpha Chi Omega as the Top Woman in Communications in the United States. In 1975, the Radio and Television Council of Greater Cleveland honored her for her 27 years in broadcasting. In 1976, she was given the Governor's Award for Excellence in Broadcasting from the National Association of Television Society. She was further honored at an American Women in Radio and Television luncheon as a "Broadcast Pioneer." Another award followed for a special report on eye care for seniors on *Lorain Conversations*. In 1983 she received the Lighthouse Award presented by the Cleveland Chapter of the Public Relations Society of America. In 1995 she was honored by Kent State as she was presented the William Taylor Distinguished Alumnus Award.[25]

Summary and Conclusions

Alice Weston showed the pioneer spirit in many ways. She overcame a speech impediment and developed an ability to ad-lib. She was the first woman to have her own television show in Cleveland, a cooking show geared toward women. As she stated later, "I would have preferred to do news, but those positions were not open to women then."[26] Through her hard work, ability and education, she eventually was able to do news and help to open many doors for women.

She developed an intimate and friendly style, a style that is commonly seen on television today. This style emerged because she really knew and liked the people in her community. She once said, "The most exciting thing about life is being able to communicate with other people. There is more excitement in people than in events."[27]

One of her most important skills was the ability to ad-lib. That is an essential skill on television today. However, much of what is done today is planned to sound like an ad-lib. Although she used notes, she never used a teleprompter and her comments and responses were based on her interest and knowledge of the guest or topic. Her genuine concern for people was shown in her interviews with her ability to make people feel comfortable and to relate to them on the human level. Weston once remarked that the only thing missing from television today is a "sense of intimacy, a personal touch."[28] Her commitment to the community, her knowledge about the people and her training and talent gave her the opportunity to set the standard for what we expect to see from television performers. She is truly one of the pioneers of local television.

Notes

1. Beadle, M.E. (1977). *The First Ten Years of VHF Television in Cleveland: 1947-1957*, p. 99. Unpublished master's thesis, Kent State University, Kent, Ohio.
2. Weston, A. (1994). The life and times of Alice Bater Schowalter aka Alice Weston. John Carroll University Media Archives, University Heights, Ohio.
3. Snook, D. (1987, Dec. 13). Alice was wonder in videoland. *The Plain Dealer*, p. 4-H.
4. Weston, A. (1999, Mar. 2). Oral-history interview. John Carroll University Media Archives, University Heights, Ohio.
5. Beadle, 1977, p. 99.
6. Weston, 1994, p. 13.
7. Beadle, 1977, p. 99.
8. Weston, 1994, p. 13.
9. Beadle, 1977, p. 100.
10. Beadle, 1979, p. 100.
11. Bydafka, M. (1954, June 10). Letter to Alice Weston. Personal papers of Alice Weston.
12. Weston, A. (1955, Apr. 25). *Inside Eight*, 5(13), p. 1.
13. Weston, A. 1955, p. 1.
14. Snook, 1987, p. 4-H.
15. Weston, 1994, p. 14.
16. *Luncheon* returns to WIIC. (Aug. 1961). *Channel 11 Tele-log*, p. 1.
17. Weston, 1994, p. 15.
18. Carter, J. (1979, June 24). Recipe for longevity. *The Cleveland Plain Dealer*, p. 1.
19. Plas, P. (1988, Aug. 14). Alice Weston retires from television with 40 years of happy memories. *Elyria Chronicle-Telegram*, p. G-2.
20. Carter, 1979, p. 13.
21. Weston, 1994, p. 37.
22. Carter, 1979, p. 1.
23. *Senior Report.* (nd). Newspaper clipping. Personal papers of Alice Weston.
24. WKYC-TV hires seniors' reporter. (1994, Sept. 13). Press Release, WKYC-TV. John Carroll University Media Archives, University Heights, Ohio.
25. Mlincek, J. (1979, July 27). TV's Alice Weston can talk—so she travels the world. *Elyria Chronicle-Telegram*, pp. B-1, B-2; Broadcast pioneer Alice Weston to receive William Taylor Award. (1995, Summer). *Jargon*. Kent State University, Kent, Ohio, p. 1.
26. Carter, 1979, p. 13.
27. Mlincek, 1969, p. B-2.
28. Snook, 1987, p. 4-H.

Bobbie Wygant. (©The Dallas Morning News; *Natalie Caudill, photographer*)

Bobbie Wygant
"They Poured Me in With the Foundation"

When film critic and entertainment reporter Bobbie Wygant spoke at a 1998 tribute to her 50 years in television, all at the same Texas station, she noted that she had been on the air as long as her station had. "They poured me in with the foundation" is how she put it.[1] Bobbie began her television career in 1948, when WBAP-TV, now KXAS-TV and NBC 5, went on the air in Fort Worth. She calls her career "a remarkable journey."[2]

Bobbie was the first woman in the Fort Worth–Dallas area to produce and host a general-interest talk show and the first TV critic in the Southwest to review both theater and film.[3] Over the years she has interviewed celebrities ranging from 1940s leading man Jimmy Stewart to 1990s heartthrob Matt Damon. She has interviewed Bob Hope, Bette Davis, George Clooney, Paul McCartney, Ethel Kennedy, Bruce Willis, Julia Roberts, Harrison Ford, Clint Eastwood, Tom Cruise, and thousands of others. Bobbie owns one of the most recognizable faces and voices in the North Texas region,[4] and she is frequently called upon to emcee area fund-raisers and celebrity tributes. But she is not a native Texan; she came to Texas as a bride.

French, Irish, and Texan

Bobbie was born Roberta Frances Connolly in Lafayette, Indiana, on November 22, 1926. She was the first child of Ella Louise Toner Connolly and Robert Loren Connolly. Her mother was a homemaker of French-Irish heritage; her father was a letter carrier of Irish heritage. Her father and granddad, Robert Emmitt Connolly, were both avid readers who could talk about anything with anybody. Bobbie says she probably got some of her verbal skills from them since she spent a lot of her growing-up years trying to keep up with their conversations. She sometimes likes to kid celebrities she's interviewing when they start giving her a bad time. She tells them, "You need to know, I'm French, Irish and Texan, so don't mess with me."[5]

Bobbie was raised Roman Catholic in Lafayette and considers her childhood quite typical of a midwestern college town. She describes her family as solid, very rooted in their Catholicism. Her mother was a movie fan and used to take her to the movies.[6] Bobbie says she gets much of her joie de vivre from her mother.[7]

As Bobbie was entering her senior year at St. Francis Academy, her mother died of cancer. It was 1943, during World War II. Bobbie was 16 years old and with her dad ran the household that included her two younger brothers, Gordon and Carl.

After graduating from high school, Bobbie enrolled at Purdue University in 1944 and majored in broadcasting, taking nearly enough hours to double-major in psychology. The idea to go into broadcasting came from listening to Purdue University's radio station; she was impressed that it had women announcers. Bobbie was one of about four women enrolled in the broadcast curriculum, which had 40 or 50 men in the program.[8] She took only two years and seven months to complete her degree and graduated with honors in June 1947.

Purdue is where she met her soul mate, the joy and love of her life, Philip Warren Wygant. They met while working at Purdue's 5,000-watt campus radio station, WBAA. They married in 1947 after a two-year courtship. Philip landed a job as an announcer at WBAP Radio in Fort Worth, where he worked while Bobbie completed her senior year at Purdue.[9]

WBAP planned to launch a companion TV station in Fort Worth, and in the fall of 1948 when WBAP-TV went on the air, Bobbie was hired as a writer in the continuity department. She would write everything and anything that needed to be written. She had experience writing and producing shows at the radio station at Purdue.[10]

WBAP: We Bring a Program

WBAP-TV officially went on the air in Fort Worth, Texas, on September 29, 1948. It was the first television station in Texas and the first in the Southwest.[11] It was owned by Carter Publications, which also owned WBAP Radio and the *Fort Worth Star-Telegram.* Carter was Amon G. Carter, Sr., and the call letters WBAP stood for "We Bring a Program."

When Bobbie started working at WBAP-TV, the station was producing nine or 10 television programs a week.[12] These programs were broadcast live in the evenings. Bobbie did many different things during these early days of television. In addition to her writing duties, she appeared on programs and helped produce the shows. She and others practically invented programming day by day. There was a lot of learning on the job for everyone. One of her earliest shows was called *Stump Us.* Viewers would call in with songs for the show's organist. If the organist failed to play a few bars, the viewer would win a prize.[13]

She was the only woman on the WBAP-TV staff writing and doing live, on-air entertainment programs in 1948. She remembers a number of women in office/clerical jobs such as traffic and bookkeeping. She and Margret McDonald Rimmer, who was hired in the 1950s to plan, produce and do a cooking show, were the only on-air women on staff in those early days. Two other women did commercials on a free-lance basis. Entertainers such as singers and dancers appeared on the station's *Barn Dance* program on a free-lance basis. Bobbie remembers a woman named Lynn Trammell who headed the station's music and film library. She says there were no other women in managerial or midmanagerial jobs during those years.[14]

Bobbie pitched products, co-hosted a variety of quiz and fashion shows, presided over afternoon movies and rode her horse, Suzie, in the annual Fort Worth Stock Show parade. She held up cans of Spam and canned turkey, interviewed local merchants, tried new recipes, modeled clothes and kept smiling and talking,[15] mostly about "girl things."[16]

Bobbie was something of a "Girl Friday" on a lot of these live shows. "Any program needing an attractive woman to help the talent or announcer used Wygant. . . . At one time Wygant was doing eleven shows a week, but she was never a hostess."[17] Management did not want to create stars out of staff people in those days because they were afraid that if one person became too well liked by viewers "that person would want more money."[18]

Bobbie worked in this capacity for 12 years, until the fall of 1960 when the host of Channel 5's locally produced afternoon interview program *Dateline* took a week off and recommended that Bobbie fill in. Bobbie filled in splendidly, was offered the job full time, and *Dateline* and Bobbie Wygant became inseparable for the next 15 years. She was the first woman at WBAP-TV to be in charge of the continuity department when the *Dateline* assignment began.[19]

Dateline

Dateline became a way to promote color television in the 1960s. Bobbie produced a fashion segment for which local department stores furnished models and colorful clothes;[20] a host interviewed guests. She became the first woman in the Fort Worth–Dallas area to be producer and host of a general-interest talk show. She usually had five segments in every 30-minute show. This involved telephoning and making herself available for people to reach her—lots of each—and making a run down of the show. The director didn't have to do anything except make sure the proper chairs were out there; she made sure the show was ready when she brought it to him.[21] Her philosophy, as a woman producing a general-interest show, was to put together a program that would appeal to all viewers, male and female, young and old, no matter what their education level or economic status.

Bobbie loved doing *Dateline* but there were days when it was difficult. One day they had live animals, a couple of interviews, and a choir. The choir was at one end of the studio. The live animals were at the other end of the studio. The interviews were scattered around out of the way. She was just running madly during the commercial from one set to the other set to find out what these people were doing. Mostly, she said they just flew by the seat of their pants.[22]

She remembers one unsettling time when she was interviewing an orthopedic surgeon and she began to smell something like burning wires. She looked out and there was smoke coming out of one camera. There was nothing to do but continue the live interview while engineers were out there taking the panels off the side of the camera and looking in it.[23]

Bobbie was hosting *Dateline* live on her 37th birthday, November 22, 1963, when news broke that President Kennedy had been shot in Dallas. For the next 30 minutes, she was Channel 5's anchor in residence. She got through it by going on automatic pilot and crying later. When she finished that day, she knew she could get through anything in the broadcasting business. "I was not nervous, I was not shaking, but when I got off the air, then the tears came. I didn't get teary eyed [on air], well it was just not the time to do it."[24] She credits years of training that gave her strength to broadcast that day.

There was never any subject Bobbie would not discuss. She had a simple formula for conducting an interview successfully: be curious, be prepared and get to the point.[25] *Dateline* ran daily during the week from 1960 until 1975. During some of those 15 years, Bobbie also did a WBAP radio show called *The World of Bobbie Wygant.*

When Bobbie started covering Fort Worth's Casa Manana and the Dallas Musicals in the 1960s, she began doing a segment called *Midnight Reviews* on Channel 5's midnight news. These were the first theatrical reviews she ever did. She would attend the opening night's performance at the theater, rush back to the station to write her review, read it on the air and ad-lib the rest. Cast members and "first nighters" were particularly interested in learning as soon as possible what Bobbie had to say about an opening performance. The midnight reviews also let Channel 5 beat the morning newspaper's review.

KXAS-TV

By the 1970s, as network programming grew, NBC's demands on affiliate stations' airtime eventually whittled *Dateline* from a half-hour show to a six-minute segment of the news.[26] Channel 5 also acquired a new owner, LIN Broadcasting. Carter Communications sold WBAP-AM-FM and the *Star-Telegram* to Capital Cities Communications in 1974. WBAP-TV was spun off to LIN Broadcasting and became KXAS-TV.[27] Bobbie's husband, Philip, in charge of the station's promotion and publicity department, came home on New Year's Eve 1974 with news that he'd been fired by the new station manager. Philip had been with Channel 5 for 26 years. The couple agreed that Bobbie would continue without him. A few days later, Bobbie was called into the new general manager's office and informed she was being transferred from the program department to the news department.[28] Until then, the only woman in the newsroom was the news director's secretary.[29] Bobbie would co-anchor a new 5 p.m. news magazine program named *Inside Area 5*. WBAP, now KXAS, Channel 5, was the prime NBC affiliate for a 36-county area that the station called Area 5.[30]

Bobbie was 49 years old and instantly clicked with her 28-year-old co-anchor, Chip Moody. The chatty, magazine format of their show suited them. Chip wanted to do any story that had an aviation or racing angle. Bobbie wanted the show business stories. Bobbie had interviewed countless celebrities during her 15 years hosting *Dateline* and when studios began providing film clips to stations, she added film reviews. Bobbie thus became the first TV critic in the Southwest to review both theater and film. Bobbie and Chip worked together for two years, from 1975 until 1977.[31]

In 1977, management decided that they wanted the 5 p.m. time slot for hard news. Bobbie told the news director that she did not want to anchor hard news but would like to do an entertainment segment for the news. She had often traveled to Los Angeles and New York, interviewing actors and various people and knew that some cities now had people doing movie reviews and interviewing actors in an entertainment segment. Management agreed and Channel 5 was the first in the market to do an entertainment segment. So Bobbie carved out a new niche for herself; she was now the station's entertainment reporter and film critic.

Her entertainment reviews became distinctive for their scholarship and compassion.[32] Her former *Dateline* co-anchor, Chip Moody, calls Bobbie the original *Entertainment Tonight,* Siskel and Ebert, and Leonard Maltin all wrapped up into one person.[33] For a number of years, her reports have been sent to NBC affiliates to use in their own newscasts and shows.

Her co-workers say Bobbie invented how to do movie and theater reviews for TV. They are awed by her energy and stamina. They describe her as "relentlessly youthful," as "effervescent" and "indomitable."[34] Until the end of 1999, Bobbie flew to New York or Los Angeles at the end of almost every week, and she worked many weeknights until midnight logging her tapes and writing her reviews when the news staff was not using the editing equipment. For years, she was producing six entertainment stories a week for the news and a 30-minute entertainment "special" once a month.[35]

Her philosophy is to be fair in these reviews, not nasty. Bobbie feels people really wouldn't accept it very well from her if she were suddenly up there "being Joan Rivers." She says that would be out of character for her, a still-devout Catholic who spends time each morning and evening in prayer and meditation because it keeps her calm.[36]

Bobbie is one of only a few women nationally who write critiques about the movies.[37] She considers herself a traditionalist, is a "sucker" for a sweeping epic,[38] and likes filmmaking techniques that break new ground. Her basic guidelines for judging a movie or play are "Is the story cohesive? Are the actors believable? Is the direction solid? Is it technically sound? Is it creative? And bottom line, would I pay $7.50 to see it?"[39] Her film ratings range from a rare five stars for an excellent movie to four stars for a highly recommended movie to one star for a movie that is not well made.

NBC 5

More changes came to Channel 5 in 1998 when the station was bought by the NBC Network and became an NBC owned-and-operated station. This ownership change led to a significant change in station policy about "junkets" or free trips. Unlike LIN Broadcasting policy, NBC network policy forbids employees to take junkets. Wygant's reports often were based on such trips.

The NBC policy change meant Bobbie would no longer be able to do her job in the way she had in the past. Her access to the stars and the industry now would be curtailed because the station had no budget to pay for her to travel as extensively as she had in the past. She was offered the opportunity to remain and do local entertainment stories, but she declined.[40]

Bobbie announced her retirement from Channel 5 in December 1999. She stepped aside with confidence, grace and a smile. Her "last" day on the air was December 7, 1999. The station's general manager described Bobbie as a "household name in the Dallas–Fort Worth community, an outstanding journalist and critic, and one of the hardest-working people in the field."[41]

In her farewell message to co-workers at the station, Bobbie mentioned that other opportunities might open for her. When one door closes, she said, another door often opens. With characteristic wit, she added that she thought everyone should change jobs every 51 years or so, whether they want to or not.[42]

Even though she was retiring, she still wanted to work and she did not want to leave the Fort Worth–Dallas area. Six months into her "retirement," she was back on the air at Channel 5, doing what she had often done: entertainment reports and interviews. This time, she was doing two stories a week on a free-lance basis and covering the local theater scene. The station had started a new 4 p.m. newscast, and the show's young anchors wanted Bobbie's reports to help build their audience in a now fiercely fought news ratings race. She had been missed.

Home and Community

Bobbie Wygant, a household name in the Dallas–Fort Worth community,[43] chose to keep her private life private. Because her husband, Philip, became promotion manager at Channel 5 and because he was a somewhat shy and retiring person himself, there was no competition between them over Bobbie's inevitable and growing celebrity. Actually, the more famous she became, the better for the station and its promotion department. It was a terrible blow to Bobbie when Philip died after a brief illness in April 1986 of a rare form of liver cancer.[44] They had been partners in work and at home for nearly 40 years. They did not have children. It took months for her to adjust to the loss.

In the greater Fort Worth–Dallas community, Bobbie is frequently the master of ceremonies and a featured speaker at fund-raisers. These events include the Susan G. Komen Breast Cancer Foundation, the Women's Shelter of Tarrant County, the Alzheimer's Association, and the Jerry Lewis Labor Day Muscular Dystrophy Telethon. Besides numerous charity events and her television work, Bobbie actively participates in the operation of her East Texas tree farm, which produces timber.

Bobbie has received numerous awards over the years. In 1966, she was selected, as one of the top 10 women in broadcasting in the United States, to attend the Asian-American Women Broadcasters' Conference in Honolulu, Hawaii. The local chapter of the International Toastmistress Clubs awarded her its first annual Woman of Excellence Award in 1973.[45] The Fort Worth Zonta Club named her Woman of the Year in 1983. Also in 1983, she was honored in Austin, Texas, by Women in Communications and received a Headliner's Award as one of the top communicators in Texas. In 1999, she was honored by the Dallas–Fort Worth chapter of the Association for Women Journalists for Lifetime Achievement in Television. And the local chapter of Women in Film gave her the group's Achievement

Award in 1999, an award "honoring a female role model who's made significant contributions to the local industry."[46]

In January 1999, Bobbie was given the first Critics Award by the National Broadcast Film Critics Association in Los Angeles. The award was presented at a luncheon at which Steven Spielberg received the Director of the Decade Award. Bobbie first met Spielberg at a luncheon in Los Angeles when he was a director-in-training at Universal Studios. Spielberg remembered her, and when he stood up to receive his award (after Bobbie had received hers), Spielberg said Bobbie was the first broadcast film critic he ever got to know.

Many of the actors, directors, and filmmakers she had interviewed over the years sent video tributes and letters of congratulations when Bobbie was the guest of honor at a 50th anniversary luncheon and tribute gala at a downtown Fort Worth hotel in October 1998. The letters came from Tom Cruise, John Travolta, and Patrick Swayze, among others. Jack Lemmon, who described Bobbie as "the best" in her field, wrote that he had been interviewed a number of times by people he had "totally, completely, forgotten." He could never forget her because, he wrote, "You are bright and extremely knowledgeable . . . a lovely lady and great fun to be with and talk with."[47] Charlton Heston wrote, "Accuracy and the art of asking interesting and intriguing questions counts in interviews particularly when one has done as many as I have. You were always both of those graciously mixed with a sense of humor and I appreciated the care you took to get it right."[48] Actress Ruta Lee wrote that Bobbie "has the magical ability to give an honest review—tempered with human kindness." She said, "Bobbie is respected and admired and, yes, loved by her peers the critics and by the criticized as well."[49]

The president and managing director of the Dallas Summer Musicals called her a "bright and shining star." He wrote, "How fortunate we are, those of us in arts organizations who have been the lucky recipients of your insightful reviews and interviews."[50] Gary Cogill, movie critic at WFAA-TV in Dallas-Fort Worth and one of her major competitors, called Bobbie "the Cal Ripkin of film reviewers" when he introduced her at the 50th anniversary party.[51]

At this tribute gala, a group of Casa Manana actors performed an original musical about Bobbie's career and their recollections of it. The stage backdrop was "Bobbie" written out in spangly pink letters. Every U.S. film company sent a representative, and many of the people she had interviewed on the air over the years were among the 350 guests who attended. The event was also a benefit that raised money for scholarships established in her honor at Casa Manana Children's Theatre School in Fort Worth.

"I Just Want to Go to Work Everyday"

Bobbie loves the broadcasting business and she has worked hard at it for more than 50 years and hopes to continue in this endeavor. She has been blessed with tremendous energy and she is grateful to everybody who has made it possible for her to do this work. She says she believes very much in the power of prayer, that she prays everyday, and that she believes that for the most part, her prayers have always been answered.[52]

Television takes commitment in time and energy. Bobbie made that commitment and navigated many changes for 51 years and counting. "I always give it my best shot," she says. "That's why I've lasted this long. I always give it my best shot every day." And that's what she wants to keep doing. She says she just wants "to go to work everyday."[53]

In January 2001, Bobbie was offered the unexpected opportunity to appear in a major motion picture as a movie critic. Although she spent her entire life saying she would rather interview an actor than be one, she was invited by director Joe Roth to play an interviewer in his upcoming film *America's Sweethearts*. Bobbie was flown first-class to Hollywood in January 2001 and was filmed in a scene with Catherine Zeta-Jones and John Cusack. The film is expected to be released in 2001.[54]

Notes

1. Stewart, P. and Philpot, R. (1999, Dec. 15). Channel 5 film critic Wygant will retire. *Fort Worth Star-Telegram*, pp. 1A, 8A.
2. Bark, E. (1998, Oct. 25). Bobbie Wygant: After 50 years on Channel 5, she's primed to keep on ticking. *Dallas Morning News*, pp. 1E-4E.
3. Stewart and Philpot, 1999.
4. Stewart, P. (1998, Sept. 30). Bobbie Wygant: A half-century on television. *Fort Worth Star-Telegram*. Fort Worth Public Library, Local History Collection, Bobbie Wygant clipping file and WBAP clipping file.
5. Baker, A. (1998, Apr. 28). Transcribed oral history interview with Bobbie Wygant, p. 3. Arlington, Texas: The University of Texas at Arlington University Archives, Division of Special Collections.
6. Baker, 1998, pp. 3, 18, 19.

7. Bark, 1998.
8. Wygant, B. (2001, Jan. 18). Personal communication.
9. Baker, 1998, p. 7.
10. Baker, 1998, p. 7.
11. WBAP. (1974, Feb.). *Fort Worth Magazine, 50*(2), p. 30.
12. Baker, 1998, p. 9.
13. Schroeder, M.R. (1983, Dec.). *The History of WBAP-TV: The First Ten Years, 1948-1957,* pp. 84, 85. Unpublished doctoral dissertation, East Texas State University, Marshall, Texas.
14. Wygant, 2001.
15. Bark, 1998.
16. Wygant, B. (2000, July 18). Personal communication.
17. Schroeder, 1983, p. 162.
18. Schroeder, 1983, p. 162.
19. Baker, 1998, p. 9; Wygant, 2001.
20. Baker, 1998, p. 9.
21. Baker, 1998, p. 13.
22. Baker, 1998, p. 11.
23. Baker, 1998, p. 12.
24. Baker, 1998, pp. 21-24.
25. Baker, B. (1969, Mar. 7). The Wygant formula. *Dallas Morning News.* Dallas Public Library, Local History Collection, Bobbie Wygant clipping file and WBAP clipping file.
26. Baker, 1998, p. 13.
27. Schnurman, M. (1997, Aug. 13). KXAS TV, LIN Corp. to be sold. *Fort Worth Star-Telegram,* pp. 1A, 13A.
28. Baker, 1998, p. 32.
29. Wygant, 2000, July 18.
30. WBAP, 1974.
31. Baker, 1998, pp. 16, 20.
32. Stewart, 1998.
33. Moody, C. (1995). *Moments: The Life and Career of a Texas Newsman,* p. 230. Dallas, Texas: Taylor Publishing Company.
34. Bark, 1998, p. 1E.
35. Wygant, 2000, July 18.
36. Bark, 1998.
37. Smith, R. (1990, Sept. 1). Stalking the female voice in criticism. *Dallas Morning News,* p. 5C.
38. Bark, 1998.
39. Wygant, B. (2000, Aug. 2). Personal communication.
40. Stewart and Philpot, 1999.
41. Stewart and Philpot, 1999, p. 8A.
42. Stewart and Philpot, 1999.
43. Stewart and Philpot, 1999.
44. Services set for Philip Wygant, ex-Channel 5 promotion director. (1986, Apr. 26). *Dallas Morning News.* Dallas Public Library, Local History Collection, Bobbie Wygant clipping file and WBAP clipping file.
45. Bobbie Wygant to receive award. (1973, Oct. 23). *Dallas Morning News.* Dallas Public Library, Local History Collection, Bobbie Wygant clipping file and WBAP clipping file.
46. Sumner, J. (1999, Apr. 30). Women in Film taps Richardson, Wygant for honors. *Dallas Morning News,* p. 5C.
47. Lemmon, J. (1998, Oct. 31). Letter to Bobbie Wygant. Personal papers of Bobbie Wygant.
48. Heston, C. (1998, Oct. 31). Letter to Bobbie Wygant. Personal papers of Bobbie Wygant.
49. Lee, R. (2000, Aug. 11). Personal correspondence with Suzanne Huffman.

50. Jenkins, M.A. (1998, Oct. 31). Letter to Bobbie Wygant. Personal papers of Bobbie Wygant.
51. Wygant, 2001.
52. Baker, 1998, pp. 33, 35.
53. Wygant, 2000, Aug. 2.
54. Wygant, 2001.

Other Sources

Bobbie Wygant. (2000, June). Bio sheet. Personal papers of Bobbie Wygant.
Carter, A. (1948, Sept. 29). Talk, Opening WBAP-TV, The Star-Telegram Station.
    Folder #11, Archives box, Amon Carter/WBAP papers at the Amon Carter Museum,
    Fort Worth, Texas.
Flemmons, J. (1978). *Amon: The Life of Amon Carter, Sr., of Texas.* Austin, Texas: Jenkins
    Publishing Company.
WBAP. (1972, Sept.). *Fort Worth Magazine,* pp. 16, 17.

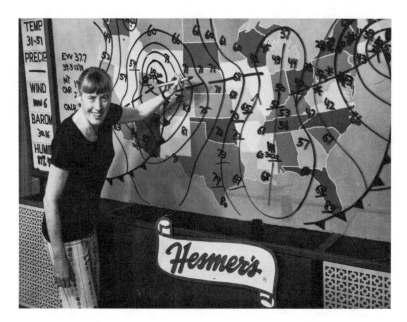

Marcia Yockey on the weather set at WFIE-TV

Marcia Yockey

A Force of Nature in Evansville, Indiana

It is difficult to describe the effect of Marcia Yockey on the Evansville market. It is, however, safe to say that she was more than the weather to Evansville. In her 35 years on the air, she became a true icon for the spirit and values of her audience. A 1996 video profile of her states: "To see an old weathercast, you would be amazed how this person could keep your attention so long with her back turned to the camera. Yet Marcia managed it by being Marcia."[1]

Yockey started weathercasting as part of the first day of programming on November 15, 1953, on WFIE-TV.[2] She retired in July 1988, over the objection of her audience.[3] In April 2000, the Indiana Associated Press named her to the Indiana Broadcasters Hall of Fame.[4] Her first station owner, Jerry Fine, declared her "an instant success."[5] Her last general manager, Conrad Cagle, also gave Yockey much of the credit for ratings leadership.[6]

Yockey started her broadcasts during the early wave of "weathergirls."[7] The novelty of the female weather reporter became quite fashionable in the 1950s. Most of these weathergirls were hired for looks and had little to no training in meteorology. The 31-year-old Yockey was athletic, energetic, and fun to watch, but she was not the beauty queen (literally) typical of the era.[8] Yockey was brash, plainly attired and well known for unladylike behavior. Although she had no degree, she is identified as one of a "tiny number of bona fide female meteorologists" in the country.[9]

Early Years

Yockey was born September 6, 1922 in Muncie, Indiana. Her family moved to Evansville, where Yockey attended grade school and high

229

school.[10] She continued her schooling as a pre-med major for three years at Evansville College.

In part due to a lack of money for medical school and in part to serve her country, Yockey gave up her dream to become a doctor in 1943 and joined the U.S. Weather Bureau. Because the men had gone to war, the Weather Bureau was asking women to serve. After three weeks' training in Chicago, Yockey was placed in the Evansville airport extension office.[11] By 1951, Yockey was the last woman serving in the Evansville weather bureau. It would be more than 30 years before another woman would work for the Evansville bureau.[12]

She was transferred to the weather bureau in Grand Island, Nebraska. She earned her pilot's license in 1951 in Nebraska and flew home to Evansville on a regular basis. On one of these trips, Ed Mitchell, a former senator and the owner of Hesmer's Foods, asked Yockey to be on television.[13]

A Life in Broadcasting

Hesmer's Foods produced, prepared and canned foods in the Evansville area. Owner Ed Mitchell knew that women made the purchase decisions for foods and he was willing to experiment with television advertising. He wanted a female spokesperson and had decided on weather as his vehicle. A bartender at the local country club suggested Yockey. Originally, Yockey refused.

Yockey finally agreed and Mitchell demanded that her 5-minute segment go at the beginning of the newscast.[14] At the age of 31, Yockey nervously started her new career in weathercasting on November 15, 1953. However, Yockey's long blonde hair was getting in the way of her face. She didn't care and stated, "You're not suppose to look at me. You're supposed to look at the fronts."[15] Mitchell wanted her to tie her hair back into a ponytail. She eventually agreed and maintained that trademark hairdo throughout her years on air.

In 1957, Yockey was upset over changes made in her weatherboard, announcer and theme music without her approval. Her old music needed updating because the recording was physically worn out. However, Yockey liked it and was resistant to change.[16] Ritt reported when it was first changed, she refused to go on air. A public service film aired in place of the weather. Eventually, Yockey took the aluminum transcription disk of the new recording and threw it down a hill. Another person was on hand to do the weather that night, but Yockey threatened to disrupt the show and again a public service film aired.[17]

Yockey had previously been approached by Bob Ossenberg, a WTVW sales representative, to move to WTVW, the only VHF station in the market.[18] So after three years on WFIE, Yockey moved to WTVW and was sponsored by Weil's within three days.[19] There was no clear connection but the very day Yockey announced her departure to WTVW, WFIE's general manager, Ted Nelson, resigned.

WTVW was a VHF station and had a much larger audience. WFIE was in the process of increasing its tower height and changing channel allocation from 62 to 14. However, it still did not have the audience reach of WTVW, and WVTW had a swimming pool.[20] This gave Yockey the chance to develop one of her trademark stunts: giving the Fourth of July weather forecast and then jumping into the pool.

At both WFIE and WTVW, Yockey worked only the 10 p.m. newscast (after prime time in Evansville). At WFIE, she began the newscast,[21] but WTVW managers moved her weathercast later into the news program. While the changes were probably done to retain audience, Yockey did not like the seemingly less important position.

To compound the problem, staffing changes at WTVW caused station management to ask Yockey to do the earlier 6 p.m. news as well. While Yockey was under the impression that she would be paid an additional $10 to do the early show, the money was never paid. In September 1964, after nine months of early newscasts, Yockey refused to do any more. She publicly threatened to go off skiing and not tell anyone where she had gone.[22]

Eighteen months later, in February 1966, Yockey made good on her threat. She was angered by the decision of the program director, Ulysses Carlini, not to let her go on a ski trip during ratings period. Yockey simply did not come to work. However, she had agreed to speak to a group of pilots for 15 minutes before work. When she arrived Yockey told them, "Boys, I'll talk to you as long as you want me to because I have got nothing else to do."[23] Carlini did both weathercasts that night. Three days later, E. Berry Smith, the station manager, announced Yockey's return to the air.

The immediate dispute had been settled but not forgotten. Over the next five years, Yockey came as close as she ever would to leaving the Evansville market. By 1971, she was in serious discussions with an

Atlanta television station. Eventually, the news director turned her down saying simply, "Atlanta was not ready for her."[24] There were also possibilities in St. Louis and Cleveland. Yockey often cited her parents as a reason why she stayed in the Evansville market.[25]

In August 1971, Yockey was again asked to do the 6 p.m. news. Since she was not paid the first time she did this newscast, she quit WTVW. But in less than two weeks, Yockey was back on the air at WFIE-TV. She continued to do the 10 p.m. newscast Sunday through Friday from September 1971 to December 1987. In 1987, she was moved from the evening newscast to a midday news segment at 11:30 a.m.[26] Station management and corporate executives felt it was necessary to use more technology, but Yockey was not willing to change her format. Other station managers suggested that her demographics were starting to skew toward an older, less desirable audience.[27]

Seven months later, Yockey found a reason to retire. She got angry when her annual July 4 jump into a pool was not allowed. Her habit was to record the event in the afternoon for play on the late news. It was apparent that station management was clearly going for a more professional image and Yockey's style was no longer wanted.

Presentation Style

As a 10-year veteran of the weather bureau, Yockey took pride in her forecasts.[28] She went out to the weather bureau herself and analyzed the information. Yockey and the weather bureau worked independently to develop their forecasts. In the early days, the bureau would draw maps every six hours; Yockey would draw the maps every three hours. In later days, bureau personnel created a computer file called Marcia that contained the data she would want before every night's forecast.[29]

Depending on the complexity of the weather, Yockey would spend between one and two hours at the weather bureau before each night's report.[30] It would take a half-hour to drive from the airport to the station. In the studio, her map was covered with a sheet of glass and she would use a large water-based marker to draw essential weather elements such as fronts, isobars, temperatures and precipitation levels. Studio staff were expected to clean it before the next weathercast. The process took only about 20 minutes, but it was messy and easy to neglect. A fear emerged around the studio that Yockey would come in to the station and the map would not be clean.[31] No one wanted to face her if the map was not ready.

For the 5-minute weathercast, Yockey would attack the map, left-handedly scrawling in temperatures and precipitation levels as she explained the weather and what was likely to happen. Most of the time, she had her back to the camera. Every once in a while, she would lean into the camera like a bookie giving you a personal tip on the weather. Often, she would rattle on about something that had nothing to do with the weather and then fly through the forecast. On other evenings, she would get right down to work and talk only about the weather. On big sports nights, the pressure was palatable in the studio (sometimes even audible from the sportscaster) to get her off the air on time.[32]

Yockey loved to entertain. She did all she could to be spontaneous, fun and unpredictable. As one longtime resident put it, "You can go to the other channels for the weather. You go to Marcia for the show."[33] Marcia loved to do stunts. When the United States landed on the moon, she created a parody for the weather report. On other nights, she rode a horse on the set or did her weather out in the snow or brought the weather inside, decorating the studio with snow or leaves.

Holidays were important to Yockey. She would wear a special skirt at Christmas, come in costume at Halloween, and go swimming (in a bikini for many years) on the Fourth of July. One year on Halloween, she appeared as a spider over her map. She remembered watermelon season, hunting season, and fishing season. She knew every annual festival and went to most of them. In effect, she was a part of each celebration in the community.[34]

Yockey was known for hard drinking and hard language off camera, but she kept her on-air presentation clean "because my mother's watching."[35] Many viewers often assumed she was drunk on the air, and she drank tea from a thermos bottle on air, which fed the rumors. Those that worked with her unanimously refuted her drinking prior to airtime.

Yockey's forecasts were scientifically sound. Her map contained extreme detail. She talked freely about winds at various levels, pressure systems and specific weather front patterns. She supported weather education by talking to groups across the region. Yockey's name appeared on two weather guides.[36] The guides contained scientific information, charts, graphs and explanations on how to read the weather map. "It took me thirty-five years to educate people. . . . You don't ever want [viewers] to know you're educating them . . . but if you sneak it in on them, then they can't live without it."[37]

Public service entered her forecast two ways. First, she would actively plug community events by talking about them, wearing T-shirts, or giving a special forecast for people going to them. Her home contained literally hundreds of old T-shirts for on-air promotions. Second, people would call in with weather requests. She would give a personal forecast for a family traveling to another state. As Yockey put it, "I put all those temperatures on there [the map] because people are always calling about them. Somebody may be flying to Tucson and want to know what the weather is like there."[38]

Yockey scornfully ignored the ratings. "I tend to believe that if you try to do your best every night, that you don't have to worry about them. Why worry about them if you are doing your best? I mean I care in June and July so I don't do anything differently in February and November."[39] Yockey did not need to worry. WFIE General Manager Conrad Cagle reported, "When I got here, we were number one at ten with Marcia and number three (out of three) at six without her. In the time that she was on the air, we lost only one rating period. That was when the competition gave away a truck."[40]

Yockey never asked for a raise from WTVW and she never got one in the years she worked there. In 1977 when Conrad Cagle became general manager of WFIE, he quickly noted that Yockey had no system for valuing herself in the commercial market.[41] She would accept whatever people wanted to pay. In a desire to increase both the station's and Yockey's income, Cagle converted Yockey from a straight contract to a "personal services agreement." Under the new arrangement, station management worked with Yockey to set parameters and values for her work as commercial talent. It was a difficult transition for those that were comfortable with Yockey's previous whatever-you-think-is-fair style.[42] It did increase her income dramatically, limited her "working appearances" and reduced the number of free plugs she gave people.

Public Life

Yockey easily became one of the most recognized figures in the region. After 34 years on the air, few people had not seen Yockey in person. People who traveled with Yockey would consistently tell a story of someone recognizing her in all parts of the world.[43] On the occasion of her 76th birthday, 10 years after she retired, *The Evansville Press* devoted half of the front page and 36 inches inside the paper to her birthday party.[44]

Perhaps the real power behind Yockey's success was her off-camera activities. Yockey was never shy with the public and she dressed the same on or off the air. Known for drinking, cussing, flying and skiing, she was also known for her tireless devotion to the community. She would visit schools, hospitals, nursing homes, and local events and would actively support benefits for multiple sclerosis, muscular dystrophy, Humane Society, Evansville Philharmonic Guild, Cancer Society, Girl Scouts and Special Olympics.[45]

Yockey's personal appearances were great promotion for her and the station. However, she did them because she loved to do them. She was driving women to the YWCA years before she became a public figure.[46] Her celebrity expanded her ability to provide public service. When she did attend an event, she became part of the event. A popular stunt was her Lady Godiva horse ride at local parades. She did this stunt at least eight times across the region.[47]

Yockey was also sensitive to her audience. Jerry Birge worked with Yockey in the 1960s and recounted a typical example. Yockey had traveled about 50 miles out of Evansville to visit a friend in the hospital. Word traveled quickly that she was there. Yockey understood that she could be a disruption, so she took the time to visit every patient in the hospital.[48]

She visited many places on a regular basis, but she particularly loved children. Yockey had a special place in her heart for the residents of the Wendell Foster Campus for Developmental Disabilities in nearby Owensboro, Kentucky. She would visit every Valentine's Day to judge an event and would get down on the floor to play with the children. She would accept no assignments on Thursdays; it was her day to visit the area nursing homes.[49]

Yockey presented herself as an "everywoman." A WTVW employee, John Schuta, observed, "If she went out with the boys, she could get along with the boys. If she was with kids she could get along with kids. She fit in wherever she went. In my opinion, that's why she was so popular."[50] Despite her acknowledged skill as a meteorologist and pilot, she maintained a self-effacing air. When she formally thanked people, she was fond of saying "mercy buckets," her adaptation of the

French phrase.[51] She also enjoyed mispronouncing words to give them a suggestive nature, such as pronouncing the "x" in grand prix.

Her co-workers sometimes experienced a different side to her and feared her anger. In one case, Yockey felt the sportscaster at WTVW was making fun of her while she was on the air. She retaliated by disrupting his postnewscast talk show by throwing balls into the set. The next day, separate meetings were held with station management and the sportscaster. The sportscaster resigned.[52] Even Yockey's closest friends would give her a wide berth when she was mad.[53] While it was difficult to anticipate her reaction, Yockey expected others to work as hard as she did. She had little patience with people that could not or would not help.

David James, her news anchor for several years, called her "very gentle."[54] Co-workers Larry Vonderah and Hugh Whittenbraker agreed in separate interviews that you could get her to do a lot if you talked to her plainly about it.[55] Cagle was able to successfully move her from her 10 p.m. news to an 11:30 a.m. slot with minimal fuss (however, with considerable financial concessions). He maintained, "I treated her like a person."[56] On the other hand, memos rarely worked well. She was often seen angry in the studio over a memo. She quit in 1966 and 1988 in part over the contents of a managerial memo.

Flying

Yockey loved flying and this became part of her public persona. She had an extensive collection of kites. She would watch and try to photograph birds. She attended the annual experimental aircraft show in Oshkosh, Wisconsin every year. She often flew to personal appearances and talked about flying on the air. When asked why she flew, her favorite reply was, because there's a bunch of blithering idiots on the highways and they won't let you go but 55 MPH. I've got more important things to do in this world than go 55."[57]

Yockey wanted to be one of the first hundred women in the world to be licensed to fly a helicopter and she was; her license was number 100. A dramatic helicopter crash in a local shopping center destroyed her helicopter, killed her instructor and a person dressed as Santa Claus in full view of waiting children.[58] After that, she maintained her membership in a Whirly Girls association but stopped flying helicopters.[59]

No matter what type of aircraft she flew, she would fly by visual flight rules without radio. She was once seen throwing a radio out of a hot air balloon she was piloting. She would follow an authorized airplane in and out of an airport. If she needed to stop at a busy airport, she might fly to a nearby airstrip and phone the control tower for permission to land. She liked to fly without a compass as well. Her skills in geography allowed her to follow roads, rivers and other landmarks.[60]

Conclusion

Yockey died on September 28, 2000, at the age of 77. Her memorial service echoed the life she led. Thousands of pictures from her years in broadcasting resulted in just as many stories from friends and fans. Mike Blake, longtime WFIE-TV sportscaster, mused, "Heaven is a lot livelier place tonight."[61]

Yockey joyfully broke the rules and succeeded in doing so. Her success may never be duplicated. However, it demonstrated the power of doing the job for the love of the job and public service for the love of people. The absence of men because of World War II gave Yockey a chance to receive meteorological training and the opportunity to be on the air. She took those opportunities and did her best. Her caring nature took care of the rest.

Notes

1. Rhodes, R. (producer). (1996). *A Profile of Marcia Yockey,* in three parts. Videotape, WTVW-TV Archive. Evansville, Indiana.
2. Siems, W. (1953, Nov. 16). Groucho Marx tardy but WFIE opens on schedule. *Evansville Press,* p. 18.
3. Cobb, A. (1988, July 6). Yockey retires from station after dispute. *Evansville Press,* p. A1; Davis, R. (1988, July 6). Yockey storms out on Ch. 14 in swimsuit tiff. *Evansville Courier,* p. A1.
4. Davis, R. (2000, Apr. 16). Marcia. *Evansville Courier,* p. C1.
5. Wick, N. (1978). 25 years for WFIE-TV. *Evansville Press,* p. 16.
6. Cagle, C. (2000, Aug. 29). Personal communication.
7. Henson, R. (1990). *Television Weathercasting: A History,* p. 79. Jefferson, N.C.: McFarland and Company.
8. Hauge, J. (2000, Aug. 25). Personal communication.
9. Henson, 1990, p. 81.
10. Lant, K. (2000, Aug. 6). Personal communication; James, D. (1978) An interview with Marcia Yockey on WFIE's 25-year anniversary. WFIE archives, Evansville, Indiana.

11. James, 1978; Martin, H. (1978, Apr. 16). Marcia! *The Sunday Look,* p. 16.

12. Davis, R. (1992, Aug. 24). Weather watchers. *Evansville Courier,* p. B1.

13. Hauge, 2000; Payne, J. (2000, Aug. 3). Personal communication; Martin, 1978.

14. James, 1978.

15. Davis, R. (1987, May 24). Miss Yockey still flies high in wacky weather world. *Sunday Courier,* p. 2.

16. Ritt, C. (1966, Feb. 16). TV weather girl Marcia Yockey quits to keep date for ski trip, *Evansville Press,* p. 11A.

17. Wormald, R. (1966, Feb. 16). Marcia Yockey quits station "skied off." *Evansville Courier,* p. 1.

18. Davis, 2000.

19. WTVW. (1957, Feb. 8). Advertisement. *Evansville Courier,* p. 13.

20. Birge, J. (2000, Aug. 4). Personal communication.

21. Ritt, 1966.

22. Wormald, 1966.

23. Ritt, 1966, p. 1.

24. Yockey, M. Personal papers. Evansville, Ind.

25. James, 1978.

26. Knipe, S., and Swanson, P. (1987, Nov. 10). Marcia to move to midday news after 34 years. *Evansville Press,* p. A1.

27. Knipe and Swanson, 1987.

28. Hauge, 2000.

29. Carroll, N. (2000, Aug. 5). Personal communication.

30. Author's personal experience, 1978–1985.

31. Author, 1978–1985.

32. Whittenbraker, H. (2000, Aug. 4). Personal communication; author, 1978–1985.

33. Martin, 1978, p. 16.

34. Rhodes, 1996.

35. Davis, 1987, p. 2.

36. Yockey, M. (c.1953). *Whether the Weather.* Evansville, Ind.: Hesmers; Yockey, M., and Barnhill, B. (1977). *United States Weather.* Oklahoma City: United States Weather Company.

37. Henson, 1990, p. 41.

38. Mathews, G. (1987, Nov. 5). The Yock: A tri-State institution. *Evansville Courier,* p. 15.

39. Roberts, M. (1980, May-June). EVV talks to Marcia Yockey. *Evansville Close-up,* p. 16.

40. Cagle, 2000.

41. Cagle, 2000.

42. Cagle, 2000.

43. Eaton, R. (1997, Mar.). Life in the fast lane. *Maturity Journal,* p. 14-18.

44. Brown, A. (1998, Nov. 9). A legend turns 76. *Evansville Press,* pp. 1, 10.

45. Eaton, 1997.

46. Yockey, M. Personal papers. Resume 1971.

47. James, 1978.

48. Birge, 2000.

49. Birge, 2000; Lant, 2000; Redinou, C. (2000, Aug. 15). Personal communication.

50. Eaton, 1997, pp. 14-15.

51. Brown, 1998, p. 10.

52. Cagle, 2000.

53. Birge, 2000; Vonderah, L. (2000, Aug. 3). Personal communication; Whittenbraker, 2000.

54. Davis, 2000, p. C1.
55. Vonderah, 2000; Whittenbraker, 2000.
56. Cagle, 2000.
57. Davis, 2000, p. C1.
58. Trevathan, W. (1967, Dec. 10). Santa stand-in and pilot dead. *Evansville Sunday Courier and Press,* pp. 1, 18.
59. Author, 1978–1985; Hague, 2000; Lant, 2000.
60. Birge, 2000; Dick, T. (2000, Aug. 1). Personal communication; Whittenbraker, 2000; Yockey, M. (1982). Personal communication.
61. Blake, M. (2000, Oct. 1). Personal communication.

Other Sources

Accuweather.com. (2000). Virtual Weather Hall of Fame. *Meteorologist Entertainment Awards* [On-line]. Available: http://www.acuweather.com/iwxpage/adc/popup/halloffame/awards.htm. Retrieved 2000, Sept. 4.

Coudret, R. (1987, Nov. 13). Marcia's fans think television weather switch stinks. *The Evansville Courier,* p. 21.

Coudret, R. (1993, Dec. 11). Local TV veteran Conrad Cagle is leaving WFIE. *Evansville Courier,* p. C6.

Davis, R. (1996, June 21). That's a wrap. *Evansville Courier,* p. B1.

Hall, R. (1975, Dec. 21). Local TV at age 22. *Sunday Look,* p. 4, 8.

Kramer, T.J. (1995, Jan. 8). In changing world, newspaper women stepping up. *Evansville Courier,* p. H28.

Mathews, G. (1991, Mar. 7). Ex-weather gal, sportscaster, actor are lively set. *Evansville Courier,* p. A3.

Nelson resigns WFIE-TV post. (1957, Feb. 5). *Evansville Courier,* p. A1.

Ritt, C. (1971, Aug. 17). Around town: Weather girl Marcia Yockey clouds up, quits Channel 7. *Evansville Press,* p. 21.

Rose, B. (1987, Nov. 16). WFIE's shift of Marcia precipitates opposition. *Newspaper,* p. 1.

Ted Nelson resigns as manager at WFIE. (1957, Feb. 5). *Evansville Press,* p. 1.

"Weather Girl" changes TV jobs. (1957, February 5). *Evansville Courier,* p. 13.

Index

Page references in italics refer to photographs.

Able, George, *142,* 146
About People, 193
Academy of Television Arts and Sciences
  (ATAS), internship program, 94–96
Addams, Jane, 52
Advertisers, effect on news, 122
Alice Weston at Home, 206
Alice Weston Show, The, 206, 207. *See also*
  Weston, Alice
Allen, Spencer, 151
All for You, 207
American Association of School
  Superintendents (AASS), 66,
  70, 72
American Council on Education, 78
America's Sweethearts (film), 224
Angelou, Maya, 174
Arakawa, Adele, xi, 9, *14*
  co-anchor at KUSA, 15–16, 17–19,
  20–23
  early years, 16–17
  educational background, 19–20
  honors and awards, 22
Armchair Planning, 205
Ashley, Beth, 158
Asia Now, 45
Association of Land Grant Colleges and
  Universities, 78

Ball, Lucille, 9, 135
Banks, Lyle, 122
Barn Dance, 217
Barrett, Joan, 111
Barton, Darryl, 100
Baze, Ted, 210
Beck, Dave, 33
Ben-Gurion, David, 209
Berdahl, Robert M., 112
Bersohn, Martin, 56
Besse, Ralph, *202*
Birge, Jerry, 235

Birth of Tommy Rohlfing, The, Concept
  program, 170
Bishop, Anne, 184
Bitter Harvest, 33
Blake, Mike, 237
Blattner, Buddy, 146
Bradley, Dan, 180, 184
Brekke, Gail, 198–199
Bremner, Eric, 42, 46
Breslin, Jim, 54–55, 57
Brett, Elizabeth, 199
Bridgeways Communications, 195–199
Broadcasting
  educational, 8
  roles of women in, 4
Broadcasts, remote, 30
Bronson, Marty, 146
Bullitt, Dorothy Stimson, ix, 10, *26,* 39
  background, 28–29
  early years, 27–28
  and KING-TV, 30–36
  radio broadcasting, 29–30, 36
Bullitt, Scott, 28
Bullitt, Stimson, 33, 40–41
Burbach, George, 144

Cable television, women in, 9–10
Cage, The, 162
Cagle, Conrad, 229, 234, 236
Campbell, Paul, 149
Carlini, Ulysses, 231
Carole Kneeland Project for Responsible
  Television Journalism, 117–118
Carter, Anon G., Sr., 217
Carter, Jimmy, 174, 175
Carter, Rosalynn, 210–211
Casa Manana, 223–224
CBS Evening News with Dan Rather, 128
Champlin, Charles "Chuck", 90, 91
Channels, UHF/VHF, 8, 80
Charlotte Peters Show, The, 144–148. *See also*
  Peters, Charlotte
Chasan, Daniel Jack, 41

Cherry, Jean, 197
Children's programming, KING-TV, 31–32
Chou-en-Lai, Madame, 174
Citizens' Summit, A, 35
Citywatchers, 90–93
Coffee Shop, 210
Cogill, Gary, 223
Cohen, Betty, 10
Cohen, D., 127
Cohen, Steve, 112
College Press Conference, 166, 167
College Student Internship Program,
    The, 95
Columbine High School shootings, 15–16
Concept, 168–170
Connecticut Voices for Children, 199
Connolly, Ella Louise Toner, 215
Connolly, Robert Emmitt, 215
Connolly, Robert Loren, 215
Coolidge, Peggy, 210
Cope, Betty, 203, 205
Copyright Law, 68
Corporation for Public Broadcasting,
    establishment of, 69
Corr, O. Casey, 42, 43
Couric, Katie, 10
Craft, Christine, 18
Crime news, coverage by KVUE, 110–112
Croly, Jane Cunningham, 3
Cronkite, Walter, on Carol Marin, 127
Cross, Bettie, 111
CSUN, 89
Curtis, Cyrus H., 3

D'Addario, Francis, 196
Dateline, 217–219, 220
Davis, W.T., 82
Dean, Dizzy, 146
DeHaven, Walt, 127
Desilu Productions, 9
Detroit Free Press, 204
Detroit News, 205
Dialogue with Laurel Vlock, 192–193
Diller, Phyllis, on Wanda Ramey, 164
Directors Guild of America, 135
Disney, Walt, 138
Distaff, 206
Documentaries
    KING-TV, 32
    Laurel Vlock, 192–193
Donahue, Phil, 35
Douglas, Mike, 152
Duquesne Beer, television sponsor, 53

Educational television, 8
    and copyright laws, 68

creation of, 75–76
Donna Matson and, 133–140
establishment of noncommercial
    channels, 77–82
FCC and, 67–69
"large classroom" approach, 69–70
Martha Gable and, 65, 66, 69–70
Eighth Day, 192
Ellerbee, Linda, 116
    on Carole Kneeland, 109
Ellsworth, Annie, 4
Emerson Corporation, 81
Enersen, Jean, ix, 8, 10, *38*
    early years, 39–40
    educational background, 40
    honors and awards, 45, 47
    at KING-TV, 34, 39–47
    on *120 Minutes,* 45
    programming values, 44
    Telescope co-host, 41–42
Eschen, Frank, 144, 145
ESPN, 183
Everson, George, 5
Eyewitness News at Noon, 171

Falcone, Paul, 198, 199
Family Fare, 206
Farbman, Harry, 146
Farnsworth, Elma G. "Pem" Gardner, 4–6
Farnsworth, Philo T., 5–6
Farnsworth Television Incorporated, 6
Faulder, Bud, 183
FCC. *See* Federal Communications
    Commission
Federal Communications Commission
    (FCC)
    channel allocation hearings, 77–82
    commercial television, 8
    educational television, 67–69
    EEO rules, 9, 10–11
    licensing freeze, 7, 67
Feder, Robert, 127
Feinstein, Diane, 163
Feldman, Bob, 101–102, 103
Feltis, Hugh, 30
Fili-Krushel, Pat, 10
Fine, Jerry, 229
Fisher, O.D., 32
Fitzgerald, John, 203
Fontaine, Pat, 151
Forever Yesterday, 194
48 Hours, 128
43 a.m., 210
Fox, John, 191
Fox, Rose, 191
Francini, Bruce, 91

Francis, Vinnie, 158
Fredrick, Pauline, 9
Frigidaire, television sponsorship, 207
Fuldheim, Dorothy, ix, 7, *50,* 51–52, 203
  book reviews, 52, 54, 57
  community service, 56
  early broadcasting career, 53–56
  early years, 52, 56–57
  family life, 56–58
  honors and awards, 56
  impact on news reporting, 58
  interviews, 55
Fuldheim, Dorothy (daughter), 57–58
Fuldheim, Milton, 57
Furness, Betty, 9

Gable, Martha (Marty), ix, 8, *62*
  AASS Atlantic City show, 70
  early years, 63–64
  and educational television, 65, 66, 69–70
  FCC hearings and, 67–69
  "large classroom" approach to
    educational television, 69–70
  Olympic gymnastics judge, 63–64
  Penn State show, 66–67
  public relations, 72
  sports reporting, 64–65
  and WHYY, 71
Gardner, Jim, 103
General Electric, 7
Giamatti, Bartlett, *190, 194*
Glennon, John, 145
Golshmann, Vladimir, 146
Gordon, Bill, 53–54
Gorrell, Leslie, 5
Gottlieb, Carl, 126
Gray, Nancy, 55
Greeley, Andrew, 123
Greeley, Horace, 3
Grief's Children, 122
Griffin, Merv, 152
Groogan, Greg, 111
Guerin, Leona, 207

Haag, Marty, 112, 113–114
Hadlock, Kathy, 115–116
Haller, Sherry, 200
Hanrahan, James, 51–52, 53
Harriott, Jim, 43
Harris, Bill, 192
Harvest of Shame, 33
Hausser, Katsuko Arakawa, 19
Hayward, Bruce, 151
Heffron, Norm, 42
Heldman, Ernie, 146
Hennock, Frieda, ix, 9, 67, *74*

appointment to FCC, 75–76
early years, 76
educational background, 76
FCC channel allocation hearings, 77–82
and KUHT, 75, 82
Henry, Susan, 4
Henry, Ted, 58
Herp, Ed, 208
Herring, Charles, 31
Hicks, Leslie, 88
Hicks, Pamela, 88
Hicks, Paul, 88
Hicks, Price, x, 8, *86*
  and ATAS internship program, 94–96
  early years, 87–88
  educational background, 88–89
  producer at KCET, 89–94
History of Jews in Hartford, The, 193
Hite, Bob, 180, 183, 184
Holloway, Diane, 117
Hollywood Video Center, 133
Holocaust Survivors Film Project, 194
Holt, Lester, 20
Homeless Man, The, Concept program, 170
Hood, Lee, 18
Howard, Lisa, xi, 9, *98*
  early career, 100–101
  educational background, 99–100
  ethical standards, 104
  honors and awards, 100
  news anchor at WPVI, 101–106
  professionalism, 105–106
Howard, Marc, 103, 105
Hubbard, Ray, 159
Hughes, Jerry, 91
Hull, R., 78
Humphrey, Hubert, *166*
Hunter, Emma, 4
Husted, Bill, 22
Hyman, Valerie, 114

Inside Area 5, 219
Ivins, Molly, on Carole Kneeland, 111, 113

Jacobs, Alma, 72
Jacobs, Andrea, 20
James, David, 236
Jean Loach Public Relations Company, 210
Jewish News and Views, 192
Jewish Spectrum, 193
Jewish Television Institute, 193
Johnson, Geraldine, 195–196
Johnson, Lady Bird, 10
Johnson, Steve, 127
Joint Committee on Educational Television
  (JCET), 78, 79, 81

Joint Council for Educational Television
    (JCET), 68
Journalism, online, 186

Kann, Stan, *142,* 146, 147
KAUM-FM, 109
KCBS-radio, 158
KCET-TV (Los Angeles), 89–94
KeFauver, Estes, 144
Kelly, John B., 64
Kemmerer, W.W., 79–80, 81–82
Kennard, Cinny, 114, 115
Kennedy, Susan, 123
Kent, Lorrainne, 115
Kent, Sanford, 115
Kent State University shootings, 55
Kerekes, J., 55–56, 58
KETC-TV (St. Louis), 81
KEYE-TV (Austin), 112
KGO-TV (San Francisco), 158, 163
KGW-radio, 32
Kinescopes, 71
KING's Clubhouse, 31
KING-TV (Seattle), 30
    and Dorothy Stimson Bullitt, 30–36
    hiring policies, 40–41
    and Jean Enersen, 34, 39–47
    management of, 33–36
    programming, 31–32, 35
Kitchen Clinic, 206
KMBC-TV (Kansas), 18
Kneeland, Carole, x, xi, 10, *108*
    background, 109–110
    character, 115–116
    early years, 115
    honors and awards, 113
    journalism mentor, 113–114
    KVUE crime project, 110–112
    legacy of, 116–117
    management style, 114–115
    news director/vice president at
        KVUE, 109
    views on broadcast journalism,
        112–113, 116
Komma, Fred, 149
KOMO-TV (Seattle), 32
Koplovitz, Kay, 10
KPIX-TV (San Francisco), 40,
    158–162
KPRC-TV (Houston), 109
KQED-TV (San Francisco), 66, 162
KROW, 158
KRSC-TV (Seattle), 30
KSD-radio, 144
KSD-TV (St. Louis), 7, 143–153
KSFO-AM, 158
KTVI-TV, 150–152

KTVY-TV (Oklahoma City), 100
KUHT-TV (Houston), 8
    creation of, 75–76, 81–82
Kuralt, Charles, 150
Kurlander, Regine, 54
Kurtis, Bill, 20
KUSA-TV (Denver), 15, 20–23
KVUE-TV (Austin), 109–118
KWBR-radio, 158
KXAS-TV (Fort Worth), 219–221
KYW-TV (Philadelphia), 167–175

Laclede Little Symphony, 146
Ladies' Home Journal, The, 3, 56
Lassen, Leo, 30
Laub, Dori, 194
Laury, William, 103
Laybourne, Geraldine, 10
Leberman, Palmer K. (P.K.), 30–31
Lee, Ruta, on Bobbie Wygant, 223
Leonard, Bill, 170
Lerner, Greda, 3
Life, 3
LIN Broadcasting, 219
Loesch, Margaret, 10
Lonely Sickness, The, 211
Lorain Conversation, 210, 212
Lost Cargo, 32
Luce, Clare Booth, 3
Luncheon at the Ones, 208
Lupino, Ida, 9, 135

MacNamara, Margaret, 174
MacNamara, Robert, 174
Madsen, Arch L., 5
Magers, Ron, 123, 124, 128
Malloy, Les, 158
"Marciarose" (column), 167, 174–175
Marciarose, x, *166*
    community service, 175–176
    educational background, 167
    honors and awards, 167, 170, 175
    at KYW, 168–175
    reporting from China, 174
    and *Sunday,* 175
Marciarose Show, The, 167, 174
Marin, Carol, xi, *120*
    background, 121
    early career, 121–122
    and ethics in journalism, 122, 124
    honors and awards, 122, 124, 125, 128
    at WBBM, 125–127
    at WMAQ, 121–125
Martin, Mike, 183, 186–187
Matson, Donna, x, 8, *130*
    community service, 140
    early years, 131–132

educational background, 132
producer/director, instructional
    programs, 133–140
teaching career, 132–133
Max Factor, 6
Mayer, Herb, 207
McElhatton, Dave, 158, 159
McFeaters, Cathy, 110, 111
McMichael, Steve, 122
Meet Me at Mannings, 158
Meet the Press, 168
Meir, Golda, 191
Mendilow, Miriam, 191
Meteorologists, female, 8
Meyers, William, 136
Midday with Wanda, 158
Midnight Reviews, 219
Mihuta, Dan, 137
Mike Douglas Show, The, 171
Miller, John, 115
Miller, Julius Sumner, 138
Mitchell, Ed, 230
Moody, Chip, 220
Moore, Garry, 148
Morfit, Mason, 148
Moritz, Marguerite, 18
Morse, Samuel Finley Breeze, 4
Mrs. Roosevelt Meets the Public, 79
Muir, Allan, 91
Muny Preview, 146
Mutual of Omaha's *Wild Kingdom,*
    146

National Association of Educational
    Broadcasters (NAEB), 78
National Education Association, 78
National Geographic Magazine, 132
NBC 5 (Fort Worth), 221
Nelson, Ted, 231
Nesbitt, Alan, 103–104
Neustadt, Stanley, 77
Newsbeat, 163
Newton, Dwight, 162
New York Illustrated, 175
New York Times, 3
New York Tribune, 3
New York World, 3
Noon News, 159–160
Northwest Cable News, 36
Now I Lay Me Down to Sleep, 122

Ober, Eric, 20
O'Brien, Jim, 102
Ochs, Adolph, 3
Ohio Network, 206, 208
Oklahoma City bombings, 16
120 Minutes, 45

One O'clock Club, 53–54
Operation Alphabet, 71
Ossenberg, Bob, 231
Ostrow, Joan, 15, 21

Pauley, Jane, 9
Payne, Ancil, 34–35, 46
    hiring policies at KING-TV, 41
Pendergrass, John, 87
Pendergrass, Maude, 87
Penn State, Martha Gable show at, 66–67
Perkins, Carol, 146
Perkins, Marlin, 146
Perris, Don, 56
Peters, Bill, 143
Peters, Charlotte, x, 7, *142*
    awards and honors, 152–153
    early years, 143
    at KSD, 144–150
    at KYVI, 151–152
Philadelphia Franklin Institute, 5–6
Philadelphia schools, public service
    programming, 65
Philbin, Regis, 180
Philco Corporation, 7
    sports programs, 64
    television demonstration at University of
        Philadelphia, 66
Photographs, early transmission of, 5
Player, Laura, 6
Poverty in the Land of Plenty, 45
Pozner, Vladimir, 35
Price, Hank, 125, 126, 127
Professor Wonderful on Why Is It So?, 138
Programming
    children's, 31–32
    noncommercial, 65, 77–82. *See also*
        Educational television
Public Broadcasting Laboratory, The, 162
Public Broadcasting System, 69
Public Eye, 125
Public service programming, Philadelphia
    schools, 65
Public television, and Martha Gable, 65, 69
Pulitzer, Joseph, 3
Pulitzer Publishing Company, 7, 144

Queirolo, Kristie Louise, 161
Queirolo, Richard "Dick," 161–162

Ramey, Wanda, x, 8, *156*
    celebrity interviews, 161
    community service, 162
    early career, 157–158
    educational background, 157
    honors and awards, 161, 163
    at KPIX, 158–162

RCA, 6–7
Reagan, Ronald, *156*
Rickett, Adele, 56
Rimmer, Margret McDonald, 217
Robertson, James, 71
Rodenberg, Howard, 110
Roedel, John, 146
Rosati, Alison, 124

Salhany, Lucie, 10
Salter, Nancy, 91–92
Sanders, Marlene, 9
San Quentin Prison, 162, 163
Sardella, Ed, 19, 21–22
Sarnoff, David, 32
Sawyer, Diane, 9
Schneider, Michael, 114
Schnell, Bertha, 57
Schoenbrun, David, 193–194
Schowalter, Arthur, 205
Schulman, Lee, 30
Schulman, Robert, 32
Schuta, John, 235
Schwarz, Patricia Peters, 152
Schwarzwalder, John, 82
Scripps-Howard Broadcasting Company,
  51
Seidenbaum, Art, 90, 91
Senior Report, 211
Severin, Russ, 143–144
Sheldon, Linn, 210
Sheridan, Terrence, 55
Sherwood, Charles, 148
Shestack, Jennifer, 172
Shestack, Jonathan, 173
Shestack, Marciarose. *See* Marciarose
Shultz, Ernie, 100
Sierens, Betty, 181–182
Sierens, Gayle, x, *178*
  community service, 187
  early years, 181
  family life, 186–188
  honors and awards, 182, 185
  sports announcer, 179–180
  at WFLA, 180, 182
Silber, Jeanette, 57
Simpson, Carole, 9
Sixteen in Webster Groves, 150
Sixth Report and Order, 8
60 Minutes, II, 125, 128
Smith, Dave, 100
Smith, E. Berry, 231
Snyder, Tom, 171, 172
Society of Professional Journalists Ethics
  Committee, on Carol Marin, 124
Sonnenberg, Joel, 125

Sorkin, Dan, 146
Speak Up, 168–169
Speilberg, Steven, 223
Spencer, Milt, 182
Spivak, Larry, 168
Springer, Jerry, 122–124
Stahl, Lesley, 9
Stargell, Willie, 182
Steeple, Ralph, 68
Step, Bev, 54
Step, Charlie, 54
Stewart, Martha, 10
Stimson, C.D., 27
Stimson, Frederick, 29
Stoddard, Alexander, 65, 69–70
Stump Us, 217
Sullivan, Leonor K., 152
Sunday, 175

Tarses, Jamie, 10
Telecommunications, ATAS internship
  program, 94–96
Telescope, 41
Televenture Tales, 31
Television
  commercial/noncommercial, 8
  equal opportunities for women,
    8–11, 173
  first live broadcast, 5
  makeup, 6
  women in management, 10
Television channels, UHF/VHF, 8, 80
Television in America: Local Station History
    From Across the Nation, ix, x, xi, 4
Television programming
  children's, 31–32
  noncommercial, 65, 77–82. *See also*
    Educational television
Television stations
  first educational, 8
  first sale of, 31
  owned by women, 10, 195–199
Television systems
  Farnsworth, 5
  RCA, 7
Ten O'clock News, 211
They Came to America, 193
Thomas-Laury, Lisa. *See* Howard, Lisa
Thomas, Lisa. *See* Howard, Lisa
Tonight's Radio Dinner, 205
Too Old, Too Ugly, and Not Deferential
    to Men, 18
Toscanini, Arturo, 146
To The Ladies, 143, 144–148
Town Meeting of the Air, 79
Trammell, Lynn, 217

28 Tonight, 93
Tyler, Keith, 67

UHF channels, 8, 80
Ulmer, William, 57
U.S. Weather Bureau, women in, 230
University of New Haven, 198
University of Philadelphia, television
    demonstration at, 66
Urman, Hal, 57
Urman, Halla, 57

Van Ells, Neal, 170
Venice Town Council, 91
VHF channels, 8, 80
Visions, 103
Vissepo, Patricia McCann, 199
Vlock, Jay, 191
Vlock, Laurel, xi, 10, *190*
    and Bridgeways Communications, Inc.,
        195–199
    community service, 199–200
    Dialogue with Laurel Vlock, 192–193
    documentaries, 193–194
    early years, 191
    educational background, 191
    honors and awards, 193, 194
Vlock, Michael, 197
Voice of America, 162–163
Volcano Named White, The, 33
Vonderah, Larry, 236

Wagner, Chris, 103
Walker, Paul, 68
Walters, Barbara, on Dorothy Fuldheim, 58
WBAA-radio (Purdue), 216
WBAP-TV (Fort Worth), 216–218
WBBM-TV (Chicago), 17, 20, 125–127
WBIR-TV (Knoxville), 121
WBNE-TV (New Haven), 192, 198
Weathergirls, 8, 229
Weisman, Michael, 179, 180
West, Ann, 199
Western Instructional Television, 134,
    137–139
Western Video Industries, 133
Westinghouse, 7
Weston, Alice, ix, 7, *202*
    ad-lib ability, 204, 205, 208, 212
    early years, 204
    educational background, 204
    honors and awards, 211–212
    interviews, 209
    at WEWS, 7, 203, 205–206
    at WIIC, 208–209
    at WUAB, 210–211

at WXEL, 207
Weston, John, 159–160
WEWS-TV (Cleveland)
    Alice Weston at, 7, 203, 205–206
    Dorothy Fuldheim at, 7, 51–58
WFAA-TV (Dallas), 109, 115
WFIE-TV (Evansville), 229, 231–232
WFIL-TV (Philadelphia), 65
WFLA-TV (Tampa), 179–180, 183–186
WFSB-TV (Hartford), 193
WHAI-TV (Bridgeport), 192, 197–198
*What Every Woman Should Know About
    Breast Cancer,* 116
When Women Call the Shots, 4
Whiteaker, Bruce, 113, 116
White, Betty, 135
Whittenbraker, Hugh, 236
WHYY-TV (Philadelphia), 71
Wiedemann, Charles G., 143
WIIC-TV (Pittsburgh), 208–209
Wild Kingdom, 146
Williamson, Martha, 10
Winfrey, Oprah, 10, 100
Wing, Julia, 102
WJW-TV (Cleveland), 53, 207
WKYC-TV (Cleveland), 203, 211
WLAF-AM, 19
WMAQ-TV (Chicago), 121–125
WNBC-TV (New York), 175
WNEW-TV (New York), 194
WNHC-TV (New Haven), 192
Wolper, David, 134
Woman Behind the Man, The, 158
Women
    employment opportunities in television,
        8–11
    historical roles in broadcasting, 4
    as meteorologists, 8
    as station owners, 10
    in television management, 10
*Women and American Television: An
    Encyclopedia,* 4
Women Behind the Camera, 4
Women Pioneers in Television, 4
Women's Press Club of New York, 3
World of Bobbie Wygant, The, 219
World War II, effect on television, 6–7
WPLG-TV (Miami), 184
WPVI-TV (Philadelphia), 101
WRAL-TV (Raleigh, NC.), 20
WRJZ-AM, 19
WSM-TV (Nashville), 121
WTIC-TV (Hartford), 193
WTNH-TV (New Haven), 192
WTVK-TV (Knoxville), 20
WTVW-TV (Evansville), 231–232

WUAB-TV (Lorain), 210–211
Wunda Wunda, 32
WXEL-TV (Cleveland), 203, 207
WYBC radio, 192
Wygant, Bobbie, x, 10, *214*
  in *America's Sweethearts,* 224
  celebrity interviews, 215
  community service, 222
  and *Dateline,* 217–219, 220
  early years, 215–216
  educational background, 216
  family life, 222
  honors and awards, 222–224
  at KXAS (formerly WBAP), 219–221
  movie/theater reviews, 220–221
  retirement from NBC, 5, 221
  at WBAP, 216–218

Wygant, Philip Warren, 216, 219, 222
WYSH-AM, 19

Yockey, Marcia, ix, 7–8, *228*
  early years, 229–230
  flying, 236–237
  presentation style, 232–234
  public life, 234–236
  stunts, 233, 235
  at WFIE, 230–232
  at WTVW, 231–232
You Count on Your Country, 158
You Learn to Adjust, 193
Your Community Speaks, 192

Zahn, Paula, 9
Zoo Parade, 146